PRE-PUBLI(

"Why hasn't someone done this before? I don't need a daily horoscope that lumps me together with 1/12 of the world's population, then presumes to predict my most intimate hopes, fears and anxieties. Instead the Celestial Forecaster offers an accurate, easy-to-understand picture of what's going on in the universe and how I and everyone else around me are likely to be affected."

Lon Milo DuQuette, author of *"Tarot of Ceremonial Magick"*

"Annie Bones has a good grasp of the basics, as well as the all-important capacity for creative thought so lacking in today's astrological community. While my own astrological ethos does not agree with the notion of the physical planets governing or influencing our earthbound fates, the writing in the Forecaster is quite good and it is likely to be a popular item with lay astrologers."

Antero Alli, author of *"Astrologik"* www.verticalpool.com

"You are the ANATOMICAL BONES of astrology" - Kira Gayle

"I run an astrology/psychotherapy practice on Maui, and so far your daily forecasts are the BEST I have run into on the net."
- Lorraine Bennington

"I enjoy your perspectives so much. They really help me understand my moods and those of the people around me, as well as what's going on in the news." - Violet

"One of my personal favorites" - www.psychicprediction.com

"Annie's perspective is spiritual, metaphysical, and thoroughly informed by Western mysticism... so you get the good stuff, not the silly commercial tripe."
- Astropro's WOW Website of the Week Award 11/2000

Athena

ANNIE BONES

CELESTIAL FORECASTER 2003

DAILY ASTROLOGY GUIDE

To Bohdi Jon Waterman —

"The stars are matter.
We're matter.
But it doesn't matter."
— Captain Beefheart

Love to you, and yours!
Annie Bones

Loon Feather Publications
Box 47031
Victoria, B.C. V9B 5T2
Canada
www.metaphysical.ca/forecaster

DEDICATION

To the King and Queen in all of us,
To whom I write sweet words

ACKNOWLEDGEMENTS

Thanks to:

Soror SSH, for editing dawn to dusk under ridiculous pressure,
Frater 72, who as my agent, husband, and publisher
believed in me and made this book possible
And to all my teachers and guides – who are myriad, especially Leon Reed and
Silver Wolf, and to Joel Radcliffe, who introduced me to astrology.

Special Thanks also to Quicksilver Productions, publishers of the Celestial Guide® for providing the astrological aspects and times on which this book is based, and to Jim and Jane Maynard, for all their support and encouragement.

Printing & Binding:	Hignell Press, Manitoba, Canada
	www.hignell.mb.ca
Production:	Frater 72
Editing:	Soror SSH
Inside Graphics:	Merx-Toledo International Ltd.
	www.exoticillustrations.com
Front cover:	M. Ridgley Clark
Frontispiece &	Linda Macfarlane
Back piece	
ISBN:	0-9731518-0-3

Written material Copyright © 2002 Annie "Bones" Sheeler, excepting quotes as noted. All Rights Reserved. Graphics Copyright by the individual artists.

TABLE OF CONTENTS

Athena		frontispiece
Overview – Aspects at a glance	Page	1
Detailed Forecasts		
January	....	9
February	....	26
March	....	42
April	....	62
May	....	80
June	....	99
July	....	123
August	....	138
September	....	157
October	....	171
November	....	188
December	....	207
Mother's Day Moon Guide		229
Sekhmet		back piece

ABOUT THE AUTHOR:

Annie "Bones" Sheeler has been immersed in astrology for 29 years. A native of Pennsylvania, she moved to the West Coast in 1984 and to Victoria B.C. in 1991. In the past she has studied astrology with Jacci Fulton, Deborah Stachowic and Antero Alli. From 1991-2001 Annie was co-owner of Avalon Metaphysical Center Ltd., a new-age book-store in Victoria B.C.. In 1995 she started writing the monthly guide "Astrology Aspects and Meditations", which grew over the years into the Celestial Forecaster. In addition to astrology, Annie also teaches tarot and metaphysics. She is an ordained Gnostic Priestess, and regularly celebrates Mass in her community.

DISCLAIMER

Find a mistake? It is Annie Bones' policy to include something for everyone. Since some people like to find errors, she regularly includes a few in her publication to meet this need. Further, she is known to state "I am so mutable, I can agree with almost anybody who disagrees with me."

PREFACE

The small volume you are holding in your hands is a rare jewel. It is not to be confused with yet another generic astrological guide. Rather, it is a signpost leading to a set of truths uniquely experienced by each of us. This is a divinatory work! It is a tool for the pure of heart.

Annie Bones has been my friend, mentor and guide for over eighteen years. As a layman, at first confused by the vast canopy of the heavens and their relationship to my own personal life, Annie's clear, astrological instruction has brought me home to the proposition that every man and every woman is a star. I have learned, as her student, the rare art of being able to place one foot firmly upon the template of destiny or kismet, while at the same time, have the other rest, with a conviction of heart, upon direct experience. In the several years I have been reading her guide, I have learned to distinguish the map of symbols and signposts from reality. This distinction has allowed me, as well as other students, to enjoy a greater sovereignty in our own unique nature and true will.

Annie significantly illuminates, with wit, kindness and a rare level of vivaciousness, the necessity of being conscious of our surroundings in a universe that often seems like a cosmic joke.

As you read, her work will shed light upon blind spots, illuminating and making exquisite sense out of a world that often seems confusing, and, even meaningless.

Her divinatory and scintillating oracle-like insight brings to readers a type of inner clarity that allows a set of circumstances, which at one time made no sense at all, to resonate almost like the strings of a sitar, whereby an entire melody becomes revealed and new chords and octaves are discovered.

The message from a cosmic celebration engages the reader with thoughts of new possibilities and visions never before experienced. The reader may seek a navigational path of individuation through the chaotic and uncharted sea of life itself.

It is with joy that my friend celebrates your life with this rich volume. She invites you to write to her as you read her predictions, apply them to your own life, and engage in an inquiry that provides an opportunity to beautifully make a difference upon this precious planet.

Mounir (Jabriel) Hanafi III°

OVERVIEW OF SIGNIFICANT ASPECTS IN 2003

JANUARY

			PST	EST	
2nd,	Thursday	New Moon in Capricorn	12:23p	3:23p	
		Mercury goes retrograde	10:19a	1:19p	
3rd,	Friday	Venus square Uranus	12:36p	3:36p	
5th,	Sunday	Mercury sextile Venus	12:00a	3:00a	
7th,	Tuesday	Venus enters Sagittarius	5:08a	8:08a	
8th,	Wednesday	Mercury sextile Mars	4:18p	7:18p	
10th,	Friday	**First Qtr. Moon in Aries**	5:15a	8:15a	
11th,	Saturday	Sun conjunct Mercury	12:02p	3:02p	
		Mars square Uranus	8:44p	11:44p	
16th,	Thursday	Mars enters Sagittarius	8:23p	11:23p	
17th,	Friday	Venus sextile Neptune	2:36a	5:36a	
18th,	Saturday	**Full Moon in Cancer**	2:48a	5:48a	
20th,	Monday	Sun enters Aquarius	3:53a	6:53a	
21st,	Tuesday	Venus trine Jupiter	7:35a	10:35a	
22nd,	Wednesday	Mercury goes direct	5:08p	8:08p	
25th,	Saturday	**Last Qtr. Moon in Scorpio**	12:33a	3:33a	
		Venus conjunct Pluto	9:57a	12:57p	
		Sun sextile Mars	9:26p	12:26a	(1/26)
28th,	Tuesday	Venus opposite Saturn	4:13p	7:13p	
30th,	Thursday	Sun conjunct Neptune	3:34p	6:34p	

FEBRUARY

			PST	EST	
1st,	Saturday	**New Moon in Aquarius**	2:48a	5:48a	
2nd,	Sunday	**Candlemas / Imbolc**			
		Sun opposite Jupiter	1:12a	4:12a	
		Venus sextile Uranus	9:25a	12:25p	
		Mars sextile Neptune	1:40p	4:40p	
4th,	Tuesday	Venus enters Capricorn	5:27a	8:27a	
5th,	Wednesday	Mars trine Jupiter	11:25a	2:25p	
8th,	Saturday	Sun sextile Pluto	7:28a	10:28a	
9th,	Sunday	**First Qtr. Moon in Taurus**	3:11a	6:11a	
11th,	Tuesday	Sun trine Saturn	1:45a	4:45a	
12th,	Wednesday	Mercury enters Aquarius	5:00p	8:00p	
16th,	Sunday	**Full Moon in Leo**	3:51p	6:51p	
		Jupiter opposite Neptune	1:12a	4:12a	
		Mars conjunct Pluto	7:55a	10:55a	
17th,	Monday	Sun conjunct Uranus	1:36p	4:36p	
18th,	Tuesday	Sun enters Pisces	6:01p	9:01p	
20th,	Thursday	Mars opposite Saturn	6:13a	9:13a	
		Mercury opposite Jupiter	11:12a	2:12p	
		Mercury conjunct Neptune	10:55p	1:55a	(2/21)
21st,	Friday	Saturn goes direct	11:40p	2:40a	(2/22)
23rd,	Sunday	**Last Qtr. Moon in Sagittarius**	8:46a	11:46a	
26th,	Wednesday	Mercury sextile Pluto	10:32a	1:32p	
27th,	Thursday	Mercury trine Saturn	10:51p	1:51a	(2/28)

1

OVERVIEW OF SIGNIFICANT ASPECTS IN 2003

MARCH

			PST	EST
2nd,	Sunday	New Moon in Pisces	6:35p	9:35p
		Venus enters Aquarius	4:40a	7:40a
3rd,	Monday	Mars sextile Uranus	11:27p	2:27a (3/4)
4th,	Tuesday	Mercury conjunct Uranus	1:16p	4:16p
		Mars enters Capricorn	1:17p	4:17p
		Mercury enters Pisces	6:04p	9:04p
		Mercury sextile Mars	9:01p	12:01a (3/5)
9th,	Sunday	Venus opposite Jupiter	8:17p	11:17p
10th,	Monday	First Qtr. Moon in Gemini	11:15p	2:15a (3/11)
		Uranus enters Pisces	12:54p	3:54p
		Sun square Pluto	1:47p	4:47p
12th,	Wednesday	Venus conjunct Neptune	10:40a	1:40p
13th,	Thursday	Sun square Saturn	3:38a	6:38a
15th,	Saturday	Mercury square Pluto	11:17p	2:17a (3/16)
17th,	Monday	Mercury square Saturn	9:34a	12:34
18th,	Thursday	Full Moon in Virgo	2:35a	5:35a
19th,	Wednesday	Venus sextile Pluto	12:26a	3:26a
20th,	Thursday	Vernal Equinox		
		Sun enters Aries	5:00p	8:00p
21st,	Friday	Mercury enters Aries	4:16a	7:16a
		Venus trine Saturn	10:31a	1:31p
		Sun conjunct Mercury	3:35p	6:35p
22nd,	Saturday	Pluto goes retrograde	9:12p	12:12a (3/23)
24th,	Monday	Last Qtr. Moon in Capricorn	5:51 p	8:51p
25th,	Tuesday	Mercury trine Jupiter	6:27a	9:27a
27th,	Thursday	Mercury sextile Neptune	9:39a	12:39p
		Venus enters Pisces	10:14a	1:14p
28th,	Friday	Venus conjunct Uranus	4:43a	7:43a
		Mercury square Mars	6:12p	9:12p
		Sun trine Jupiter	9:31p	12:31a (3/29)
31st,	Monday	Mercury trine Pluto	1:12a	4:12a

APRIL

			PST	EST
1st,	Tuesday	New Moon in Aries	11:19a	2:19p
		Mercury sextile Saturn	8:29p	11:29p
2nd,	Wednesday	Sun sextile Neptune	12:34p	3:34p
3rd,	Thursday	Jupiter goes direct	7:03p	10:03p
5th,	Saturday	Mercury enters Taurus	6:38a	9:38a
6th,	Sunday	Daylight Savings time begins turn clocks ahead 1 hour at	2:00a	2:00a
		Mercury sextile Uranus	12:26p	4:26a (EDT)

			PDT	EDT
9th,	Wednesday	First Qtr. Moon in Cancer	4:40p	7:40p
		Sun trine Pluto	8:28p	11:28p
10th,	Thursday	Mercury square Jupiter	4:08a	7:08a
12th,	Saturday	Venus square Pluto	11:00p	2:00a (4/13)
13th,	Sunday	Mercury square Neptune	4:32p	7:32p
14th,	Monday	Sun sextile Saturn	1:37p	4:37p

OVERVIEW OF SIGNIFICANT ASPECTS IN 2003

APRIL (cont'd)

			PDT	EDT
16th,	Wednesday	**Full Moon in Libra**	12:36p	3:36p
		Venus square Saturn	11:51p	2:51a (4/17)
17th,	Thursday	Sun square Mars	6:55p	9:55p
20th,	Sunday	Sun enters Taurus	5:03a	8:03a
21st,	Monday	Venus sextile Mars	1:50a	4:50a
		Venus enters Aries	9:18a	12:18p
		Mars enters Aquarius	4:48p	7:48p
22nd,	Tuesday	Sun sextile Uranus	5:55a	8:55a
23rd,	Wednesday	**Last Qtr. Moon in Aquarius**	5:18a	8:18a
26th,	Saturday	Mercury goes retrograde	4:59a	7:59a
28th,	Monday	Venus trine Jupiter	8:19p	11:19p
29th,	Tuesday	Sun square Jupiter	12:32p	3:32p

MAY

1st,	Thursday	**Beltane / May Day**		
		New Moon In Taurus	5:15a	8:15a
2nd,	Friday	Venus sextile Neptune	6:02a	9:02a
3rd,	Saturday	Sun square Neptune	5:19p	8:19p
7th,	Wednesday	Sun conjunct Mercury	12:21a	3:21a
		Venus trine Pluto	10:33a	1:33p
8th,	Thursday	Mars opposite Jupiter	10:35a	1:35p
9th,	Friday	**First Qtr. Moon In Leo**	4:53a	7:53a
12th,	Monday	Mercury square Neptune	9:31a	12:31p
13th,	Tuesday	Mercury square Mars	10:20a	1:20p
14th,	Wednesday	Venus sextile Saturn	2:15a	5:15a
		Mars conjunct Neptune	7:37a	10:37a
15th,	Thursday	Lunar Eclipse		
		Full Moon in Scorpio	8:36p	11:36p
		Neptune goes retrograde	5:50p	8:50p
16th,	Friday	Venus enters Taurus	3:58a	6:58a
18th,	Sunday	Venus sextile Uranus	8:38a	11:38a
19th,	Monday	Mercury square Jupiter	4:47p	7:47p
20th,	Tuesday	Mercury goes direct	12:33a	3:33a
21st,	Wednesday	Sun enters Gemini	4:12a	7:12a
22nd,	Thursday	**Last Qtr. Moon In Pisces**	5:31p	8:31p
23rd,	Friday	Mercury square Jupiter	6:26p	9:26p
24th,	Saturday	Sun square Uranus	12:35a	3:35a
		Mars sextile Pluto	11:52p	2:52a (5/25)
26th,	Monday	Venus square Jupiter	12:29a	3:29a
		Mercury conjunct Venus	5:04p	8:04p
27th,	Tuesday	Venus square Neptune	12:06a	3:06a
		Mercury square Neptune	9:18a	12:18p
30th,	Friday	Solar Eclipse		
		New Moon In Gemini	9:20a	12:20a (5/31)

JUNE

2nd,	Monday	Jupiter opposite Neptune	7:58p	10:58p

OVERVIEW OF SIGNIFICANT ASPECTS IN 2003

JUNE (cont'd)

			PDT	EDT
3rd, Tuesday		Saturn enters Cancer	6:32p	9:32p
		Sun trine Neptune	7:28p	10:28p
4th, Wednesday		Sun sextile Jupiter	12:13a	3:13a
5th, Thursday		Venus square Mars	4:54p	7:54p
6th, Friday		Uranus goes retrograde	11:59p	2:59a (6/7)
7th, Saturday		**First Qtr. Moon in Virgo**	1:28p	4:28p
9th, Monday		Sun opposite Pluto	1:41p	4:41p
		Venus enters Gemini	8:32p	11:32p
10th, Tuesday		Mercury square Mars	10:49p	1:49a (6/11)
12th, Thursday		Venus square Uranus	3:54a	6:54a
		Mercury enters Gemini	6:34p	9:34p
14th, Saturday		**Full Moon in Sagittarius**	4:16a	7:16a
		Mercury square Uranus	3:03p	6:03p
16th, Monday		Mars enters Pisces	7:25p	10:25p
20th, Friday		Venus trine Neptune	9:57a	12:57p
		Mercury trine Neptune	1:36p	4:46p
		Mercury conjunct Venus	8:53p	11:53p
21st, Saturday		**Last Qtr. Moon in Pisces**	7:45a	10:45a
		Summer Solstice		
		Sun enters Cancer	12:11p	3:11p
22nd, Sunday		Mercury sextile Jupiter	10:55a	1:55p
		Mars trine Saturn	9:17p	12:17a (6/23)
23rd, Monday		Mercury opposite Pluto	9:44a	12:44p
		Venus sextile Jupiter	11:07a	2:07p
		Mars conjunct Uranus	1:03p	4:03p
24th, Tuesday		Sun conjunct Saturn	6:39a	9:39a
		Sun trine Uranus	8:06a	11:06a
		Saturn trine Uranus	4:34p	7:34p
		Venus opposite Pluto	6:57p	9:57p
		Sun trine Mars	8:55p	11:55p
29th, Sunday		**New Moon in Cancer**	11:39a	2:39p
		Mercury enters Cancer	3:17a	6:17a
30th, Monday		Mercury trine Uranus	8:26a	11:26a
		Mercury conjunct Saturn	6:14p	9:14p

JULY

			PDT	EDT
1st,	Tuesday	Jupiter trine Pluto	5:40a	8:40a
		Mercury trine Mars	5:06p	8:06p
4th,	Friday	Venus enters Cancer	10:39a	1:39p
5th,	Saturday	Sun conjunct Mercury	3:21a	6:21a
6th,	Sunday	**First Qtr. Moon in Libra**	7:32p	10:32p
		Venus trine Uranus	11:19a	2:19p
8th,	Tuesday	Venus conjunct Saturn	1:30a	4:30a
11th,	Friday	Venus trine Mars	12:28a	3:28a
13th,	Sunday	**Full Moon in Capricorn**	12:21p	3:21p
		Mercury enters Leo	5:10a	8:10a
19th,	Saturday	Mercury opposite Neptune	2:02p	5:02p
21st,	Monday	**Last Qtr. Moon in Aries**	12:01a	3:01a

OVERVIEW OF SIGNIFICANT ASPECTS IN 2003

JULY (cont'd)

			PDT	EDT
22nd,	Tuesday	Mercury trine Pluto	2:36p	5:36p
		Sun enters Leo	11:04p	2:04a (7/23)
25th,	Friday	Mercury conjunct Jupiter	8:17p	11:17p
28th,	Monday	**New Moon in Leo**	11:53p	2:53a (7/29)
		Venus enters Leo	9:25p	12:25a (7/29)
29th,	Tuesday	Mars goes retrograde	12:37a	3:37a
30th,	Wednesday	Mercury enters Virgo	7:06a	10:06a
31st,	Thursday	Mercury opposite Uranus	11:22a	2:22p

AUGUST

1st,	Friday	**Lammas**		
4th,	Monday	Sun opposite Neptune	7:01a	10:01a
		Mercury sextile Saturn	8:12p	11:12p
5th,	Tuesday	**First Qtr. Moon In Scorpio**	12:28a	3:28a
6th,	Wednesday	Mercury opposite Mars	6:13a	9:13a
7th,	Thursday	Venus opposite Neptune	9:23a	12:23p
10th,	Sunday	Sun trine Pluto	1:39a	4:39a
11th,	Monday	**Full Moon In Aquarius**	9:48p	12:48a (8/12)
		Venus trine Pluto	10:17p	1:17a (8/12)
12th,	Tuesday	Mars trine Saturn	7:56p	10:56p
		Mercury square Pluto	8:00p	11:00p
18th,	Monday	Sun conjunct Venus	11:04a	2:04p
19th,	Tuesday	**Last Qtr. Moon In Taurus**	5:48p	8:48p
21st,	Thursday	Venus conjunct Jupiter	3:23a	6:23a
22nd,	Friday	Sun conjunct Jupiter	3:08a	6:08a
		Venus enters Virgo	4:36a	7:36a
		Venus opposite Uranus	9:47p	12:47a (8/23)
23rd,	Saturday	Sun enters Virgo	6:08a	9:08a
24th,	Sunday	Sun opposite Uranus	3:01a	6:01a
26th,	Tuesday	Venus opposite Mars	3:18p	6:18p
27th,	Wednesday	**New Moon In Virgo**	10:26a	1:26p
		Jupiter enters Virgo	2:27a	5:27a
28th,	Thursday	Mercury goes retrograde	6:42a	9:42a
		Sun opposite Mars	10:59a	1:59p
		Pluto goes direct	8:34p	11:34p
29th,	Friday	Jupiter opposite Uranus	9:38p	12:38a (8/30)
30th,	Saturday	Venus sextile Saturn	4:23p	7:23p

SEPTEMBER

3rd,	Wednesday	**First Qtr. Moon in Sagittarius**	5:34a	8:34a
		Sun sextile Saturn	11:48a	2:48p
5th,	Friday	Venus square Pluto	2:29a	5:29a
7th,	Sunday	Mars opposite Jupiter	1:01p	4:01p
		Mercury conjunct Venus	10:35p	1:35a (9/8)
10th,	Wednesday	**Full Harvest Moon in Pisces**	9:36a	12:36p
		Sun square Pluto	2:34a	5:34a
		Sun conjunct Mercury	6:57p	9:57p
11th,	Thursday	Mercury square Pluto	10:46p	1:46p

OVERVIEW OF SIGNIFICANT ASPECTS IN 2003

SEPTEMBER (cont'd)

			PDT	EDT
14th,	Sunday	Uranus enters Aquarius	8:48p	11:48p
15th,	Monday	Venus enters Libra	8:58a	11:58a
18th,	Thursday	**Last Qtr. Moon in Gemini**	12:03p	3:03p
20th,	Saturday	Mercury goes direct	1:53a	4:53a
23rd,	Tuesday	**Autumnal Equinox**		
		Sun enters Libra	3:47a	6:47a
		Venus trine Neptune	10:08p	1:08a (9/24)
25th,	Thursday	**New Moon in Libra**		
		Moon conjunct Sun	8:09p	11:09p
		Venus square Saturn	8:20a	11:20a
27th,	Saturday	Mars goes direct	12:52a	3:52a
28th,	Sunday	Mercury square Pluto	9:28a	12:28p
29th,	Monday	Venus sextile Pluto	10:50a	1:50p

OCTOBER

2nd,	Thursday	**First Qtr. Moon in Capricorn**		12:09p	3:09p
3rd,	Friday	Sun trine Neptune		8:23p	11:23p
6th,	Monday	Sun square Saturn	6:40a	9:40a	
		Mercury enters Libra	6:28p	9:28p	
8th,	Wednesday	Venus trine Uranus		9:47p	12:27a (10/9)
9th,	Thursday	Venus enters Scorpio		11:56a	2:56p
10th,	Friday	**Full Moon in Aries**		12:27a	3:27a
		Venus trine Mars		1:32p	4:32p
11th,	Saturday	Sun sextile Pluto		4:31a	7:31a
12th,	Sunday	Mercury trine Neptune		6:57p	9:57p
14th,	Tuesday	Mercury square Saturn		7:49a	10:49a
17th,	Friday	Mercury sextile Pluto		1:25a	4:25a
		Venus square Neptune		8:47p	11:47p
18th,	Saturday	**Last Qtr. Moon in Cancer**		5:31a	8:31a
		Venus sextile Jupiter		2:32a	5:32a
20th,	Monday	Venus trine Saturn		2:48a	5:48a
22nd,	Wednesday	Sun trine Uranus		1:17p	4:17p
		Neptune goes direct		6:55p	9:55p
23rd,	Thursday	Sun enters Scorpio		1:09p	4:09p
		Mercury trine Uranus		1:56p	4:56p
24th,	Friday	Mercury enters Scorpio		4:20a	7:20a
25th,	Saturday	**New Moon in Scorpio**		5:50a	8:50a
		Sun conjunct Mercury		2:58a	5:58a
25th,	Saturday	Saturn goes retrograde		4:43p	7:43p
26th,	Sunday	**Daylight Saving Time ends**		**PST**	**EST**
27th,	Monday	Mercury trine Mars		4:29p	7:29p
30th,	Thursday	Sun trine Mars		7:55a	10:55a
		Mercury square Neptune		11:46a	2:46p
31st,	Friday	**Halloween / Samhain**			
		First Qtr. Moon in Aquarius		8:25p	11:25p

OVERVIEW OF SIGNIFICANT ASPECTS IN 2003

NOVEMBER
			PST	EST
1st, Saturday		Mercury sextile Jupiter	4:48a	7:48a
		Mercury trine Saturn	5:17a	8:17a
		Jupiter sextile Saturn	9:11a	12:11p
		Venus square Uranus	4:42p	7:42p
2nd, Sunday		Venus enters Sagittarius	1:42p	4:42p
		Sun square Neptune	10:56p	1:56a (11/3)
5th, Wednesday		Sun trine Saturn	3:24p	6:24p
6th, Thursday		Sun sextile Jupiter	12:33p	3:33p
8th, Saturday		Lunar Eclipse		
		Full Moon in Taurus	5:13p	8:13p
		Uranus goes direct	4:45a	7:45a
11th, Tuesday		Venus sextile Neptune	12:36a	3:36a
		Mercury square Uranus	6:04a	9:04a
		Mercury enters Sagittarius	11:20p	2:20a (11/12)
12th, Wednesday		Venus square Mars	9:27a	12:27p
13th, Thursday		Mars trine Saturn	9:26p	12:26a (11/14)
14th, Friday		Venus square Jupiter	7:34p	10:34p
16th, Sunday		**Last Quarter Moon in Leo**	8:15p	11:15p
17th, Monday		Venus conjunct Pluto	5:48p	8:48p
18th, Tuesday		Mercury sextile Neptune	11:48p	2:48a (11/19)
20th, Thursday		Mars opposite Jupiter	5:59a	8:59a
21st, Friday		Sun square Uranus	9:13a	12:13p
22nd, Saturday		Sun enters Sagittarius	9:44a	12:44p
		Mercury square Jupiter	7:10p	10:10p
23rd, Sunday		Solar Eclipse		
		New Moon in Sagittarius	2:59p	5:59p
		Mercury square Mars	7:14p	10:14p
24th, Monday		Mercury conjunct Pluto	6:12p	9:12p
25th, Tuesday		Venus sextile Uranus	10:20p	1:20a (11/26)
26th, Wednesday		Mars square Pluto	3:17p	6:17p
		Venus enters Capricorn	5:07p	8:07p
30th, Sunday		**First Quarter Moon in Pisces**	9:16a	12:16p

DECEMBER
1st,	Monday	Mercury sextile Uranus	9:53p	12:53a (12/2)
2nd,	Tuesday	Mercury enters Capricorn	1:34p	4:34p
3rd,	Wednesday	Sun sextile Neptune	3:35a	6:35a
6th,	Saturday	Venus opposite Saturn	4:03a	7:03a
8th,	Monday	**Full Moon in Gemini**	12:37p	3:37p
10th,	Wednesday	Sun square Jupiter	2:59a	5:59a
11th,	Thursday	Venus trine Jupiter	6:22a	9:22a
		Sun conjunct Pluto	9:26p	12:26a (12/12)
13th,	Saturday	Mercury opposite Saturn	6:14a	9:14a
16th,	Tuesday	**Last Qtr. Moon in Virgo**	9:42a	12:42p
		Mars enters Aries	5:24a	8:24a
		Mercury-trine-Jupiter-Non-Exact	N/A	N/A
17th,	Wednesday	Mercury goes retrograde	8:01a	11:01a
20th,	Saturday	Venus enters Aquarius	10:33p	1:33a (12/21)

7

OVERVIEW OF SIGNIFICANT ASPECTS IN 2003

DECEMBER (cont'd)

			PST	EST
21st. Sunday		**Winter Solstice**		
		Sun sextile Uranus	3:33p	6:33p
		Mercury opposite Saturn	10:35p	1:35a (12/22)
		Sun enters Capricorn	11:04p	2:04a (12/22)
22nd.	Monday	Jupiter-square-Pluto-Non-Exact	N/A	N/A
23rd.	Tuesday	**New Moon in Capricorn**	1:43a	4:43a
25th.	Thursday	Venus sextile Mars	5:29a	8:29a
26th.	Friday	Mercury square Mars	12:53a	3:53a
		Sun conjunct Mercury	5:11p	8:11p
29th.	Monday	Sun square Mars	9:57p	12:57a (12/30)
30th.	Tuesday	**First Qtr. Moon in Aries**	2:03a	5:03a
		Uranus enters Pisces	1:15a	4:15a
		Venus conjunct Neptune	9:24a	12:24p
		Mercury sextile Uranus	11:31a	2:31p
		Mercury enters Sagittarius	11:52a	2:52p
31st.	Wednesday	Sun opposite Saturn	12:57p	3:57p

CAPRICORN

Key phrase "I USE "
Cardinal Earth Sign
Symbol : The Goat

December 21st, 2003 — January 20th, 2004

January 1st Wednesday
New Year's Day

Moon in Sagittarius goes V/C	9:23 a.m. PST	12:23 p.m. EST
Moon enters Capricorn	3:42 p.m. PST	6:42 p.m. EST

Mercury sextile Venus begins (see 1/4)

We kick off this New Year with a darkly waning Sagittarius Moon going void-of-course for a number of hours throughout the day. At this time of dwindling lunar light, we are closer, practically on the brink of a New Moon, set to take place tomorrow. This is a dark time when our disquieted moods are sparked with flashes of vision, of hope for inspiration and a fresh outlook on life. For some this will serve as the right time to rest and listen in quiet stillness. For others there is no escaping the hyper-activity of holiday clamour and celebration. All the while, the ever popular void-of-course lunar energy creates confusion, forgetfulness, tendencies to be spacey, countless contingencies, loads of traffic, and a general quality of failing to notice important details while our moods are so easily steeped in minor distractions. Perhaps it is best to just go with the flow of the parade and party spirit, even though trying to organize the effort falls by the wayside. This holiday time is perfect for some and downright hell for others. Sorrow, illness and sadness is most difficult to face when darkness shadows the heart in the light of celebration. Deeper within the heart, the spark of life still glows. Moon in Sagittarius emphasizes the need to go beyond the usual boundaries and reach out to new insights and visions. Sagittarius focuses on expansion and captivates our interests with a bigger picture of how to expand despite the set-backs of decreasing light. Later on when the Moon enters Capricorn, the basic mood of the evening is somewhat solemn, rather serious and fraught with deep concerns. There is an air of determination with each matter under consideration. Bringing in the New Year takes a bold quality of persistence.

January 2nd Thursday
New Moon in Capricorn
Moon conjunct Sun   12:23 p.m. PST   3:23 p.m. EST
Mercury goes retrograde   10:19 a.m. PST   1:19 p.m. EST
Mars square Uranus begins (see 1/11)
Saturn opposite Pluto begins (see 4/26)

Capricorn New Moon (Moon conjunct Sun) encourages us to put out a strong and determined chin towards progress. This is a good time to initiate long term goals and to incorporate a new daily habit that will have satisfying and long lasting results. How appropriate this is for a New Year! Nurture your long-term goals with the spirit of determination. New Moon in Capricorn urges us to create productivity in our life and aim for new heights for ourselves despite the mishaps of the past. This is a demarcation period, a time where we often set a precedent in achieving progress that previously appeared very challenging. On the other hand, some find this lunar and solar conjunction foreboding and wickedly monotonous. What? Work? Now? What about recovering from the holidays? The cost of those holidays now calls to our attention the incredible clean up work (physical and financial) that the past has left us. As if all that isn't enough, now Mercury is about to go retrograde for three weeks, and this is no time to create goals and expect to launch them successfully! Yet we have got to get to work, even though we may not feel like doing it. This Moon reminds us of the importance and the immensity of that work, plain and simple. Capricorn is diligent to the core and never quits making this an excellent time to establish important personal, career, and group oriented goals and objectives. This is a grounding time for us, as much as it is uplifting and also challenging at the same time. Diligence. Persistence. Work. Patience. Thoroughly committed, tried, trodden and true is the Capricorn spirit.

Mercury retrograde in Capricorn (Mercury retrograde Jan. 2 – 22.) This New Year starts off with Mercury going retrograde, meaning that it will appear to move backwards through the degrees of the zodiac from our geocentric view as it turns around the Sun. Mercury will go retrograde four times this year, with each retrograde period occurring for approximately three weeks. In this year 2003, it is the three earth signs of the zodiac in which Mercury goes retrograde, ending with a fourth retrograde period moving into the year 2004. As Mercury goes retrograde through an earth sign, it tends to especially affect communications concerning the material things of our lives. Likely disruptions include the labelling and delivery of packages, the transfer and handling of funds, the sorting and moving of goods, the charging of accounts, and interpretations of business deals and construction projects. This may be a particularly hard time to keep track of goods during moves. Whether moving home or business, give the movers clear instructions on the correct address! Saturn rules Capricorn, so a poor sense of timing in the relaying of information, or a serious tone to communications, may cause all of those monotonous misunderstandings to be difficult to endure. Pay particular attention to what you promise and commit yourself to, as Mercury in Capricorn can bring on a manipulative tone to communications. Be aware of the tendency to be talked into doing something that might disrupt one's own harmony or personal mind-set. Ask people to confirm or repeat instructions, so that you're sure your message was properly received, agreed to, and understood. For the next three weeks it is best to make communication attempts more than once or twice. Be persistent and be patient. Don't worry about the delays. There is eventually a logical explanation with Mercury related setbacks, and things will right themselves with time.

January 3rd Friday
Quandrantids Meteors
Moon in Capricorn goes V/C	4:56 p.m. PST	7:56 p.m. EST
Moon enters Aquarius	7:56 p.m. PST	10:56 p.m. EST
Venus square Uranus	12:36 p.m. PST	3:36 p.m. EST

Throughout the day, the young virile goat energy of the newly waxing Capricorn moon kicks our senses into a serious drive to work out pent up concerns and problems. There is a determined move to get jobs tackled and tasks and deeds done. Later on, the Moon goes void-of-course for a couple hours and the determined drive to get things done is stifled by minor contingencies. The serious tone of mood fades away in the evening as the Moon enters Aquarius and our moods are opened up to new thoughts and ideas about making some progress. This makes it much easier to reflect on the feats and accomplishments of the day.

Venus square Uranus (occurring Dec 28, 2002 – Jan. 9, 2003.) Venus, the planet that governs love and magnetism, is undergoing the square aspect to Uranus, the planet of chaos and disruption. It may be difficult for love (Venus) to flourish in a spontaneous and carefree fashion, and there may be obstacles placed between love and freedom. This is a difficult time for rebels and revolutionaries to find love, or feel loved. Be careful not to become too personally affronted by these explosive or radical love matters. This influence may be testing the power of your love to withstand chaos. Be assured in self-love and empower affection with personal integrity. People are changing at a rapid rate and it is essential to let love take its course concerning issues of personal freedom. Applying pressure only increases the force of an explosion.

January 4th Saturday
Moon in Aquarius

The Moon is newly waxing in the sign of Aquarius, and there is a newness in the air that stirs us to reach out and be connected to it all. A young Aquarius Moon now touches our moods with a positive and strong appeal for human rights. Aquarius Moon reminds us that we need to face the issues that most vitally threaten our freedom. There is a spark of political controversy in the air with every newly waxing Aquarius Moon. Remember to enjoy the freedoms that we now have and share and continue to hold precious. Protect and uphold these rights! The more our rights are exercised the stronger they become. The benefits of good deeds will increase one's good karma threefold.

January 5th Sunday
Moon in Aquarius
Mercury sextile Venus   12:00 a.m. PST   3:00 a.m. EST

Moon in Aquarius opens us to the awareness of our own built-in genius as human beings. Deep thought is stirred and the magnified desire for innovation and clarity brings out the radical and less subtle aspects of our moods. Most of our western system is now based on technology. When technology throws curve balls, the dance to set things strait can be tedious. Once more, all of this can happen, even on a Sunday. Meanwhile since Mercury is newly retrograde (see Jan. 2nd), communication related problems and setbacks are starting to become more apparent . Sometimes it pays to take the more practical approach, even though our moods may lead us into uncertain terrain, logic will eventually prevail.

Mercury sextile Venus (occurring Jan. 1 – 7.) This aspect brings good news and opportunities concerning love, music, and the arts. There are opportunities to sell art or valuables. This is a good time to get the message of love across where it is needed most. This is surely a time to share love messages and spread them like seeds. Love will come back to sustain the heart and this is a good time to call it to the attention of those people we treasure.

January 6th Monday
Moon in Aquarius goes V/C   12:44 a.m. PST   3:44 a.m. EST
Moon enters Pisces   2:57 a.m. PST   5:57 a.m. EST
Mercury sextile Mars begins (see 1/8)

Overnight the Moon enters Pisces and our moods shift into a more flexible expression as we ease up on mental tension. Pisces Moon puts us in touch with our intuitive sense and suddenly our language is adaptable to so much more perception. With this perception we talk and communicate in a rhythmic flow of dance, pantomime, and the use of symbols. There are answers in focusing on the use of symbols. There is an art in the use of light and space. The density of matter creates an atmosphere, a mood within which we transform ourselves. This is the art of applying the language of symbols. Symbols represent our beliefs. Clothes, jewellery, and material objects that we possess are a part of this language on a surface level, and we must choose how to present these symbolic gestures of ourselves to the world. Choose your symbols and apply your language well: it is a reflection of the self. Waxing Pisces Moon encourages us to build on our imagination and to brighten the possibilities for greater inspiration. Activating the imagination enhances the mood.

January 7th Tuesday
Moon in Pisces
Venus enters Sagittarius   5:08 a.m. PST   8:08 a.m. EST

Pisces Moon entices our attraction to art and music as well as escapism and dreamy distractions. Pisces Moon, now waxing, creates the opportunity for many to access an internal part of their own being. This is a time of reverie and reflection. Pisces Moon puts us in touch with our belief systems and the trials that we must endure individually concerning our own particular beliefs. For some, there is a creative process unfolding, for others there is a battle going on with addictive behavior or the need to escape. For most, the dreamlike quality of this time drifts in a timeless fashion, connecting us with our past as well as showing us the future as we open ourselves up in the now.

Venus enters Sagittarius (occurring Jan. 7 – Feb. 4.) The planet of love and the expression of affection now travels through the sign of Sagittarius, bringing out a love of the arts, philosophy, travel, cultural exploration, outer space, and sports achievements. Expect an extroverted spirit of camaraderie among people in general, spreading affection beyond the usual bounds. Sagittarius people will find their affections and love life strong, and relationships can be enhanced and made whole as Venus crosses over their natal sun. Pisces and Virgo people may notice that love related focal points are causing tension in their personal lives with Venus squaring their natal sun at this time. Gemini people may be made acutely aware of their personal need for love and beauty in their lives while Venus now opposes their natal sun. On the other hand, it may be best to take measures not to oppress our busy minded Gemini folks with petty love related spats while Venus is in Sagittarius. There are so many variations possible on the themes that love reveals; don't sweat the small stuff.

January 8th Wednesday
Moon in Pisces goes V/C   3:55 a.m. PST   6:55 a.m. EST
Moon enters Aries   1:15 p.m. PST   4:15 p.m. EST
Mercury sextile Mars   4:18 p.m. PST   7:18 p.m. EST

Throughout this morning the void-of-course moon in Pisces creates a very spacey and blithely uninhibited quality of expression to our moods. There is a tendency to forget things and get started off slowly. By early PST / late EST afternoon the moon enters Aries and the general course of our moods become more upbeat and self confident. Waxing Aries Moon generates energy and gives many of us the impetus to carry on with personal needs and projects requiring attention.

Mercury sextile Mars (occurring Jan. 6 – 10.) Clear communications concerning actions being taken may make this a superb time to seek employment. Mercury sextile Mars brings out opportunities that can be received, recognized, communicated and acted upon. News or information may lead to the taking of immediate action. People are likely to back up their statements with action during this period, and it would be a good time to apply diplomacy. Bear in mind that Mercury is currently retrograde and communications have the potential of being misunderstood. This aspect will repeat on March 4th with Mercury direct, helping to reconcile (through action) any information that may have been misinterpreted at present. In the meantime, be sure to cover all bases regarding communications before taking action during this aspect. Applying active communication does have the potential for a very favorable outcome.

January 9th Thursday
Moon in Aries

Throughout the day the Moon remains in Aries and the general course of our moods are outgoing and forward looking. There may be a bit of anxiety in the air, possibly the need to get out and about is affecting our moods, and this is a common symptom of what we often call "winter fever." Restless and anxious souls are not always willing to be patient and as a result may be somewhat accident prone in their haste. Winter activities do not have to be dull. Some folks are just reacting to the post holiday quiet. As a result people may appear testy and unsettled and may take their hasty moods out on others. It is just a symptom of what some people experience this time of year, particularly with Moon half full in Aries.

January 10th Friday
First Quarter Moon in Aries
Moon square Sun	5:15 a.m. PST	8:15 a.m. EST
Moon in Aries goes V/C	7:10 p.m. PST	10:10 p.m. EST

First Quarter Moon in Aries. Waxing Aries Moon generally activates our moods and the first quarter moon of Aries inspires our moods in an active, upbeat manner. This is the time to get in tune with personal levels of energy, strength and vitality. There is a self starter energy in the air and the active ones among us are on the prowl. Aries Moon brings on an expression of courageous vigor, as well as a sense of bold adventure. As a general rule moods are marked by confidence and sometimes cantankerous forcefulness. First Quarter Moon in Aries brings on a certain kind of drive to make a lasting impression. Moon in Aries squaring to the sun in Capricorn serves as a good time to apply diligence to your inspired abilities.

January 11th Saturday
Moon enters Taurus	1:48 a.m. PST	4:48 a.m. EST
Sun conjunct Mercury	12:02 p.m. PST	3:02 p.m. EST
Mars square Uranus	8:44 p.m. PST	11:44 p.m. EST
Jupiter opposite Neptune begins (see 2/16)		

Overnight the Moon enters Taurus and the general course of moods become settled on practical concerns and desires. Some may be hung up on overspending and may feel the crunch of needing to be more prudent. Taurus Moon often brings out financial concerns and focuses. Others are feeling indulgent, and the need to relax and be absorbed in the luxuries of life brings out the indolent side of our moods. Throughout today the waxing Taurus Moon focuses our moods on beauty and pleasure, and creates joy in the practical nature of simplistic beauty as well as functionality. Those who didn't get what they really needed for Christmas are sure to feel the need by now. Taurus Moon emphasizes the importance of *having*, particularly having those elements and practical needs of our life which serve as a vital part of existence. What we don't have that we truly need is likely to be noticed today and this is a good time to take care of practical needs.

Sun conjunct Mercury in Capricorn (occurring Jan. 8 – 14.) This aspect which creates a much more thoughtful, communicative, and expressive year ahead for those Capricorn born people celebrating birthdays Jan. 8th to the 14th this year. This is your time (Birthday Capricorns) to record ideas, relay important messages, and pay close attention to your enterprising thoughts as they are touched by Mercury, creating the urge to speak and be heard. Your thoughts now will reveal a great deal about who you are and where you are heading in the year to come.

Mars square Uranus (occurring Jan. 2 – 21.) The potential for harsh action is very strong with this aspect, and we may encounter such disasters as earthquakes, the fires of war backfiring, arson, explosive tempers, and possibly even atrocious hate crimes against minorities and underdogs. Of course, hard lessons concerning explosives are also very possible with this aspect so be especially careful to avoid accidents of any kind! It is wise to completely avoid extremely risky undertakings that may rock the boat of fiery activity while Mars is square Uranus.

January 12th Sunday
Moon in Taurus

Taking in a picture of absolute beauty brings wonders. The sun is in Capricorn and the Moon is in Taurus; there is an earthy expression of awareness penetrating our moods and concerns. Throughout the day, the waxing Taurus Moon focuses our moods on material luxuries and the need to create beauty and comfortable surroundings. On the other hand, the Capricorn sun persists in keeping us busy pressing through the winter boldly and with determination towards making achievements happen in our lives. This is a good time to focus on making financial breakthroughs and to tackle money management with some clarity and purpose. There will be much on which to focus concerning money matters in the months to come. As for now, this is the time to organize a working business plan and to apply our monetary efforts with diligent care. Don't forget, Mercury is retrograde in Capricorn until the 22nd. It may be best to keep plans simple and to postpone communicating complex ideas and launching big business plans until after that time.

January 13th Monday

Moon in Taurus goes V/C	9:44 a.m. PST	12:44 p.m. EST
Moon enters Gemini	2:08 p.m. PST	5:08 p.m. EST

Venus sextile Neptune begins (see 1/17)
Sun sextile Mars begins (see 1/25)

The moods of the day start off practical and clear but eventually begin to try our patience and sense of endurance. For several hours the moon is void-of-course during the day. There may be a midday phase of frequently misplacing objects, of hesitating, and perhaps for some folks, of sheer laziness occurring. When the Moon enters Gemini, moods begin to pick up with more talk and discussion. Gemini Moon brings out the need to talk about what's going on. By evening, a full fledged series of conversations begin to put the day into perspective. Interactive moods open up frivolous and curious thoughts and ideas.

January 14th Tuesday
Moon in Gemini

The steadily waxing Gemini Moon puts our focus on communicating and receiving information. Activities center on writing, speeches, conversations, and secretarial duties. On the surface a lot of the information drifts past our ears. Through seemingly meaningless detail, eventually becoming more significant, useful and practical information is obtained. Sifting through details seems costly for some, but not to the trained investigator who is not hasty to draw conclusions, and just connects all the pieces of the puzzle wherever they snap into place. As you go along, the details of the day will fall into place swiftly. Be careful not to overly tax the nervous system with too much coffee, caffeine products or sugar. Remember also, Mercury is retrograde; this means there is a lot of misinformation going around. Anything worth understanding correctly requires more careful study, particularly at this time.

January 15th Wednesday

Moon in Gemini goes V/C	6:16 p.m. PST	9:16 p.m. EST
Moon enters Cancer	11:56 p.m. PST	2:56 a.m. (1/16) EST

Throughout the morning and day Gemini Moon brings dual viewpoints to the foreground of our thoughts, and represents a prime opportunity to express our thoughts freely through writing, speaking, and holding discussions. Gemini Moon brings out our curious and communicative side, and there is a lot of talk and social focus taking place. A myriad of details requires concentrated work. The need to be in more places at once requires the clarity to wisely choose how time is spent. By evening the Moon goes void-of-course creating mental havoc. There is a tendency to become preoccupied, resulting in slow-moving progress and general confusion. Mindless activities are probably the safest.

January 16th Thursday

Moon in Cancer
Mars enters Sagittarius   8:23 p.m. PST   11:23 p.m. EST
Venus trine Jupiter begins (see 1/21)

The Moon is in Cancer and, throughout the entire day, gears up our senses with deep emotional expressions, and focuses our attention on nurturing and instinctual urges. This serves as a good time to brighten up the home and make it feel more comfortable. Deep feelings run through our moods with a strongly waxing Moon in Cancer, and there may be a tendency for some people to be distracted and moody. For the most part this is simply a time when many of us need a little more reassurance and love.

Mars enters Sagittarius (occurring Jan. 16 – March 4.) Mars in Sagittarius will affect our lives by giving us great shifts of energy and vitality and, in some cases, will bring about anguish and anger where life situations aren't harmonious. For the next six weeks, people (especially Sagittarians) are likely to apply some extra energy towards creative and outgoing projects. Mars is a fiery influence, and Sagittarius serves this energy very well as a mutable fire sign. Philosophers, athletes and travelers are particularly open to experiencing vast amounts of output and energy as the forces of Mars activate the Sagittarian perspective. For a large portion of 2001 Mars was in Sagittarius stirring up war-like events until the week of 9-11 when Mars (the god of war) proceeded into Capricorn - the week the unthinkable happened. For all of 2002, Mars did not pass through Sagittarius at all. It was over that fateful year of 2001 that Mars in Sagittarius rocked and stirred our philosophical outlook. Active philosophies were suddenly stifled by the act of war, which forced many of us to examine our feelings of anger around the issues and reasons that brought war to North America. Mars in Capricorn then forced us to take our actions and reactions very seriously. As for now, Mars in Sagittarius will no doubt stir more philosophical debate over the actions taking place in the world at this point in time.

January 17th Friday

Moon in Cancer
Full Moon Eve
Venus sextile Neptune   2:36 a.m. PST   5:36 a.m. EST

Mother Moon is at home in the sign of Cancer, and while it waxes up this evening on a Full Moon Eve, it builds up our emotional core with a sense of fullness and depth. Whatever feelings are happening around a full Cancer Moon tend to be amplified. This means that if pent up feelings have escalated to uncontrollable heights, they're gonna blow like a whale's spout! While Mercury is retrograde and feelings are running strong, it is best not to push the envelope by saying the wrong thing. When in doubt, keep silent, but be sure to find a safe outlet for those pent up emotions. The emotional realm is full and round like the Moon, and it is best not to challenge people too much concerning their comfort zones. Cancer Moon emphasizes the nurturing qualities of mom and the comfort and safety of the home environment. Elaborate foods and "comfort foods" are emphasized. Cancer Moon puts us in touch with the archetype of the Mother: the nurturer, provider and emotional tone setter. Those who have trying relationships with their Mother (generally speaking), have a difficult time with the moodiness of Full Cancer Moon. Self-love, reconciliation, and reacquaintance with one's true needs help a person acknowledge and come to terms with the kinds of feelings that can surface through this energy. This also allows us to serve our own (or other's) maternal needs. The Moon is Full this very eve, this is a time to celebrate the bounty of our emotional pleasures, and to honor Mother Moon in all her splendour. Happy Full Mooning!

Venus sextile Neptune (occurring Jan. 13 - 21.) Love, art, beauty and feminine expression enhance spirituality. Love is given an opportunity to infiltrate in a spiritually enhanced fashion. Venus sextile Neptune is a good time to focus love on spiritual beliefs. This aspect can have a strong healing effect on the soul, and reaches into the feminine parts of our being with a calm fortitude. This serves as an excellent aspect to reach out spiritually to those we love as well as to our spirit guides. This aspect also holds the potential for one to realize the profound beauty and the depths of which true love is capable. Faith and belief in love matters may be rewarded at this time, and love matters may be enhanced where similar beliefs are shared. This is a time to persist with loving expression and devotion towards one's beliefs.

January 18th Saturday
Full Moon in Cancer
Moon opposite Sun   2:48 a.m. PST   5:48 a.m. EST
Moon in Cancer goes V/C   2:48 a.m. PST   5:48 a.m. EST
Moon enters Leo   6:29 a.m. PST   9:29 a.m. EST

The **Full Cancer Moon** (Moon opposite Sun) emphasizes Mom and maternal energy throughout the land, and there is a tendency for people to be moody and somewhat preoccupied with their feelings. Although today marks the Full Moon, it happened overnight and most of its energy was unleashed last night. This morning the Moon enters Leo and the general course of our moods become self absorbed. Family related events and children are emphasized, but as the Moon now begins to wane, the energy level, although upbeat, is somewhat lazy and kicked back.

January 19th Sunday
Moon in Leo

It's a lazy Leo Moon Sunday, some are lazy by the sheer fact that they still exhibit signs of a post Full Moon lunar hangover. Today is the last day of the Sun in Capricorn. We are now a third of the way through winter and the spirit of this time likens to an awakening. We are on the brink of the Aquarius sun days.

Today's Leo Moon brings out the need to relax and keep warm in the midst of winter. Leo moon brings out the catlike qualities of our moods, and in case you haven't heard, cats love to hibernate on a winter day winter just as much as bears do (though for shorter periods.) This is nothing that a warm tropical sun wouldn't cure, and assuredly many folks are feeling the desire to get away from it all and play. Nonetheless, the stoic Capricorn sun, while it still exists, urges us onward to persist through this quiet time of winter with diligent determination. Leo Moon magnifies personal desires as well as family needs. This is a good time to treat oneself to something that will encourage the heart, particularly the childlike aspects of the heart.

AQUARIUS

Key phrase " I KNOW "
Fixed Air Sign
Symbol : The Water Bearer

January 20th through February 18th

January 20th Monday

Sun enters Aquarius	3:53 a.m. PST	6:53 a.m. EST
Moon in Leo goes V/C	5:46 a.m. PST	8:46 a.m. EST
Moon enters Virgo	10:32 a.m. PST	1:32 p.m. EST

Venus conjunct Pluto begins (see 1/25)

Throughout the morning there is a tendency for moods to be mindlessly selfish and perhaps disoriented due to the void-of-course Moon in Leo. Later in the morning PST early afternoon EST, the Moon enters Virgo and our moods are more focused and grounded throughout the day. Virgo Moon emphasizes cleanliness and perfection.

Sun enters Aquarius (Jan. 20 – Feb. 18.) Happy Birthday Aquarians! Aquarius is the 'water bearer'. Perhaps this is why it is often mistaken as a water sign, even though it is actually the 'fixed air' sign of the zodiac, and deals specifically with human intelligence, hence the phrase: "I Know." The Aquarius influence emphasizes reaching out towards a body of light and information that will benefit everyone. Aquarius focuses on the raising up and enhancement of human consciousness. This is a time for opening up to new ideas and possibilities. We started out the calendar year with the Sun in Capricorn emphasizing the crystallization of goals and the fulfillment of responsibility. Now the Sun in Aquarius changes our concepts, ideas, and work ethics as we begin to see how much easier we can make life and our workload through an innovative approach to our work. Aquarius calls for the need to break through outmoded methods of achieving progress and the use of what we accept as fixed or scientific knowledge. Freedom is the real key behind what inspires Aquarians most. Despite the established systems, we are free as humans to influence the wave of the future. Aquarians are often eccentric and dynamic, and even when they are common and complacent in their outlook on life, they manage to surprise us on many levels. They are usually adept in some unexpected way. They're often up to date on complex systems, or have a keen understanding of the bureaucracies and how to approach the unimaginable puzzles of human existence. Aquarians know - they know all - and to dispute anything with them is to be duly tested, if not surprised in a manner least expected. Aquarians are usually clever people who enjoy a challenge. The movement of the future will dismiss our current fears as outmoded forms of ignorance. The Aquarian wave of the future will continue to battle the unfeeling aspects of scientific research. This is called humanitarianism; it is the key to human survival and also a very big part of the Aquarian drive. Human rights issues are Aquarian issues and Sun in Aquarius will help us to differentiate between true humanitarianism and the humanitarian posturing that is actually a deceitful ploy to gain political and economic control. This is why we must adhere to the Aquarian concept of learning to think and act for ourselves and not relying exclusively on scientific methods or the brainwashing of politics to see to our needs. This also means we must speak up for our rights whenever necessary, and dispel those controversies concerning our chosen ways of living or dying. Aquarius is the fixed air sign that examines absolute knowledge with fixed clarity, and then initiates a new reign of knowledge based on brilliant breakthroughs of time's most significant inventors and observers of nature, our world, and our universe: the scientists and scholars that shape our viewpoints. The important thing to realize is that we humans do have a choice concerning the directions our lives take. Today's celebrated inventors and visionaries were yesterday's heretics and heathens. The voice of modern day heretics, eccentrics and rebels will continue to challenge and awaken our understanding. Aquarius is ruled by the enigmatic planetary force of Uranus, often the strange provocateur that forges new clarity and hope through the storms of chaos and disruption. Freedom fighters will remind us that we must find a solution to every great atrocity that dampens the human spirit. We must always take measures to prevent tomorrow's health crises, to insure the perpetuity of our species. The Aquarius sign, the fixed sign of air represents the sum of human knowledge used to determine the direction humanity will take. Big planetary influences (such as Uranus and Neptune) have been gracing the skies of Aquarius, creating changes that reflect overall global awareness. It is time for us to turn our minds to the vision of utopia – to create a positive picture of the future - while we face up to and vigorously protest the oppression that makes our lives difficult and inhumane. It is the old world oppression of greed and ignorance that we must address in this Aquarian time; through knowledge we will succeed. This is the time for Aquarians to apply their brilliance and be heard.

January 21st Tuesday

Moon in Virgo
Venus trine Jupiter   7:35 a.m. PST   10:35 a.m. EST

Virgo Moon emphasizes the need to focus on such things as accounting, dieting, research and analysis. Sun in Aquarius and Moon in Virgo brings out the need to get the technical world of communications in order. Meanwhile Mercury is still retrograde for just one more day, and the efforts to put confusing details into order might take a few more days to sort out. There is a definite need to access and manage resources (or a lack of them) more wisely at this time but a bit more patience will be required also. This is a time to get down to earth and apply a nose-to-the-grindstone philosophy in order to appease the demanding qualities of this January winter day.

Venus trine Jupiter (occurring Jan. 16 – 26.) Venus trine Jupiter is a favored and prized aspect that allows for greater potential to receive and expand gifts of love. Love (Venus) is harmoniously placed with prosperity and opportunity (Jupiter.) This is a great time to use love to expand your outlook on life. Commonly, this translates to the act of adorning beauty with riches, so it's not a bad time to adorn your loved ones with jewellery or trinkets. In those cases where people are not feeling so prosperous, at least this aspect allows for the hope of getting through those tight financial situations by appreciating beauty. Creating the illusion of wealth can be a very powerful way to uplift one towards a sense of persistent fortune, and a lot of this has to do with simple aesthetics and quality moments. Innovative gifts of love have a strong effect on loved ones at this time.

January 22nd Wednesday

Moon in Virgo goes V/C   1:34 a.m. PST   4:34 a.m. EST
Moon enters Libra   1:23 p.m. PST   4:23 p.m. EST
Mercury goes direct   5:08 p.m. PST   8:08 p.m. EST

Overnight the Moon goes void-of-course in Virgo and throughout the morning there is a tendency for our moods to be overly critical and nit picky about the imperfections of simple daily tasks. Be aware of the tendency towards morning quarrels. By afternoon the Moon enters Libra and the mood of the day shifts over to an emphasis on making decisions and adjustments, particularly concerning social affairs and balancing out relationship concerns.

Mercury goes direct in the sign of Capricorn (Mercury direct: Jan. 22 – April 26.) If the past three weeks (since January 2nd) have seemed very difficult with regard to relaying simple messages, Mercury retrograde in Capricorn is the likely culprit that has put a damper on communications. Now that Mercury moves forward, this will be a better time to settle any misunderstandings or disputes that have cropped up this past month. Unsettled contracts can be corrected and negotiated more clearly and swiftly now, and there is likely to be much less difficulty interpreting and translating. Mercury is the planet that carries the message and for the past few weeks this retrograde planet has been leaving us clueless as to how communications have been so mixed up. Now at least the majority of us that are so strongly affected by Mercury retrograde can move forward in our thinking and our way of presenting our thoughts. We can interpret others better and get on with business. For now, it's down to the business of celebrating that Mercury has gone DIRECT!

January 23rd Thursday
Moon in Libra
Venus opposite Saturn begins (see 1/28)

As the Moon wanes down in Libra, we focus on balancing the inconsistencies of relations with partners, loved ones and friends. Libra Moon emphasizes the need for teamwork. There are a number of adjustments being made throughout the entire day and evening. This may also be a crucial time of decision, particularly in making decisions that affect the people that share our life and work. This waning Moon phase of Libra emphasizes the need to clear up any troubling imbalances that exist between friends. This is a good time to drop grudges and attempt diplomacy with others, particularly now that Mercury has finally gone direct (see yesterday.)

January 24th Friday
Moon in Libra goes V/C	11:48 a.m. PST	2:48 p.m. EST
Moon enters Scorpio	4:09 p.m. PST	7:09 p.m. EST
Sun conjunct Neptune begins (see 1/30)		

Throughout a good portion of the day the Moon is void-of-course in Libra causing a lot of issues around making decisions, and a tendency for people to disagree on the various matters at hand. Despite the confusion, the mood finally breaks and changes over to the sign of Scorpio. Waning Scorpio Moon emphasizes the need for release of tension and emotional build ups must be discharged. This is a good time to work on allowing emotional expression to flow, however harsh it may appear on some levels, and trust that the release will bring a greater sense of healing.

January 25th Saturday
Last Quarter Moon in Scorpio
Moon square Sun	12:33 a.m. PST	3:33 a.m. EST
Venus conjunct Pluto	9:57 a.m. PST	12:57 p.m. EST
Sun sextile Mars	9:26 p.m. PST	12:26 a.m. (1/26) EST

Last Quarter Moon in Scorpio (Moon square Sun) is often an intense time for the emotions. Issues that matter deep down are likely to come up to the surface today. Scorpio rules passion and compassion and it is likely that the dark secrets of our lives will be touched on in some way. The Last Quarter Moon in Scorpio urges us to release stored up tension. Try to find a way to experience emotions without imposing them on others. Safety conscious physical workouts may work really well for some folks. Safety consciousness of any kind is particularly important. Don't forget to keep an eye out for suspicious activity at this time, and beware of thieves, smooth talkers, and the potential for violent outbreaks. It may be best not to let anyone try to talk you into something that goes beyond your personal limits. Stand your ground.

Venus conjunct Pluto (occurring Jan. 20 – 30) This aspect represents a love or fascination at work concerning matters of fate as well as power. This is the place where the influences of love and power merge into one, and may help to create a breakthrough for those who are having difficulty accepting the work of fate or higher powers. There is hope for those who acquire an appreciation for the not so glamorous aspects of existence. A lot of what seems uncontrollable these days is really in our mind and not our heart. What is in our heart speaks the truth, and the unpredictable facets of the hardships of loss or death are often brought to light with this aspect of Venus conjunct Pluto. Facing difficult power issues with loving affection gives us strength to face the hardships more easily.

Sun sextile Mars (occurring Jan. 13 – Feb. 8.) Sun sextile Mars brings a surge of favorable and also challenging energy and activity into our lives, particularly energizing those Capricorn and Aquarius folks celebrating a birthday this year January 13th through February 8th. These birthday people are undergoing the sextile aspect of their natal sun to the planet Mars. There are opportunities at work that must be acted upon in order for all of this extra energy to pay off. There may also be a lot of anguish and pressure concerning the direction the self-image is taking, and the heat that is being stirred requires direction and assertiveness. Now is the time, especially for these Capricorn/Aquarius born birthday folks, to take some action with their lives and continue throughout the coming year. This aspect was also influential for many of these cusp born people last year, and it is evident that a trend is occurring in these people's lives, bringing milestones and loads of active opportunities.

January 26th Sunday

Moon in Scorpio goes V/C	3:14 p.m. PST	6:14 p.m. EST
Moon enters Sagittarius	7:26 p.m. PST	10:26 p.m. EST

Throughout today the waning Moon in Scorpio intensifies our moods concerning heavy kinds of emotional energy that needs to be dealt with on some level. By 3:14 p.m. PST / 6:14 p.m. EST, the Moon goes void-of-course for more than four hours, at which point it is important not to get all bent out of shape concerning annoying but minor setbacks. In the evening the Moon enters Sagittarius, emphasizing the need to let go of emotional hurdles and progress forward beyond the usual bounds. Sagittarius Moon reminds us to develop and enhance our vision of what we hope to create for ourselves.

January 27th Monday
Moon in Sagittarius
Mars sextile Neptune begins (see 2/2)

Throughout the day, the waning Moon in Sagittarius brings our moods to a place of introspective awareness. Star gazing is a special sport on Sagittarius Moon nights, especially with the constellation Orion so bright and large in winter. Cold winter nights are upon us and the need to stay warm and comfortable keeps us busy on numerous levels. It is important to keep fit and not to overextend oneself at this time. For many this is a time of being stretched thin, either financially and/or with basic levels of energy. Sagittarius Moon encourages us to push on and this spirit takes us beyond the usual bounds and allows us to find resources in unexpected places.

January 28th Tuesday

Moon in Sagittarius goes V/C	7:26 p.m. PST	10:26 p.m. EST
Moon enters Capricorn	11:30 p.m. PST	2:30 a.m. (1/29) EST
Venus opposite Saturn	4:13 p.m. PST	7:13 p.m. EST

Sun opposite Jupiter begins (see 2/2)

Waning Sagittarius Moon continues and throughout the day there is a forward moving drive to work off energy and give the mind and body some philosophical as well as physical exercise. There is an extraordinary push at work to make ends meet. By 7:26 p.m. PST / 10:26 p.m. EST, the Moon goes void-of-course, creating a lull of minor uncertainty at times throughout the evening. Later the Moon enters Capricorn and the overall mood setting becomes more focused and grounded.

Venus opposite retrograde Saturn (occurring Jan. 23 – Feb. 2.) Love, beauty, and magnetism is opposed to restrictive discipline. While the need is very strong to attain a sense of beauty, to stop and smell the roses, there is a constantly compelling and obsessive awareness to press on with work and vital responsibilities. Love matters and concerns are subjected to unavoidable trials and restrictions. Love is opposed to and estranged by restrictive limitations and covenants. There will be folks among us thrust into the challenge of facing jealousy, guilt, offensive outbreaks, anguish, oppression, defeat or despair. There are always lessons where our sheltered passions lie. We must be careful how our passions are stirred or handled. To stir up such passion at this time, one is likely to be all too quickly confronted by his or her own personal demons. Hold steadfast to all principles of wisdom. Be careful not to bite off more than you can chew, especially concerning irresistible attractions.

January 29th Wednesday
Moon in Capricorn
Mars trine Jupiter begins (see 2/5)

Today all of the personal and outer planets are in the fall and winter signs of the zodiac, while the two social planets, Jupiter and Saturn, are in summer and spring signs. Much of the drive to serve the world may feel somewhat self imposed or self imposing. This is to say that the overall need to get out and do the work, and do it right, feels truly personal. Capricorn Moon wanes and always gives a sobering edge to our moods, forcing us to cast a more serious eye on matters at hand. Meanwhile, those social planets, Jupiter and Saturn are spelling out a whole different picture. Jupiter in Leo reminds us that prosperity can be found on the stage and in the world of entertainment, and there are grand opportunities for those leading personalities that stand out in our culture. Saturn in Gemini demands structure and discipline that are backed with time honored facts and are examined by a second opinion before being taken for a test drive. Don't get caught taking the workload all too seriously; but the darkly waning Moon in Capricorn is here to give us the incentive to work, not to argue our way out of it. Be sure to do it today. Tomorrow's long void-of-course Moon day and evening will make the workload seem uncontrollable.

January 30th Thursday

Moon in Capricorn goes V/C   2:34 a.m. PST   5:34 a.m. EST.
Moon V/C all day and night
Sun conjunct Neptune   3:34 p.m. PST   6:34 p.m. EST
Venus sextile Uranus begins (see (2/2)

Capricorn Moon emphasizes the need to keep everything together and in control, though accomplishing it may be more difficult. Today's illusion of being in control is thwarted by time itself. The void-of-course Capricorn Moon has many folks in a relentless tail spin to make deadlines that are seemingly impossible to make, and to make ends meet even though the flow of capital is not panning out the way it should. Keep up the good working spirit as best as is possible, and expect to make better work progress by tomorrow, particularly in the area of having to figure out solutions.

Sun conjunct Neptune in Aquarius (occurring Jan. 24 – Feb. 6.) This aspect particularly affects Aquarius people celebrating birthdays January 24th through Feb 6th this year. You are the lucky ones being affected this upcoming year by intuitive inclinations and spiritual desires. Your visions (Aquarius birthday folks) will inspire great feats, and the higher, more spiritually refined parts of the soul are going to be speaking to you this upcoming year. Listen! This may be a time to let go of personal attachments and outmoded desires that appear to be going nowhere. As each year evolves, your highly complex Aquarian idealism will work up your spiritual beliefs into a kind of peak performance level, even if you don't believe you have such a thing as spiritual beliefs. Since 1998 Neptune has been crossing over the early degrees of Aquarius; early born Aquarius folks have been strongly affected by Neptune's belief-altering influence. Aquarians will continue to encounter a kind of spiritual catharsis and by the time you've been through this you'll know what that means. This is your time (Aquarius people born during the above noted dates) to integrate a listening pattern concerning the Great Spirit in your life. This means concentrating and focusing on the spiritual part of the self (or higher self) that rules over personal destiny and guides the self with the true desires of the soul. Can you handle that, birthday folks?

January 31st Friday

Moon enters Aquarius   4:44 a.m. PST   7:44 a.m. EST

The darkly waning Moon enters Aquarius and now reaches the balsamic phase, the darkest before the completely dark New Moon taking place tomorrow. Deep contemplative thoughts require brilliant solutions to brighten the mood. Yesterday's void-of-course Capricorn Moon may have slowed many of us down, especially since running on thin lunar light and requiring the best possible solutions to serve the demanding world is a difficult post for those who must serve. This requires superhuman forces of spirit. This requires know-how and renewed confidence. It is sometimes difficult to believe that others will come through for us when we need to rely on them. Aquarius demands faith in humanity. The celestial forces are busy right now. Sun, Moon and Neptune hover together in Aquarius, bewildering many of us about our ability to believe in humanity despite its foibles. Although there is little comfort in the old saying that it is always darkest before the dawn, do not be disquieted by moments of doubt. We have nearly reached the mid-point of winter: this is no time to mull in the dark even though the light seems dim. The all encouraging light will return as it always does in the next couple of days, both in the renewal of the lunar light (New Moon February 1st) and the coming of Candlemas (see February 2nd.)

February 1, Saturday
Chinese New Year – Year of the Goat
New Moon in Aquarius
Moon conjunct Sun   2:48 a.m. PST   5:48 a.m. EST

Today the **Moon is New in the sign of Aquarius** (Moon conjunct Sun.) This is the time to open up to new feelings regarding our understanding of science, technology, and these changing times. New Moon in Aquarius is a good time to begin new social and philanthropic endeavors. Aquarius says: "I know," and humankind's knowledge is always tested: it is through what we **do** know that we persist constantly to find out what we **don't** know. New knowledge adds to our power and this is a good time to learn something new about ourselves and our ever changing world. Knowledge, after all, is power.

February 2, Sunday
Candlemas / Groundhog Day

Moon in Aquarius goes V/C	8:02 a.m. PST	11:02 a.m. EST
Moon enters Pisces	11:54 a.m. PST	2:54 p.m. EST
Sun opposite Jupiter	1:12 a.m. PST	4:12 a.m. EST
Venus sextile Uranus	9:25 a.m. PST	12:25 p.m. EST
Mars sextile Neptune	1:40 p.m. PST	4:40 p.m. EST

While the Moon is void-of-course in Aquarius this morning, it is best not to get into disputes over right and wrong. By afternoon the Moon in Pisces shifts our moods into a clairvoyant kind of awareness. A dreamy and imaginative mood fills the air. **Today is Candlemas**: a celebration of the return of the light, and a new realm of focus occurs. It is at this time that a handful of people around the globe celebrate the midpoint of winter as the time of ceremonial initiation. Out of the darkness and into the light; this represents a time of blossoming knowledge and a time to acknowledge one's own growth. We are now one half of the way through winter season. It is increasingly noticeable how much more light appears to linger as each evening unfolds in the later half of this season. This holiday is also known as Imbolc, the breakthrough of winter's darkness, physically and emotionally. The saintly lady of the Irish legends known as "Bridget" or "Bride" wears a crown of candles signifying the circle of light returning to our realms. Some may also call this the quickening of the light. To light a candle (or many candles) at this time is a powerful symbol of acknowledging this celebration. Another familiar celebration of this time is Groundhog Day, when the groundhog's shadow becomes a popular tale foretelling the fate of the final half of winter season.

Sun opposite Jupiter (occurring Jan. 28 – Feb. 8.) This aspect particularly affects the Aquarius born people celebrating birthdays Jan. 28th – Feb. 8th. These Aquarius birthday people are experiencing the opposition of Jupiter to their natal sun. This brings an acute awareness of the shift of personal economic issues, usually either for better or worse. There is a strong personal awareness (or perhaps obsession) at work concerning the struggle to obtain a sense of wealth and well being. The need for peace in the shifting economy of these times is particularly strong for these folks. This is all especially true since Jupiter is now retrograde until March 2nd this year. In order to stand your ground, it is important to remain rooted and practical in your own growth desires. Use your best techniques (birthday folks of this time) of applying wisdom concerning your expenditures, and this will bring you around to the place you instinctively know you need to be.

Venus sextile Uranus (occurring Jan. 30 – Feb. 6.) Here there is an opportunity for eccentric love to erupt. This aspect brings an attraction to the act of breaking out of useless tendencies and habits, and also brings an opportunity for love related matters to break through the imprisonment of not meeting personal needs. This is the time to work out pent up frustrations with loved ones and to reconcile differences by applying love and accepting divergence, giving freedom and slack to our loved ones, without ourselves being oppressed. For some, this approach may seem impossible or harsh, but the time is now to let go of false hopes and get back in touch with a sense of personal freedom and self-reliance. Trust, in turn, that everything that has built up our love relationships is as strong as the foundation of our love itself. Those who are meant to be attracted will return, and those who are not free, or are overly dependent on their immediate family, must occasionally break through the barriers of identity clashes. On a positive note, here's a reminder that radical kinds of love and aesthetics can be very uplifting at this time. Stand by those who uplift you. There is also an opportunity for the rebellious aspect of art to break through and be known.

Mars sextile Neptune (occurring Jan. 27 – Feb. 9.) This aspect brings the vitality of Mars into a favorable position with the spirit-awakening influence of Neptune. Those that act on their visions and the ceremonies of their particular belief systems will have an opportunity to connect with a very profound spiritual experience. This aspect brings the active work of artists, poets, and musicians into unique and very powerful statements about being in an endowed and sacred state of awareness. There is an irony at work with these two forces; Mars is active and masculine, while Neptune has a very nebulous and passive guise that affects our deeper inner sense of beliefs and spirit. When these two planets are placed in a favorable position to each other, personal spiritual breakthroughs can be made.

February 3, Monday
Moon in Pisces

Today the Moon in Pisces is beginning the waxing cycle as a newly emerging crescent. This being so, the overall mood begins to awaken our senses to a vague sense of visionary awareness and to initiate the potential for strong psychic intuition. This is a good time to use the imagination and focus on artistic and creative endeavors. All the while, a glimmer of light barely touches our winter slumber, yet something inherently special and often incommunicable to others touches the heart in the newly waxing inspiration of Pisces Moon. This is the time to recognize an inherent gift within oneself. It is best to get the better part of the workload accomplished today; tomorrow's long void-of-course Moon day will no doubt decrease any sense of making progress.

February 4, Tuesday

Moon in Pisces goes V/C	6:52 a.m. PST	9:52 a.m. EST
Moon enters Aries	9:44 p.m. PST	12:44 a.m. EST (2/5)
Venus enters Capricorn	5:27 a.m. PST	8:27 a.m. EST
Sun trine Saturn begins	(see 2/11)	

This morning's dreamy, psychic Pisces Moon reverie leads into a full day of the void-of-course Moon syndrome. The result leaves us with a veritable plethora of spaced out moods, forgetfulness, and an overall tendency throughout the day to lack concentration and focus. It is best to just expect this and not get hung up on what does or doesn't get accomplished today.

Venus enters Capricorn (occurring Feb. 4 – March 2.) Venus in Capricorn brings out an attraction for the staunch and ardent duty of accomplishing goals, and creates stable ground for the development of relationships. For the next few weeks there will be increasing attempts to make an impression with one's dedication providing well for loved ones. Venus in Capricorn creates a love of work, and people will feel motivated to hard work towards the achievement of goals. This is the time when many people are attracted to gaining momentum on getting in shape and becoming more physically attractive. This is not commonly considered a good placement for Venus to be in a person's chart, given that the nature of one's love or marriage is often a love life compromised for material and social convenience. Without a more creative set of circumstances at work, a person of this type's love is often plagued with coldness or indifference, and is somewhat calculating and with an emphasis on material concerns. As Venus crosses over the natal sun of our Capricorn friends between now and March 2nd, they are prone to be more in touch with their own need for affection and desire for beauty. Oftentimes a number of aspects and shifts are busily working to test some of us on challenging levels, while providing relief for others. Venus in Capricorn puts us in tune with the precious firmament: our sense of foundation and the security of our physical environment. It allows us to appreciate our goals and accomplishments as we evaluate the possibilities of this unfolding new year.

February 5, Wednesday
Moon in Aries
Mars trine Jupiter   11:25 a.m. PST   2:25 p.m. EST

Waxing Moon represents a time of building up, or increasing the awareness of our feelings. Aries waxing Moon is an especially important time not to let disruptive feelings brew and steam before releasing the pressure. Throughout the day our moods are beset with the constant need to handle and deal with pressure. Winter restlessness stirs our hearts. The desire to start up new projects is also a symptom of the newly waxing Aries Moon.

Mars trine Jupiter (occurring Jan. 29 – Feb. 13.) This favorable aspect may be the time to act on opportunities as they arise and to set one's visions and dreams into a feasible plan that holds the potential for favorable actions to occur. Mars trine Jupiter affects the actions taking place around us in a favorable and gifted way, concerned with the expansion of our livelihood and our awareness. Mars activates and stirs action while Jupiter represents not only our sense of economy and how to advance, but our sense of philosophic and visionary awareness as well, allowing us to realize new talents and new means of livelihood, the intake of wealth, and well being. For some people this aspect has brought gifts of inheritance and opportunities for growth. Mars trine Jupiter allows us to activate a stronger grasp of our domains and gives some people the extra energy to push past obstacles that have challenged their sense of advancement. Bear in mind that Jupiter is currently retrograde, and therefore this aspect is more likely to manifest from within, where personal attainment shines, rather than happening due to outside source.

February 6, Thursday
Moon in Aries

Th basic mood setting for today focuses on the need to stand out, and to be on top and in control of situations around us. There is an eagerness in our moods. Both the child and the warrior are geared for battle. Today's moods are filled with determination and inspiration. Sometimes the Aries Moon causes too much inspiration and the search for a good fight or release of raw aggression must come out. A lot of pushing and shoving may be evident in today's activities. Some folks may feel it's necessary to tell the first ripe candidate that comes along just how full of it he or she is. This may be a difficult time to ignore pushy aggressors; nonetheless, being aware of this behavior and attempting to avoid it by watching for the signs - before the bluster gets out of hand - may well be in your favor today.

February 7, Friday

Moon in Aries goes V/C	6:21 a.m. PST	9:21 a.m. EST
Moon enters Taurus	9:59 a.m. PST	12:59 p.m. EST
Mars conjunct Pluto begins (see 2/16)		

The Moon is void-of-course in Aries as our moods are touched by a somewhat sloppy, accident prone, or self-delusional start on the day. By later in the morning on the west coast, early afternoon on the east coast, Moon enters Taurus and our moods and sensibilities shift over into a more pragmatic and down to earth focus. Taurus Moon brings out the need to deal with financial concerns and emphasizes money and trade. It also emphasizes beauty and practicality. The fixed earth nature of Taurus inspires many folks to watch their pocketbooks, and to make sure they're getting the most value possible out of all expenditures. There is also a need to let the beauty of our surroundings be accented and appreciated.

February 8, Saturday
Moon in Taurus
Sun sextile Pluto   7:28 a.m. PST   10:28 a.m. EST

The Moon now waxes in Taurus reminding us to pay attention to the unfinished business of the physical world. Since there is no end to physical tasks and jobs, it is always best to harness the bull energy when it comes around, and to endeavor to enliven those untouched corners of our existence. To put energy where some desired result is likely to be attained, is to appease the need for comfort and beauty. This is the time to dress up winter's mask with a touch of the pending spring.

Sun sextile Pluto (occurring Feb. 3 – 13.) Sun in Aquarius is sextile to Pluto in Sagittarius, bringing opportunity that appears demanding and vast to those Aquarius folks celebrating birthdays this year; Feb. 3rd through Feb. 13th. These Aquarius birthday people are undergoing the sextile aspect of their natal sun to Pluto, giving them the opportunity to take charge and step up into positions of power, and to address multigenerational audiences in differing levels of hierarchy. This is an opportunity for these Aquarius birthday folks to undergo a powerful transformation, and empower what they identify as theirs through their lessons of the long trials of the past. Though life may have had its difficult trials, this is the time for many Aquarians to rise above! Go thee forth and conquer, master Aquarians! Those folks born towards the end of the Aquarius sun cycle have not yet been affected by this aspect; in several more years this empowering opportunity will be closer to you. In the meantime, persist with diligence self-respect, and assurance to resolve the conflicts of your life. Your time to triumph is always available when your will and persistence to achieve is balanced and intact. This holds true for all signs of the zodiac!

February 9, Sunday
First Quarter Moon in Aquarius
Moon square Sun   3:11 a.m. PST   6:11 a.m. EST
Moon in Taurus goes V/C   7:28 p.m. PST   10:28 p.m. EST
Moon enters Gemini   10:45 p.m. PST   1:45 a.m. EST (2/10)

Today we come to the **Moon's First Quarter mark in the sign of Taurus** (Moon square Sun.) Taurus is none other than a Venus ruled sign, emphasizing love, beauty, the luxuries of our world and the expression of appreciation. There is an emphasis on beauty and adoration today ringing in the spirit of a half waxed moon. Throughout this day our moods focus on physical world consciousness. There is also a basic need to get the practical matters of life handled. Taurus Moon emphasizes beauty and practicality. The fixed earth nature of Taurus leaves many folks feeling inclined to watch their pocketbooks and to make sure they're getting the most value possible out of all expenditures. There is also a need to let the beauty of our surroundings be accented and appreciated. At 7:28 p.m. PST / 10:28 p.m. EST, the Moon goes void-of-course and lazy moods may be evident.

February 10, Monday
Moon in Gemini
Sun conjunct Uranus begins (see 2/17)

The Moon is in Gemini keeping our minds and our moods busy. The emphasis on covering many details at once becomes the primary objective. Gemini Moon brings talkative, curious and inquisitive moods. While the Sun hovers in the realm of Aquarius and the Moon now sails through Gemini, the focus of the day revolves around the need to acquire and utilize important knowledge and information. This is a time of research and development, of mulling over possibilities and examining resources. Tests of the mind may be evident and ideas harnessed at this time are likely to have quality results.

February 11, Tuesday

Moon in Gemini
Sun trine Saturn   1:45 a.m. PST   4:45 a.m. EST
Mars opposite Saturn begins   (see 2/20)

Trivia Question: What are the two most common things in the universe?*... Sometimes the whirling universe is bursting with more great mystery than one can comprehend. Sometimes the vastness of knowledge cannot be stored with so much detail overloading the system. Sometimes the mind is full and the chattering world won't cease. Gemini moon playfully waxes and loves to play tricks on the mind. Don't overdo the caffeine and take it easy on the nervous system. When in doubt, apply humor. ...*Trivia Quiz Answer: Did you guess hydrogen and oxygen? – you were close! Comedy dictates that hydrogen and **stupidity** are the two most common things in the universe.

Sun trine Saturn (occurring Feb. 4 – 17.) This aspect affects, in particular, those Aquarius people celebrating birthdays Feb. 4th through the 17th this year. This is a positive time for these Aquarius folks to get a handle on their lives, and may help make it easier to take on the responsibilities of life with a lot less complication and difficulty in the year to come. Aquarius birthday folks may notice more acceptable forms of responsibility and work happening in their life throughout this year. Now is your time (birthday people) to work successfully on putting more structure into your life; the kind of structure you've truly been needing and wanting awaits you in the coming year. It is possible, time (Saturn) is on your side, and now is a good time to make your move!

February 12, Wednesday

Moon in Gemini goes V/C   6:28 a.m. PST   9:28 a.m. EST
Moon enters Cancer   9:19 a.m. PST   12:19 p.m. EST
Mercury enters Aquarius   5:00 p.m. PST   8:00 p.m. EST

A ripple of basic confusion over simple details pervades the morning as the Moon in Gemini goes void-of-course for awhile and finally slips into Cancer. Throughout the afternoon, our moods are geared towards nurturing and appeasing the emotions. Some do this with an emphasis on food, cooking, and dining. Others may choose to pamper themselves with luxury baths, while others still just need to spill the emotional core, and let off some steam in the hope that someone will listen sympathetically. There are loads of ways to nurture. Sometimes it's as simple as applying the listening ear.

Mercury enters Aquarius (occurring Feb. 12 – March 4.) Now the focus of communications shifts towards the swarm of Aquarian related events. Throughout the course of this month and through March 4th, Mercury in

Aquarius brings to light the latest in technology and the world of invention. There is talk in the air full of idealistic proportions, and there are unusual issues relating to humanitarian acts. This is the time for Aquarians to speak out and be heard. This is also a time for human rights issues to be brought to the surface of discussion. Many people now take this time to speak up and be heard on important issues which affect us all. Mercury in Aquarius is an excellent time to focus on increasing memorization skills and on learning, inputting and relaying valuable knowledge. Tomorrow the Moon is void-of-course throughout the entire day and night; be sure to get important work completed as much as possible today.

February 13, Thursday
Moon in Cancer goes V/C   4:22 a.m. PST   7:22 a.m. EST

All too early, the Moon goes void-of-course in Cancer. This day will seem to many like a day of distractions, particularly emotional or mood oriented distractions. Mood fluctuation is inescapable and this tends to slow down overall progress considerably. Sometimes the world just goes through a chain reaction of venting various kinds of moods and emotions. All of this moodiness is a natural process, but it can cause forgetfulness, oversensitive or defensive mood swings, perhaps even senseless attempts at being logical. This is the day before Valentines Day; it is very important to avoid relationship turmoil by NOT forgetting our loved ones. The aspects of this time are masculine in nature, while the lunar mood is very sensitive. Practicing a little extra tenderness and forgiveness will help to balance the spirit of our interactions.

February 14, Friday
Saint Valentine's Day
Moon enters Leo   4:04 p.m. PST   7:04 p.m. EST

Friday is a day attributed to Venus, the planet of love and beauty, and how appropriate it is that today is Saint Valentine's Day! Be grateful for the affections that genuinely exist in your life and be sure to let loved ones know how much they matter to you. Much of the day continues with the Moon void-of-course in Cancer, creating a particularly sensitive arena for disturbing and agitating minor setbacks and delays. By 4:04 p.m. PST / 7:04 p.m. EST the Moon enters Leo and focuses our moods on personal projects, family matters, and entertainment. Romance is sparked with the drama and spotlights of Leo perfectionism. This is a good time to give compliments, stroke the ego until it blushes, to dance, sing, and enjoy letting the wild and beastly side of our natures be free.

February 15, Saturday
Moon in Leo
Full Moon Eve

Tomorrow the Moon will be full in Leo in the afternoon, and throughout today the Moon builds its great energy. Tonight can be easily considered the Eve of the Full Leo Moon. The Sun rules the sign of Leo and when the Moon is full in this sign it often influences physical energy, stamina and strength, instilling a zest for life. Full Leo Moon is a good time to activate personal desires and do something good for the self. Leo Moon moods inspire a practical outlet for applying creative skills, gaining public recognition, encouragement and appreciation. On the other hand, it is wise to be aware of a tendency to tackle too much for the sake of one's own well-being; therefore, it is advisable not to overdo it when wallowing in egocentric talents. Full Leo Moon reaches into the playful side of our nature and encourages us to seek the light of our own dreams and aspirations in an uplifting, encouraging, and light-hearted manner.

February 16, Sunday
Full Moon in Leo
Moon opposite Sun	3:51 p.m. PST	6:51 p.m. EST
Moon goes V/C	5:18 p.m. PST	8:18 p.m. EST
Moon enters Virgo	7:22 p.m. PST	10:22 p.m. EST
Jupiter opposite Neptune	1:12 a.m. PST	4:12 a.m. EST
Mars conjunct Pluto	7:55 a.m. PST	10:55 a.m. EST

A **Full Moon in Leo** (Moon opposite Sun) captures our moods today, and there may be an opportunity here to enhance and harmonize friendships and family situations in a fulfilling and enriching manner. Moon in Leo brings out the playful, imaginative, and creative side of our moods. Most of us are easily drawn towards the need to find warmth and affection, or just plain attention, at this time. By evening the Moon is in Virgo creating a focus on analyzing and reflecting on the process that all of this full moon energy has brought us. Not only is the Moon full, other planetary aspects happening now are worthy of notation.

Jupiter opposite Neptune (occurring Jan. 11 – July 4.) Jupiter opposite Neptune is a relatively uncommon aspect which has been actively occurring since January 11th and continues through July 4th of this year. On June 2nd this aspect will reach its peak once again, just as it is now. This aspect occurs over this long period of time, due to both the retrograde pattern and the rate of motion of these two slower-moving planets as they travel through the celestial degrees. Jupiter affects our sense of prosperity and expansion into new realms of fulfillment and discovery. Neptune represents our experience with divine mystery and the spirit of our beliefs. Jupiter opposite Neptune may be forcing us to review our beliefs and to take on a more expansive viewpoint of life's mysteries. On the other hand, we are probably going to be tested as to the validity of our beliefs and how we project those beliefs on others, or how other's beliefs are projected on us. This aspect is bringing on a number of initiations concerning commerce and our world economy; all of this is a reflection of the integration of our beliefs. For more on Jupiter opposite Neptune, see June 2nd.

Mars conjunct Pluto (occurring Feb. 7 – 24.) Through this aspect, action and activity fall into a powerful connection with transforming forces at work. Powerful forces are likely to take some form of disruptive and very possibly destructive fiery action with Mars conjunct Pluto in Sagittarius. The philosophical viewpoints of each generation are now being activated, and there may be some forcefulness and heat between them. This is an especially important time to take precautionary measures in dealing with authorities. Let us not forget that while this aspect is happening, Mars is also about to oppose Saturn (see Feb. 20); this is a reminder that the extraordinary trouble maker known as "Saturn opposite Pluto" is still in our midst. Even though we will not see Saturn opposing Pluto at an exactness this year, this hidden aspect is still radiating its affects from January 2nd through April 26th, 2003. On February 21st of this month, Saturn (fortunately) goes direct, and Saturn opposite Pluto, which is only a couple of degrees away from repeating, will undergo a kind of standstill throughout the close of this month. Expect some definite social and political tension to escalate around this time and over the next couple of weeks. There is no doubt that crisis and war-related upsets are brewing, and that we are at the crux of a few very temperamental and unsettled forces. There is no use in worrying. It is wisest to be vigilant and clear about what is happening in our lives, and to use caution in all that we do. Like a catalyst, Mars conjunct Pluto is simply giving this fiery energy an outlet . See April 26th for the closing commentary on Saturn opposite Pluto.

February 17, Monday
Moon in Virgo
Sun conjunct Uranus   1:36 p.m. PST   4:36 p.m. EST
Mercury opposite Jupiter begins   (see 2/20)
Mercury conjunct Neptune begins   (see 2/20)

Virgo Moon emphasizes accounting, diet, research and analysis. Sun in Aquarius and Moon in Virgo brings out the need to get the technical world of communications in order. There is a definite urgency to access and manage resources more wisely. This is a time to get down to earth and apply a nose-to-the-grindstone effort in order to appease the demanding qualities of this February winter day.

Sun conjunct Uranus (occurring Feb 10 – 24.) This aspect especially affects people celebrating a birthday this year February 10th through the 24th. This is a time when these Aquarius/Pisces cusp-born birthday people have their natal sun strongly connected to Uranus. There will be much disruption and chaos in the lives of these folks, and there will also be radical breakthroughs towards a sense of freedom. Sun conjunct Uranus causes strong rebellious tendencies. There is a desire at work to get radical and take life at a different pace, to fight oppression and injustice, possibly even with an entirely off-the-wall approach towards dealing with the calamity. Where there is knowledge to back this radical new approach, there is a way to achieve a sense of freedom, and there is a good chance to make an impression in the pending year. This will be your year (birthday folks) to express yourselves and your innovative desires. Big changes are in the air this year.

Everyone, be sure to get the essential part of your workload completed as much as possible today; tomorrow's void-of-course Moon day will be likely to cause a greater potential for contingencies and delays and a slowing down of progress.

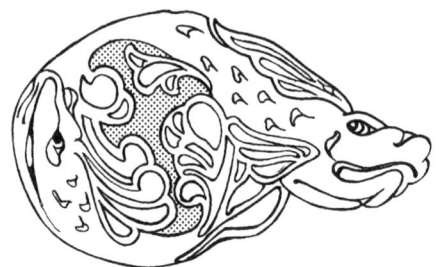

PISCES

Key Phrase "I BELIEVE"
Mutable Water Sign
Symbol: The Fish

February 18th — March 19th

February 18, Tuesday

Sun enters Pisces	6:01 p.m. PST	9:01 p.m. EST
Moon in Virgo goes V/C	7:56 a.m. PST	10:56 a.m. EST
Moon enters Libra	8:48 p.m. PST	11:48 p.m. EST

Throughout a fair portion of the day, the Moon is void-of-course in Virgo. This tends to create moods of skeptical confusion. The events of the day are best taken in stride and preferably with a sense of humor. Don't expect to get much done and all will be well. This does not mean we cannot apply at least a prudent level of effort. Strive to do better, but don't eat yourself up with criticism. Later in the evening when the Moon enters Libra, the evening mood is more geared towards harmonizing the atmosphere and interacting with a loved one or friend.

Today **Sun enters Pisces** (occurring Feb. 18 – March 20.) Now the final lap of winter is upon us. Happy Birthday to our Pisces friends! Pisces represents belief and there are many ways to believe. Some forces of belief among us are positive and some are quite negative and oppressive. Belief in science is a sign that we are emerging out of the age of Pisces and into the age of Aquarius. Within the human heart there is a fragile awareness of mortality. Strongly inherent in widely known religions and belief systems, there is a firm embrace of the belief in the soul's rebirth. The Piscean symbol of the fish(es) is a prehistoric representation of long term experience or incarnation and age old wisdom. Pisces is the last sign of the zodiac representing the completion of a cycle. This mutable water sign is adaptive and can absorb all kinds of influence. If bogged down by oppressive influences, the Piscean becomes burnt out and oversensitive. The whole Piscean character can meld and blend in to become intuitively aware of any belief system that exists. Pisces is ruled by Neptune, the planet of least resistance. Sometimes the Piscean character is like a conduit, able to take in and facilitate any influence that comes along. The art of channeling spirits is very Piscean. Skepticism is commonly noted as being the trait of Virgo, today's Moon sign is in Virgo, the polarized opposite of Pisces. Instead of choosing to believe, the Virgo chooses to analyze. The two styles, or polarities, are brought together by believing in what you analyze and analyzing what you believe. Piscean events emphasize the creation and adoration of art; linking up with and tuning into the spirit world and beyond, as well as taking up interests in the great mystery of our existence. The days of Pisces focus our attention on such Piscean activities as art, music and spiritual practices or religion. This month is a time to let the imagination fly and get the creative juices flowing in preparation for spring. Aquarius is the eccentric, Pisces is the artist. As the one expression melds into the other, the statements of brilliant, creative, sublime and even divine art and music take the stage as the emerging Pisces energy shows us how to celebrate, and to develop some kind of belief in the arts of life! Out of Aquarius we take the extraordinary knowledge and experience of humanity, and in Pisces we purify that experience and seek further insight by getting in touch with divinity.

February 19, Wednesday
Moon in Libra

Our attention today focuses on interests such as research, storehouses of information, court related matters and concerns, as well as culinary delights. Libra Moon emphasizes the pleasures of the learning and teaching process. This is a good day to focus on business as usual, to take the time to show some appreciation for good friends, and enjoy the contents of your latest favorite book.

February 20, Thursday

Moon in Libra goes V/C	8:29 a.m. PST	11:29 a.m. EST
Moon enters Scorpio	10:09 p.m. PST	1:09 a.m. EST (2/21)
Mars opposite Saturn	6:13 a.m. PST	9:13 a.m. EST
Mercury opposite Jupiter	11:12 a.m. PST	2:12 p.m. EST
Mercury conjunct Neptune	10:55 p.m. PST	1:55 a.m. EST (2/21)

The general course of today's Libra Moon moods are focused on balancing matters that arise between friends and loved ones. This will no doubt seem like a busy day since a number of planetary aspects have reached their peak.

Mars opposite Saturn (occurring Feb. 11 – March 1.) Mars opposite Saturn always makes us acutely aware of the timeliness of our actions and the importance of acting in a timely manner, or doing something about a problem before it's too late. Medical emergencies often crop up with this type of aspect when it affects people personally. There will also be an awareness of the dynamic polarity between offensive and defensive forces. In opposing forces in battle, this aspect often brings fiery and sometimes tragic endings. This is all especially true now that Mars is conjunct with Pluto in opposition to Saturn. It is always important to pay attention to those aspects of one's life that are active and hold the potential for accidents. The popular old adage of "look before you leap" is a good meditation to apply during this crucial time of Mars opposite Saturn.

Mercury opposite Jupiter (occurring Feb 17 – 24.) This aspect puts the focus of news on the opulent lifestyles of the rich and famous. Those who are experiencing an economic crunch are unable to stop talking about their financial situation, and may produce non-stop talk concerning the need for advancement, a raise, or an income. There are obsessive concerns being raised regarding the need to excel in a crunch or in a jobless market. Issues concerning wealth become controversial, and there is often an acute awareness of what expenditures are being made. People talk of wealth, and there is considerable debate as to what wealth really represents. Most of the time wealth is an illusion and people really don't know what they're talking about when they make assumptions about the apparent well being of others. Generally, those who are doing well financially will do better still, and those who are feeling the economic crunch are likely to be complaining; nearly everyone will be talking about their financial condition. One way or another it is a time of acute awareness concerning talk about and exchange of money.

Mercury conjunct Neptune (occurring Feb. 17 – 25.) This aspect brings out communications on the hypersensitive issues and matters concerning people's belief systems and domains of spirituality. Aquarius represents humanity. Neptune in the sign of Aquarius focuses on the essential need for belief to be placed in humankind; that is, we must believe in ourselves and our own capabilities in order to survive spiritually. Many folks may be feeling a strong need to speak up about their beliefs, particularly as they may be feeling thwarted by a lack of any kind of economic advancement while these two conjunct planets are opposing Jupiter. Mercury in Aquarius focuses news, talk and discussion on human rights issues, while the Neptune conjunction touches strongly on our beliefs and our spiritual experience of those beliefs. At this time many are deeply moved to speak about their convictions, especially Aquarians. None of these issues or beliefs will be necessarily new; this is simply a time when these concepts at work are becoming more spiritually activated. Mercury is always the voice and the informant. When Mercury conjuncts with Neptune, it is best to learn from the talk and the news that goes on around us concerning humanitarian topics. This aspect also represents a good time to pray, meditate, connect with the higher spirit within, and have a talk with God.

February 21, Friday
Moon in Scorpio
Saturn goes direct   11:40 p.m. PST   2:40 a.m. EST

Today's moods express a deep underlying perception, an intense awareness that laces the events of the day with strong doses of emotion. A waning Moon in Scorpio calls to us to drop and let go of strong destructive tendencies, challenges us to cease hurting ourselves and others, and to transform our lower impulses into higher aspirations. Under favorable circumstances, this is a good time to let go of the pain you've been concealing. Sexual activity is the tension reliever that many will be seeking.

Saturn goes direct (Saturn direct: Feb. 21 - Oct. 26.) After an extended four month retrograde period, Saturn now goes direct. Saturn, representing time, restriction, and acts of discipline toward responsibility, has been retrograding since Oct. 11th, 2002, and we have had to backtrack on all the obligations yet unfulfilled so we could weed out the mess of having so much to do in so little time. This has been a time of implementing, testing and correcting various kinds of security measures in our lives and there were many sacrifices made in order to feel a sense of completion and accomplishment. As Saturn resumes a forward-moving course, we can more freely organize and stabilize our priorities and disciplines, and this allows projects to get back on a productive and progressive path. Discipline is the key to perseverance. We are now a little freer to take on responsibility with less hassle and restraint. We can focus in a more timely fashion on finding solutions to classic old problems, and we stand a chance to make progress in a more practical manner with the millennium shift now well underway. Saturn being retrograde was no excuse to obscure one's will and objectives, this is the time to get back on track with personal goals and disciplines. Now it will be easier to keep a steady check on quality control. Rejoice in your lessons as the tests of today create a stronger you for the call of tomorrow. Saturn rules!

February 22, Saturday
Moon in Scorpio goes V/C   11:15 p.m. PST   2:15 a.m. EST (2/23)

Scorpio Moon gets intense and passionate, and while it is waning, the emotional current reminds us to let go of the costly passions and intensities of the past which now serve no purpose other than to create pain – unless, of course, pain is what you're into by choice and not experienced as the result of a very bad habit. Sexual inhibitions may be one source of Scorpio Moon trauma that requires release. Obsessions around the pain of loss or abuse may be another. With Scorpio Moon there are all sorts of skeletons in the closet: possibilities which require special attention and emotional release. One layer at a time allows for the healing process to deal with each level of injury as completely as possible. Be sure to express love in a peaceful environment for an optimum healing response.

February 23, Sunday
Moon enters Sagittarius   12:46 a.m. PST   3:46 a.m. EST
Last Quarter Moon in Sagittarius
Moon square Sun   8:46 a.m. PST   11:46 a.m. EST

We have now reached a **Last Quarter Moon in Sagittarius** (Moon square Sun), and a waning moon is a good time to internalize new wishes and thoughts about the upcoming season while focusing on healing disruptive feelings and letting go of unsatisfactory habits. Sagittarius Moon focuses our attention on such things as sports, philosophy and travel. This is the time to broaden the mind and allow oneself to go further than anticipated, particularly when envisioning the future.

February 24, Monday
Moon in Sagittarius
Mercury sextile Pluto begins (see 2/26)
Mercury trine Saturn begins (see 2/27)

Moon in Sagittarius puts the emphasis on endeavors such as travel and vision quests. This is the peak of the tropical holiday season and many more fortunate folks are benefiting from breaking away and getting out of the cold at this time. For most, however, the expense of such traveling is out of the question, which is why it is all the more important for these people to use the imagination, and apply the journey of visionary work and vision questing to take them to a place of bliss and comfort. Sagittarius Moon is a great time to let the imagination soar, and to apply a philosophical outlook to the abounding forces that have changed and challenged our lives this month.

February 25, Tuesday
Moon in Sagittarius goes V/C   3:50 a.m. PST   6:50 a.m. EST
Moon enters Capricorn   5:11 a.m. PST   8:11 a.m. EST
Mars sextile Uranus begins   (see 3/3)

Early this morning, the Moon goes void-of-course briefly, and then shifts over into Capricorn where a somewhat serious mood fills the atmosphere. Long term goals and concerns come into play. Keeping the foundation of our lives and our work strong and firm is the underlying theme of today's moods. When losing ground, it is difficult to maintain a sense of humor, but humor is an essential part of maintaining one's integrity. Shaky territory requires an overhaul - rebuild and start over again. Commitment to carrying on a time honored tradition, or discharging the workload with a sense of completion and accomplishment brings favorable moods today.

February 26, Wednesday
Moon in Capricorn
Mercury sextile Pluto   10:32 a.m. PST   1:32 p.m. EST

Moon in Capricorn throughout the day gives our moods a sense of diligent, persistent, and disciplined focus. There is a need today to get things done, to face up to unfinished business, and to handle whatever comes along with serious intent. There is great potential for accomplishment today as long as one remains focused on the tasks at hand and watches the clock. This is an especially important time to carry out responsibilities and to drop fears concerning financial security. Risk increases as long as nothing is done concerning one's condition. Get to work.

Mercury sextile Pluto (occurring Feb. 24 – 28.) Communications and discussions are enhanced, with an opportunity to make a breakthrough in negotiations with a strong power. Mass media may well be entranced by a notable event or by news concerning world superpowers during this aspect. Information and news at this time will be noteworthy. This serves as a good time to reach out to those of another generation and make an attempt to communicate something vital.

February 27, Thursday
Moon in Capricorn goes V/C   4:58 a.m. PST   7:58 a.m. EST
Moon enters Aquarius   11:24 a.m. PST   2:24 p.m. EST
Mercury trine Saturn   10:51 p.m. PST   1:51 a.m. EST (2/28)

Across North America, the morning is filled with the lunar affects of a void-of-course Capricorn Moon. There is a tendency towards deep moods of seriousness and feeling as though each and every matter that presents itself is heavily laden with work and responsibility. Generally, tasks are difficult to get a handle on. By late morning on the west coast and afternoon on the east coast, the Moon enters Aquarius and our moods become more oriented toward performing great tasks or solving great problems with ingenious breakthroughs in technology. Humanitarian services are myriad, and there are ways and means to make the connections necessary this afternoon.

Mercury trine Saturn (occurring Feb. 24 – March 3.) Mercury trine Saturn brings favorable dialog concerning where to draw the lines. This is a good time to make an impression, to teach and to communicate to others those important matters that must be clarified. Timely information and news represents a gift or blessing. Important news comes with this aspect. News concerning the end of a long and arduous task brings relief.

February 28, Friday
Moon in Aquarius

Moon in Aquarius affects our moods with a sense of humanitarian openness, while a scientific sense of proceeding with caution reminds us to apply our knowledge in all dealings with others. This is a good time to try experiments with one's way of life, and to apply new methods of living more boldly and freely. With the sun now in Pisces, the characteristic dreamy quality of life coupled with the Moon in Aquarius, makes for a very imaginative and interesting time.

March 1st Saturday

Moon in Aquarius goes V/C	6:30 p.m. PST	9:30 p.m. EST
Moon enters Pisces	7:26 p.m. PST	10:26 p.m. EST
Mercury sextile Mars begins (see 3/4)		
Mercury conjunct Uranus begins (see 3/4)		

The waning balsamic phase of the Moon in Aquarius brings us the awareness of our own built-in genius as human beings. Deep thought is stirred, and the magnified desire for innovation and clarity brings out the radical and less subtle aspects of our moods. The imperfect systems of conflicting bureaucracies and volumes of complex issues needing to be dealt with require a brilliant approach. The many complexities of "The System" cost us loads of frustration, and at times like this there is often a deep rooted desire to rebel and bend the rules. Repeatedly looking to The System to solve problems often leaves us feeling less than human and hard done by, as we soon realize that the channels that exist are often designed to shuffle a problem along rather than deal directly with individual cases. Most of our western system is now based on technology. When technology throws curve balls, the dance to set things straight can be tedious. In the darkness of the moon's balsamic phase there is an internal contemplation seeking miraculous answers as the dimensions of humanities' problems appear compounded. Aquarius Moon guides us towards making a breakthrough, and it is wise to remember that it is always seemingly darkest before the light, or before the New Moon. By evening, the moon shifts over into the sign of Pisces. Through the darkness of deep contemplation a stubbornness hovers where emotional depression haunts the spirit. It is only the dark side of the New Moon, and mild symptoms of depression will soon pass.

March 2nd Sunday

New Moon in Pisces		
Moon conjunct Sun	6:35 p.m. PST	9:35 p.m. EST
Venus enters Aquarius	4:40 a.m. PST	7:40 a.m. EST

Throughout the day, the dark balsamic Moon in Pisces casts a spell of frequent day-dreaming and long moments of internal reflection. Tendencies towards escapism may be strong today. By evening we reach the New Moon mark, and the light will begin to return to our outlook on the world.

New Moon in Pisces focuses our attention on the need to get in touch with our own beliefs, and to inspire these beliefs with devotion and renewed faith. A good place to begin is with the self, believing in oneself and one's own capabilities and possibilities. The world of magic exists in the melding mutable water of the Piscean expression. Crisp new psychic and intuitive inclinations lead to a spark of inspiration that carries us through the dwindling days of winter towards the renewed light of Spring Equinox. Let the intuitive and creative process begin!

Venus enters Aquarius (occurring March 2 – 27.) Venus in Aquarius creates a fondness for the pleasures of social life. Venus in Aquarius puts the focus of attraction and adoration on eccentric, brilliant or humanitarian-related causes. This is a time when the love life of Aquarius people is enhanced and made whole, while Scorpio and Taurus people may notice that love-related focuses are causing tension in their personal lives. Leo people may be made acutely aware of their own personal need for love and beauty in their life. Leo as a general rule can never get enough love, but may be particularly aware of this while Venus is opposing Leo's natal sun this month. This is the time to work out and perfect our love of humanity with Venus in Aquarius. Teach tolerance.

March 3rd Monday
Moon in Pisces
Mars sextile Uranus   11:27 p.m. PST   2:27 a.m. (3/4) EST

Throughout today the Moon in Pisces focuses our moods on the need to escape, the need to express, the need to be artistic and even profound. The Moon now waxes and a sense of renewed hope is finally upon us.

Mars sextile Uranus (occurring Feb. 25 – March 10.) Mars, which governs all activities and forces of action, is in a position of opportunity and hope with regard to the explosive and chaotic energies of Uranus. Both of these planets are charged with forceful energy and vitality as well as being violent and unsettled at times. Masculine forces are forging ahead abruptly and loudly right now, and the outlook is very fiery, although not necessarily completely destructive. There is also the potential for a vast eruption of creativity. Those who are affected by this aspect are likely to be stir-crazy and in strong need of a revolution or revolt. Anger and frustration can be stifling at times, causing the need for freedom and a definite breakthrough. Take caution with your actions and be aware of the potential for accidents when the opportunity to vent some heat arises. This aspect is not as disruptive as an opposition or square might be; therefore it is important to look for the opportunity and potential in all sources of raw masculine energy.

March 4th Tuesday
Shrove Tuesday (Mardi Gras)

Moon in Pisces goes V/C	5:04 a.m. PST	8:04 a.m. EST
Moon enters Aries	5:30 a.m. PST	8:30 a.m. EST
Mercury conjunct Uranus	1:16 p.m. PST	4:16 p.m. EST
Mars enters Capricorn	1:17 p.m. PST	4:17 p.m. EST
Mercury enters Pisces	6:04 p.m. PST	9:04 p.m. EST
Mercury sextile Mars	9:01 p.m. PST	12:01 a.m. (3/5) EST

Sun square Pluto begins (see 3/10)

The Aries Moon gets our blood pumping. There's a strong sense of needing to look out for number one - none other than the self, of course. There is a long list of celestial events altering the universe today.

Mercury conjunct Uranus (occurring March 1 – 8.) Everyone is crying for some kind of freedom. This aspect creates an element of rebellion and radical explosions in the messages being delivered. There is a great deal of controversial talk in the air at this time. Mercury being in the sign of Aquarius is likely to raise some very interesting and unusual questions about who we are and what we're up to. Consciousness raising talk is prevalent, and there is much discussion around invention and innovative methods of living. Mercury and Uranus are at the same point together in the heavens. They are in Aquarius on the cusp of Pisces, and these two planets are doing a sextile dance with Mars. Mercury magnifies the volume of explosive news, as Uranus stirs the hearts of rebels and non-conformists who are tired of the failing and chaotic system. All of this is charged with a positive sextile angle to the relentless force of Mars. There is a real opportunity here to let off some steam, and perhaps no way of stopping it.

Mars enters the sign of Capricorn (occurring March 4 – April 21.) Now through April 21st, the main thrust of activities will be inspired by the diligent push of Capricornian persistence. Mars in Capricorn is in the place where it is exalted. Activities will shift towards diligent, ambitious and enterprising endeavours. With Mars in Capricorn a sense of duty is instilled. Activities, if successfully managed, will produce long-lasting results. This is **not** a good time to create enemies; attitudes created now will produce long-lasting results, and long-standing enemies are not a good thing to have when trying to create a sense of forward moving progress. Mars is the representation of masculine force, and it is popularly associated with the God of War. It was just three days after Mars last entered Capricorn in 2001 that the attacks on the USA occurred on that fateful September day. As we have seen, the US responded with a hard driving defence against the atrocities of terrorism. Mars in Capricorn brings on a very serious and strong force of energy that is exceptionally relentless. The life-force of spring season is in full swing now. This is a wise time to be on guard.

Mercury enters Pisces (occurring March 4 – 21.) On this long day of planetary shifts, Mercury enters Pisces, causing the general focus of news, media, and communications to revolve around issues of our beliefs, spiritual growth, our cultural expression, arts and music, and our tendencies towards escapism and drug use. Today through March 21st, Mercury in Pisces brings out the mystic in all of us and adds quite a bit of color and flare to the imagination as we are relaying messages. This is a good time to immerse one's self in creative writing and music and to open up the channels to the spirit world, allowing for messages from the other side to penetrate our psyches. This is a good time to listen, and learn from the priests, holy teachers, loved ones, and spirit guides of our choosing.

Mercury sextile Mars (occurring March 1 – 8.) This aspect allows for favorable communications with regard to the actions that are taking place around us. Mercury in Pisces is sextile to Mars in Capricorn. This means people will not just want to talk about their beliefs, they will want to back up that talk with hard-driving action. This aspect last occurred January 8th and is repeating itself since Mercury was retrograde at the beginning of the year and is now moving forward through this aspect once again. Active communication has an even greater potential to get its message across now that Mercury sextile Mars occurs with Mercury moving forward.

March 5th Wednesday
Ash Wednesday
Moon in Aries

Its March; the Moon is waxing in Aries. We're now counting down two more weeks of winter season and a restless fervor captures our moods. Aries Moon activity breaks the sleepy winter lull with a sudden propensity to cut through the grey areas of life. As a general rule there is very little tolerance for vagueness or uncertainty going around. To be uncertain is to get pushed aside or perceived as being unworthy by the public. Stand up or stand out today, otherwise you might be overlooked. Unless, of course, you wish to lay low, at which point you're bound to be less noticeable.

March 6th Thursday

Moon in Aries goes V/C	5:10 p.m. PST	8:10 p.m. EST
Moon enters Taurus	5:36 p.m. PST	8:36 p.m. EST
Venus opposite Jupiter begins (see 3/9)		
Sun square Saturn begins (see 3/13)		

Throughout today, the Moon in Aries inspires our moods to push forward. There is perhaps an air of competitiveness and pushiness happening among friends and foe. There is a restless spirit in the air, a strong desire on the part of many to begin anew, to shake up and break up old business, to start up new projects in preparation for the coming season. By evening, the Moon enters Taurus and our moods settle into practical matters, creature comforts, and concerns around financing some of those new projects that are calling to us.

March 7th Friday
Moon in Taurus
Venus conjunct Neptune begins (see 3/12)

Today's Moon in Taurus focuses much of our attention on the perfection of the physical world. This is a time when getting a sense of value or pleasure from our environment and our resources means simplifying the act of beauty. When funds or resources are low, creating the illusion of beauty can have exceptional results if done well. The true Taurian will have a vested interest where real value is concerned. There is often great beauty and practical value in simplicity. The Pisces Sun coupled with the Taurus Moon of this day focuses our attention on the true value of aesthetic beauty, and the need for appreciation is strong.

March 8th Saturday
Moon in Taurus

Taurus Moon now waxes, and focuses our late winter attention on the need for some early spring cleaning. This is not to say that the flesh will be willing while the spirit is inspired. In the slumber of this late winter time, sleepy bears still snore and Taurus Moon can easily inspire tendencies towards laziness. On the other hand, some will find it within themselves to accomplish great feats of physical work. This is a good day to be resourceful with what we have and utilize our practical knowledge to create a very simple, yet awe inspiring environment that will allow us to enjoy the comfortable stillness before the relentless buzz of spring erupts.

March 9th Sunday

Moon in Taurus goes V/C	6:29 a.m. PST	9:29 a.m. EST
Moon enters Gemini	6:38 a.m. PST	9:38 a.m. EST
Venus opposite Jupiter	8:17 p.m. PST	11:17 p.m. EST

This morning the waxing Moon enters Gemini and opens up our moods with the need to communicate and talk about what has been on our minds. Gemini Moon often focuses our attention on those areas of life where we have mixed-feelings and there is a tendency to mull things over that have not been settled just right in our minds.

Venus opposite Jupiter (occurring March 6 – 14.) This aspect brings on an acute awareness of the dynamics of attraction and wealth. There is financial struggle, as artists and support groups reach out to various channels for assistance in an attempt to survive or expand. There is the potential for love being compromised by the pursuit of jobs and livelihoods. Some may be forced to give up a person or a place they love in order to work towards advancing a career elsewhere. Venus opposite Jupiter increases awareness of the need for sensual pleasures and of what determines the depth of that pleasure.

March 10th Monday

First Quarter Moon in Gemini
Moon square Sun   11:15 p.m. PST   2:15 a.m. (3/11) EST
Uranus enters Pisces   12:54 p.m. PST   3:54 p.m. EST
Sun square Pluto   1:47 p.m. PST   4:47 p.m. EST

Today brings us to the **First Quarter Moon in Gemini.** This is a day of collecting information while we look at both sides of given pictures. Gemini Moon is waxing up and allowing for changeable and adaptable moods throughout the day, giving us a busy mindset. Covering many details at once becomes the primary objective, and processing information becomes essential. Do not let gossip and idle chatter be of concern. The evening's First Quarter Gemini Moon takes place very late in the evening on the west coast and carries over into the early morning on the east coast. As it waxes up towards the first quarter mark throughout today, the Gemini Moon puts us in touch with how we feel about our thoughts. If you don't like how you feel about your thoughts; endeavor to change or alter your way of thinking. Omit thoughts which attempt to defeat your sense of purpose; encourage thoughts that uplift and inspire your spirit. Be careful not to overdo the caffeine. Bear in mind that the Moon will be void-of-course all day tomorrow. Learn to relax and stay focused and all will be well.

Uranus enters Pisces (Uranus in Pisces March 2003 – March 2011.) Radical change is the status quo of Uranus' expression in our world. From 1988-1996 Uranus was in Capricorn shaking up the operations and standards of the old stoic institutions. From this we got strip malls and chain stores galore. Then from 1996 – 2003 Uranus graced the skies in Aquarius, the sign it rules, as radical change took place in humanitarian issues and in the world of invention and technology. The internet, cell phones and compact disks took the spotlight with massive production volumes, and competition soared in the computer world. In the past seven years, Uranus in Aquarius brought the age of invention to new heights. Now the planet of chaos and rebellion forges its path in the sign of Pisces. Out of the creation of those strip malls and chain stores came the need to fill them up with innovative electronic gadgetry and tools for humanity. For the time being, radical change has been mass produced to the point of inundating the technology market. Radical change has also come in the Aquarian form of biological technology, scientific discoveries, biological warfare issues, and the mass marketing of pharmaceuticals. As production dropped off, companies downsized, and the recession moved in; the radical increase of a hunger for change has left us with technological chaos. Uranus in Pisces now sets the stage for a new brand of rebellion and chaos. Uranus in Pisces for the next eight years promises to bring storms to our institutions of religion. During this time, our consciousness awakens to examine our belief systems and spiritual lifestyles. Chaos moves through and challenges our beliefs, our spiritualism and our place of worship. A supreme awakening is now set to occur in the core of our belief structures. Uranus in Pisces will bring an explosion of creative art and computer programs to blow our minds. There may well be an unprecedented attempt at cracking down on or exploiting Piscean expressions such as addiction, escapism, and unconventional forms of worship. At the same time, war is declared on the dying old religions which no longer serve our commercially battered souls. This all takes place while emphasizing our need to free ourselves from the emotional hardships of what religion is really all about: facing our mortality. New and radical fascinations and expressions can be expected to form in the world of psychic research, occultism, art, poetry, movie making, plays, and music. Those that treasure their beliefs as an intricate part of their lifestyle are likely to see great change and challenge in their spiritual life. Metaphysical endeavours are likely to be tried and tested in ways we would never have imagined.

Sun square Pluto (occurring March 4 – 18.) This aspect particularly affects those Pisces people celebrating birthdays this month from March 4th through the 18th. These Pisces born birthday folks are undergoing the square aspect of Pluto to their natal sun. They are now the soldiers undergoing the tests of the Pluto square, and for them this brings disruptive change and many challenges to overcome the pain of loss and the severity of transformation. As well, Virgo people (born Sept. 3rd – 17th) who are at the exact opposite of this Pisces time of the year, must also change in order to progress through these tests of Pluto - necessary transformation. Pluto tests often involve dealing with illness and loss, irreparable damage and dramatic life changes. Sagittarian and Gemini people born at the mid-point of their signs, also know what these tests of Pluto are about, as Pluto continues to trace a slow moving path through the middle to later degrees of Sagittarius. With the tests of Pluto, to attempt to hold on to past realities is to cause greater destruction on your path of life. This is the time to persevere through the obstacles of hardship. Yet the hardships that are taking place now will resurface in time so do take note of the struggles going on in your life (especially those of you for which the above mentioned signs and dates of the zodiac are relevant.) Realize this trend will be repeated and will require methods of release and attitude changes towards life in order to survive the anxiety and the stress. Take it one day at a time and do not let fear and worry rule this condition! Know that you are not alone in facing these challenges. Move steadily through the required transformation, as stagnation and fear only bring extended suffering.

March 11th Tuesday
Moon in Gemini goes V/C	3:24 a.m. PST	6:24 a.m. EST
Moon enters Cancer	6:12 p.m. PST	9:12 p.m. EST

From the very start of the day the Moon in Gemini is void-of-course, creating a tendency for many of us to be scattered, distracted and frequently inaccurate while relaying thoughts and information. Annoying thoughts, senseless ideas, and pointless dialog affront the senses. Typos, dyslexia, and mispronunciation are just a common series of symptoms of the void Gemini Moon. Take heart, by nightfall the Moon enters Cancer, and the confusion of disjointed thoughts shift to a clearer sense of how we are feeling. The Cancer Moon puts us in touch with the need to be at home in a nurturing environment where a favorite comfort food easily settles the poor rattled brain.

March 12th Wednesday
Moon in Cancer
Venus conjunct Neptune   10:40 a.m. PST   1:40 p.m. EST

Throughout the day the waxing Moon in Cancer brings out our maternal instincts, and focuses our moods and feelings on the desire to nurture emotional needs.

Venus conjunct Neptune (occurring March 7 – 17.) These two very feminine planets are currently aligned as a higher and lower octave of each other, creating a very fluid and open expression of femininity. Venus represents love, magnetism, and attraction, while Neptune (the higher octave of Venus) represents spiritual love, and the melding of spiritual energies. Venus is conjunct with Neptune in the sign of Aquarius. In Aquarius, the cohesive and melding forces of Venus and Neptune manifest with original, idealistic, and inventive expressions. Beauty and art (Venus) are linked with spirituality and belief (Neptune), much of it around focused humanitarian causes and issues (Aquarius.) Science and technology are given more acceptable and aesthetic appearances with this aspect. Venus conjunct Neptune can be utilized to reach a higher vibration of feminine, spiritual love. This aspect allows beauty, femininity and personal attraction to be connected with the higher spiritual vibrations of the universe. This is an ideal time to connect with one's own guardian angel and spirit guide. Venus conjunct Neptune, if utilized, will bring great wisdom.

March 13th Thursday
Moon in Cancer goes V/C   1:13 p.m. PST   4:13 p.m. EST
Sun square Saturn   3:38 a.m. PST   6:38 a.m. EST
Mercury square Pluto begins (see 3/15)

This may be a typical time of moodiness, and the need to whine and complain is just a symptom of wanting to be heard and understood. It may be difficult to remedy this need with a simple solution since the moon will be void-of-course throughout the afternoon and into the evening. Warm bubble baths, cosmetic pampering, massage, and delicious nourishing foods are just some of the many delightful ways to soothe one's ills. Moods are best geared towards making the place we call home a place of healing.

Sun square Saturn (occurring March 6 – 20.) This aspect particularly affects those Pisces people celebrating birthdays this year from March 6th through the 20th . These birthday folks are undergoing personal challenges concerning patience, feeling out of control, losing a sense of time, having poor timing, etc. The challenge is to overcome obstacles that intrude on one's sense of discipline and accuracy. Often, false starts occur during the phase of one's life when Saturn squares the natal sun. This challenge will pass but it also forces one to take a good look at what does matter in life, and to appreciate life for what it is, and not what they are conditioned to think life is supposed to be about.

This may be a time of sacrifice, loss or compromise. This may be a time of complexity and insecurity for these Pisces birthday folks (born on the above noted dates) experiencing the Saturn square natal sun challenge. Saturn represents those things in life that we are willing to work for and maintain. Just because there is a challenge in the path does not mean that it is time to give up. Saturn represents our sense of discipline and our application of effort and focus. Here we learn about our limitations, and our strengths are also realized. This is a good time for Pisces birthday folks to conserve energies and take losses and to difficulties in stride. Through the tests of this time a stronger human being emerges to take on future tests with greater ability. Running away from hardship now will only make life more difficult later. The Pisces in you knows this!

March 14th Friday

Moon enters Leo   2:06 a.m. PST   5:06 a.m. EST
Mercury square Saturn begins (see 3/17)

Overnight, the waxing Moon enters Leo. This is a time when moods are drawn toward the self and the needs and desires of the family, which is the extension of the self. Leo Moon is a good time to enjoy entertaining friends, and a rewarding time to build on self confidence and to tend to personal needs and desires. As a general rule, moods at this time are up-beat and playful, and most people are focused on feeling good about themselves and their friends and relations.

March 15th Saturday

Moon in Leo goes V/C   5:24 p.m. PST   8:24 p.m. EST
Mercury square Pluto   11:17 p.m. PST   2:17 a.m. (3/16) EST
Sun conjunct Mercury (see 3/21) begins

Throughout the day, playful and bubbly expressions of mood take place. Leo is associated with longevity, and governs the heart and spine. Sun ruled Leo influences physical energy, stamina and strength, and instils a zest for life. By evening (5:24 p.m. PST / 8:24 p.m. EST), the Moon in Leo kicks into a void-of-course mode. There may be twinges of cranky, tired, scattered and undoubtedly childlike expressions of mood. The beast is weary and in need of some repose. This is a good time to attempt to get some rest if at all possible, or if not, it may be well to at least enjoy something entertaining to lighten the heart a bit.

Mercury square Pluto (occurring March 13 – 19.) This aspect brings obstacles with regard to communicating to those of other generations. This is a particularly difficult time to deal with harsh issues and discuss them in a manner that makes the hardships any easier. Mercury square Pluto often brings difficult and sometimes fatal news. Talk often concerns the corruption of superpowers and the setbacks this corruption causes. The effects of Mercury square Pluto focus our attention on the obstacles and difficulties of communicating about power issues and the great dangers that our own concept of threat represents. It is especially important to be aware of what we choose to say or think about powers that appear greater than ourselves. These powers are sometimes closer to us than we think.

March 16th Sunday
Moon enters Virgo   5:52 a.m. PST   8:52 a.m. EST
Venus trine Saturn begins (see 3/21)

As we shake aside the beastly concerns of a long void Leo Moon night, the morning brings a Moon in Virgo mood. Virgo is the prudent sign of the zodiac, always looking for the loopholes in everything, always questioning, always doubting, scrutinizing, and discerning. Apart from the critic that comes out in all of us, one might notice there is a strong need to pay attention to personal hygiene. Perhaps there is a need to apply some extra effort when brushing the teeth, washing the body and hair, and preparing one's overall appearance and the feeling about this appearance. The trick is to do all this without being overly critical of one's personal state of being. Virgo emphasizes health and daily maintenance, and don't forget the Moon is simply the mood and feeling tone setter of our condition. It is only a temporary state of being and not everyone is focused on their daily moods. Those that are focused on mood will be the ones to notice the true feeling of what is really going on around them. If we don't wish to appear overly judgmental, we don't always have to react to the things we observe, we can just simply be aware of them.

March 17th Monday
Saint Patrick's Day
Moon in Virgo
Full Moon Eve
Mercury square Saturn   9:34 a.m. PST   12:34 p.m. EST

By the measurement of the waxing of the Moon, tonight is technically the Full Moon Eve, as tomorrow's Full Moon in Virgo reaches its peak in the predawn morning. This means the Full Moon energy is already upon us, there is a lot of analyzing going on, and there are many critics and critical statements being made about the course of our work and use of our resources. Virgo also puts the focus on cleaning, diet, health practices, accounting and filing, preparing taxes, and handling all of life's mundane necessities. Virgo purges and purifies our surroundings with sound resourcefulness and simple logic. This serves as a good time to celebrate health and to enjoy the pure goodness of freshly harvested foods. Virgo rules the intestines and represents the process of elimination. Now is the time to focus on eliminating the used resources of our life to make room for a new focus on healing and growth. Celebrate your existing health and do something good for your body on this Full Virgo Moon. Happy FULL MOONING!

Mercury square Saturn (occurring March 14 – 20.) This aspect affects communications and information in a way that is timely, and often difficult to take or to get around. Mercury governs communications, and the square aspect presents an obstacle, making it difficult for information to penetrate very easily. Instead, information is likely to be stifled by obstacles getting in the way of deadlines, particularly given that Mercury is squaring to Saturn, which represents time and the discipline that it takes to reach a goal or to summon a response necessary to accomplish a desired effect. This may be a challenging time to try to get through to people with instructions or advertisements, and is a difficult time for teachers to teach effectively. It may be challenging right now to sell someone on a product or to request a raise or promotion. Whatever the desired effect may be, it is wise to use caution when attempting communications during Mercury square Saturn, especially concerning matters of time and timing. This aspect makes it difficult to put a message out there and be taken seriously. People may become very tongue tied and feel quite off track. Although most of us do it all the time, it is best not to offer one's opinion or advice so freely, unless it is requested. Even then one might consider giving the matter some more time... like until this aspect passes.

March 18th Thursday
Purim
Full Moon in Virgo
Moon opposite Sun	2:35 a.m. PST	5:35 a.m. EST
Moon in Virgo goes V/C	2:35 a.m. PST	5:35 a.m. EST
Moon enters Libra	6:43 a.m. PST	9:43 a.m. EST

Long before the dawn, the **Full Virgo Moon** (see yesterday) reaches its peak opposite the sun. It then goes void-of-course and, by morning, enters the sign of Libra. Though the Moon now wanes it is still very full, and as it travels through the celestial belt of Libra, it confirms our need to set things right with relationships and partnerships of all natures. A sense of clarity is restored as our moods become preoccupied with making decisions, getting on with life, and making adjustments. The newly waning Libra Moon emphasizes the need to clear up any unresolved matters with the important people in your life. This is a time to mend relationships and keep the peace. Libra Moon also emphasizes such events as reading and research, as well as teaching and learning. Libra searches for the balance between the thinking process and the application of knowledge, and uses knowledge to apply wisdom in the effort to create harmony.

March 19th Wednesday

Moon in Libra goes V/C   7:02 p.m. PST   10:02 p.m. EST
Venus sextile Pluto   12:26 a.m. PST   3:26 a.m. EST

The mood of the day on the celestial chef's menu is about balancing and harmonizing our lives while maintaining a central area of peace in which we seek to dwell. Many of us have our battles to face, while others are truly at work moulding and changing the face of justice itself. With so many moral issues at work in the justice system, there is no higher pinnacle point from which to create a sense of balance than the very center of our individual being. Here on the brink of the Vernal Equinox, the springtime fervor builds up our senses. Waning Libra Moon keeps us busy on many levels, making adjustments to all the seasonal changes happening at this time. By 7:02 p.m. PST / 10:02 p.m. EST, the Moon goes void-of-course and the general course of our moods are at a standstill when it comes to making adjustments and applying decisions. This may be an evening of continually adjusting to the misunderstandings of loved ones.

Venus sextile Pluto (occurring March 16 – 22.) Venus sextile Pluto points to the opportunity to grow and transform with love related struggles. This is best done with kind gestures of love. For some this may mean having an opportunity to seize power for the love of power. For others it may represent a favorable encounter with those in more powerful positions in life. There was a time when Pluto, the god of the underworld, seized Persephone who was a symbol of youth, fertility and Venusian beauty. Many have viewed this myth as a power play on the part of the underworld king. Others view it as the well understood destiny of Beauty and the Beast. For others still, this aspect may bring a favorable and long required breakthrough in relationships. Sometimes the death of a power figure occurs, such as one who is the beloved, and the love of that figure is empowered by the impact of the fate. Where there is lustre, there is someone willing to buy it at any cost. Power sometimes buys our love and then we are not so free or happy to have taken this opportunistic position. At any rate, the greater powers that we often do not understand can take precedence over the things of life we value, and this aspect invites creative trouble which sometimes has an unexpectedly favorable effect: the beauty's heart can be won by the beast after all. Let love be your greatest weapon, its value is priceless and no master of the universe can afford to be without it. Set your price high, and don't sell yourself short.

ARIES

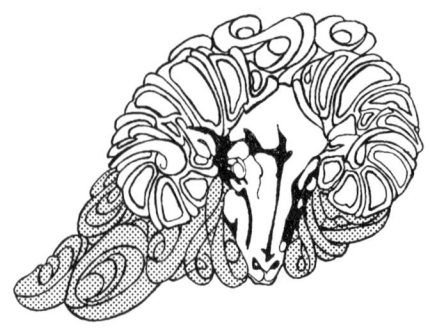

Key Phrase "I AM"
Cardinal Fire Sign
Symbol: The Ram

March 20th — April 20th

March 20th Thursday
Vernal Equinox

Sun enters Aries	5:00 p.m. PST	8:00 p.m. EST
Moon enters Scorpio	6:38 a.m. PST	9:38 a.m. EST

There is always an element of drama present with waning Scorpio Moon. Much of this drama is a reaction to the strong celestial energies that fill the air at this time.

Sun enters Aries (occurring March 20 – April 20.) Today brings the time classically known as **Vernal Equinox**, or the first day of spring. This is the time when the hours of the day are exactly as long as the hours of the night. We are on the side of the Equinox that merges toward the return of the light, as opposed to Autumnal Equinox when the sun enters Libra, the opposite of the sign of Aries. We now celebrate the lengthening of the days, and for a handful of Equinox enthusiasts this solar holiday requires ritual ceremony and acknowledgment. This time hails the focus of new growth and the return of Persephone (spring goddess) from the depths of Hades (hell, or the underworld.) Happy Birthday to our Aries friends as the Sun in Aries brings about an expression of courageous and bold new beginnings, as well as instilling confidence and forcefulness. Aries is anything but shy, as there is an inherent desire to exceed and survive, as well as make a lasting impression. Aries is the cardinal fire sign that doesn't give up easily; in fact, it notoriously never quits. This expression and style is the leader of the fiery realm, and is ruled by the active and vital planet, Mars. Aries boasts of being the first, and isn't easily offended when it comes to being criticized or misunderstood. There is a strong sense of devotion to the self and the need to excel in the Aries individual's chosen field. Sun in Aries serves as a good time to initiate new projects and apply diligence with inspired ability. The youthful vigor that Aries provides is present in the expressions of the season as the growth of living matter inspires all.

March 21st Friday

Moon in Scorpio goes V/C	8:30 p.m. PST	11:30 p.m. EST
Mercury enters Aries	4:16 a.m. PST	7:16 a.m. EST
Venus trine Saturn	10:31 a.m. PST	1:31 p.m. EST
Sun conjunct Mercury	3:35 p.m. PST	6:35 p.m. EST

Waning Scorpio Moon reminds us to keep a handle on self-criticism, as well as the tendency towards jealousy, suspicion and crimes of hate. Intense moods can be worked out through all kinds of therapy. Dealing with personal truth is important.

Mercury enters Aries (occurring March 21 – April 5.) Mercury now enters Aries, bringing out a communicative focus on selfhood, initiation, new projects, and new ways of seeing and experiencing life. We are all constantly in the process of being initiated into some aspect of selfhood, particularly given that we are constantly learning, acquiring new skills, growing and aging. Mercury in Aries helps us to discuss a focus on the newness in our lives and our personal ways of reacting and emerging through new experience. Mercury in Aries also brings news on the war activities of the world since Aries is ruled by the god of war, Mars. Wherever there is action, there is also a great deal of talk with Mercury in Aries through April 5th.

Venus trine Saturn (occurring March 16 – 26.) This aspect brings the timely gift of love. Paradoxically, it also allows for some peace in the closure of a love relationship. Venus trine Saturn brings the gift of responsive and enduring love. This is the aspect to enhance a love vow or oath with the timely application of loving energy, and is also a good aspect to better understand the importance of devotion and responsive caring. Love is a gift as well as a self-created responsibility. Remember when extending love, it is best not to have expectations concerning the need to receive it in return. This will come in due time while one is practicing the application of love's expression. Genuine love, when given without expectation, will return naturally, and bring love into your life. It is also wise to remember that the best love is given by a person who genuinely loves and respects the self foremost. Loving yourself is the first gift to give, and loving others is the most beautiful way to celebrate your own gift of love.

Sun conjunct Mercury (occurring March 15 – 28.) This is a very common aspect which creates a much more thoughtful, communicative, and expressive year ahead for those Pisces and Aries born people celebrating birthdays from March 15th through the 28th. This is your time (Birthday Pisces/Aries) to record ideas, relay important messages, and pay close attention to your imaginative thoughts as they are touched by Mercury, creating the urge to speak and be heard. Your thoughts will reveal a great deal about who you are at this time and in the year to come.

March 22nd Saturday

Moon enters Sagittarius	7:33 a.m. PST	10:33 a.m. EST
Pluto goes retrograde	9:12 p.m. PST	12:12 a.m. (3/23) EST
Mercury trine Jupiter begins (see 3/25)		
Sun trine Jupiter begins (see 3/28)		

Throughout the day, the forecast calls for moods of exploration and a desire for travel, as well as a need to stretch one's philosophical legs, so to speak.

Pluto goes retrograde (Pluto retrograde March 23 – August 28.) The greatest changes occurring in the course of history are largely the changes caused by Pluto's influence. Pluto processes take the longest time to go through since, from our perspective, Pluto appears to move very slowly. Starting today, Pluto appears to stand still at 19 degrees in Sagittarius and ever so slowly it will appear to move backwards in the degrees of Sagittarius from now through August 28th. When Pluto resumes a forward moving course this summer, it will have traveled only three degrees in the sky, which is average for a Pluto retrograde period. This means the hardships that have been created and brought to our attention in the past five months must be addressed all over again, and that we must acknowledge the evolution of humankind's current condition in order to survive the changes that are occurring on planet Earth. Pluto deals with the changes that occur in attitude concerning the overall group consciousness of each of the generations. Each generation has its own insight as to what hardship represents. This transformation is about consciousness, without which we would not be. This is a time to make life better by consciously transforming fear into determination and despair into belief in oneself, no matter what condition of fate surrounds us. The destructive habits, prejudices, sufferings and haunts of previous generations must be addressed and altered to suit our abilities to tackle the world of the future. We will all have greater challenges and tests of epic proportions to battle, and old out-dated concerns must be dealt with in order for us to address solutions to the new problems arising. With Pluto's changes we must face diseases, losses, shattered dreams, and altered or unexpected doses of reality. Pluto retrograde forces us to look within; this is a good time to confirm our greatest strengths by directing abusive patterns into constructive and useful disciplines that will reshape and bring hope to the youthful outlook that is emerging. Pluto represents the dominion of power and control, which are always in a state of flux due to our mortal tango with fate. Some endings are not a result of our choosing, yet we must face the fact that traditions, cultures and life forms on the planet are being annihilated at this phase of our evolution. Our old concepts and memories of how life once was, or is supposed to be, are dying with the times. Many ancient traditions and religions still stand tall, but even our comprehension of these traditions have undergone a major transformation. There is a worldwide epiphany that challenges the fate of which traditions will be continued, and how. We are now entering more than just a new millennium; this is a New Age, or New Aeon, that emerges. It was only in the last century that Pluto was discovered, yet throughout history the trials of mankind have borne witness to the archetypal presence of Pluto's force. Reality and normality are illusions that Pluto sweeps away as its emergence through Sagittarius opens up global awareness and our foresight of world wide struggles. There are aspects of life that are not meant to be controlled, but how we react to the shifts of this time is something we do control. While embracing the certainty of change, living consciously by example holds power.

March 23rd Sunday
Moon in Sagittarius
Venus conjunct Uranus (3/28) begins

Throughout the day, Moon in Sagittarius keeps our moods enthusiastic, and there is a tendency towards a philosophical outlook. With the Moon and the Sun both in fire signs, there is currently a great deal of electrical and lively energy waking up our senses. This is a good time to work off stored energy or to share excess energy where it is needed. Sagittarius Moon emphasizes travel and opens the pathways to connections that need to be made. Many folks may be drawn towards envisioning the type of prosperity of which they are in need. Envisioning is the first step. Once a sound vision is in place, putting the vision out where it can be reciprocated is the next step towards manifesting opportunity.

March 24th Monday
Last Quarter Moon in Capricorn
Moon square Sun	5:51 p.m. PST	8:51 p.m. EST
Moon in Sagittarius goes V/C	3:58 a.m. PST	6:58 a.m. EST
Moon enters Capricorn	10:48 a.m. PST	1:48 p.m. EST

Mercury square Mars begins (see 3/28)

Overnight the Moon goes void-of-course and remains void all morning on the east coast and up until 10:48 a.m. on the west coast. Be aware of travel delays at the start of the day. Throughout the rest of the day, the **Last Quarter Moon in Capricorn** emphasizes the need to take control as well as let go of control wherever it is needed. Capricorn Moon connects our moods with a serious undertone of needing and wanting to take hold of our goals and summon results. The Saturn-ruled Capricorn emphasizes time and the timeliness of important events. This may be a time of addressing the importance of pending deadlines. Is it time to proceed or is it time to let go? Certain quests in life may not be meeting personal needs. Is something which lacks substance taking up too much time in your life? Life is so serious with Capricorn Moon, and in its last quarter waning state it reminds us that in order to be in control we must let go of what we can't control. Attached to success? Persistence wins overall where there is a stubborn need to excel. Do it today, tomorrow's long void-of-course Moon is likely to slow progress.

March 25th Tuesday

Moon in Capricorn goes V/C   10:16 a.m. PST   1:16 p.m. EST
Mercury trine Jupiter   6:27 a.m. PST   9:27 a.m. EST
Mercury sextile Neptune begins (see 3/27)

The Moon in Capricorn in such many to rise to the occasion of feeling as though they are ready to tackle the workload ahead. Progress soon slows as the Moon goes void-of-course during the late morning PST / early afternoon EST. Though it is hard to get motivated later in the day when minor setbacks begin to come in droves, it is essential not to let a serious tone of mood turn to unconstructive flustering and useless complaining. Deal with each problem as it comes along, taking them in stride, and don't expect to finish the day's work on time.

Mercury trine Jupiter (occurring March 22 – 28.) This is a most favorable aspect that brings good news of expansion and prosperity to those who are open to broadening their awareness. Mercury brings news, while Jupiter brings wealth and prosperous change. This serves as a good time to advertise and put information out there concerning one's business endeavours, though perhaps this is best done with caution as Mercury has just started to square with Mars (occurring from March 24 – April 4.) It won't be difficult to get the attention of an audience, but it may cause some heat in how the message is reciprocated. All the while, the big billboard of life is broadcasting our thoughts. For some folks, Mercury trine Jupiter serves as an advantageous time to ask for a job or a loan, or a good time to provide a service which may have a bearing on a potential promotion. This is an especially good time to look openly for opportunity when sharing information, and to promote oneself and one's capabilities.

March 26th Wednesday

Moon enters Aquarius   4:51 p.m. PST   7:51 p.m. EST

Today, like much of yesterday, clouds our moods with the pressure to work under circumstances that make it difficult to feel like working. If there is something that needs to be removed from your life and is holding you back then this may be the time to say good-bye. Waning Capricorn Moon tends to bring out serious moods around finding some level of completion in our lives. It may be difficult to face up to disciplines and responsibilities at this time, but it is important to know deep down whether or not all these responsibilities will bring truly worthwhile results in the long run. By 4:51 p.m. PST / 7:51 p.m. EST, the Moon enters Aquarius and the focus of mood begins to shift towards pulling everything together in a much more cohesive way, giving us a glimpse at the science of the way our lives are going. Solutions are more readily available as the evening progresses.

March 27th Thursday

Moon in Aquarius
Mercury sextile Neptune   9:39 a.m. PST   12:39 p.m. EST
Venus enters Pisces   10:14 a.m. PST   1:14 p.m. EST

Waning Moon in Aquarius gives us an openness to humanity, while at the same time, puts us in touch with the aspects of humanity that we disdain and abhor. It is important to serve the public with a sense of honor. Even though not everyone appreciates these efforts, there will always be someone who does.

Mercury sextile Neptune (occurring March 25 – 29.) This short lived but beneficial aspect serves as a good time to communicate with those who are an aid in spiritual matters. Mercury sextile Neptune is an opportunistic time to apply the work of prayers and spells. Take this opportunity to internalize thoughts and beliefs and mould them into a workable understanding.

Venus enters Pisces (occurring March 27 – April 21.) The planet of magnetism, attraction and love will be placing our desires and attention on Pisces related talents and practices over the next month. Music, poetry, the arts, psychic phenomena, spiritual and religious practices will all be endearing attractions and lively pursuits now through April 21st. Venus is the feminine planet of love, and Pisces is an extremely feminine, dreamy and spiritual expression being animated by the love force of Venus. Love endeavours will emphasize passivity, tenderness, sensitivity and the need for a gentle approach towards love's expression.

March 28th Friday

Moon in Aquarius goes V/C   12:27 p.m. PST   3:27 p.m. EST
Venus conjunct Uranus   4:43 a.m. PST   7:43 a.m. EST
Mercury square Mars   6:12 p.m. PST   9:12 p.m. EST
Sun trine Jupiter   9:31 p.m. PST1   2:31 a.m. (3/29) EST
Sun sextile Neptune begins (see 4/2)
Mercury trine Pluto begins (see 3/31)

The morning begins with a sense of clarity to the mood. By 12:27 p.m. PST / 3:27 p.m. EST, the Moon goes void-of-course, and the entire rest of the day is likely to be spent on some unexpected contingency. Void Aquarius Moon sometimes brings technical failures or confusion. There are numerous aspects building up at this time. It may take another day or two to smooth over the kinks in the system.

Venus conjunct Uranus (occurring March 23 – April 2.) Venus conjuncts with Uranus for the first time since Uranus entered the sign of Pisces on March 10th. This aspect gives an added punch to the matters of love and affection. Venus conjunct with Uranus in Pisces creates potential encounters with spiritual love and psychic connections, wherein there are sometimes found a wise, though often unusual, counsel of love. Often with this aspect there is a radical or explosive attraction that takes place, or a love of making mischief and experimentation. For some this may create genuine chaos and havoc in the love life arena. Chaos is often considered a test of love. For some folks however, the power of love is so strong that chaos is just a form of exercising it, like a walk in the park. If love matters seem chaotic during this time, be positive and open to the challenge. Love affairs that are born under this aspect usually don't last long. With no foundation they are often torrid, explosive, and short-lived encounters.

Mercury square Mars (occurring March 24 – April 2.) Under the influence of Mercury square Mars, this is not a time to lose one's temper (and it could happen so very easily.) This is a good time to be especially careful and to watch what you say. Think before you speak as words can easily be taken the wrong way. This aspect is prone to rousing arguments and mental blocks concerning the actions of others. Explaining an accident right after it happens is not an easy task. Mercury square Mars makes it difficult for some to justify their actions or explain why they take a certain stand in life. Communications may easily become blocked or misunderstood if one is too caught up in the action of what is going on. It's simple: pay attention! The spoken word may arouse anger. This is a good time to hold off on making risky comments, particularly around associates, customers, and strangers, and to be careful not to misinterpret information as being hostile or personal.

Sun trine Jupiter (occurring March 22 – April 4.) This aspect is bringing those Aries people celebrating a birthday from March 22nd through April 4th to a favorable natal solar position to Jupiter. This represents a time of gifts and expansion for these Aries birthday folks, and there are good times in the works for them in the coming year. Despite Jupiter's retrograde pattern, this is a grace period for these birthday folks, and for a time now, opportunity and fortune will shine! This aspect will bring a better sense of what it means to expand and attain one's personal desire. Be sure to take the time right now (Aries birthday people) to enjoy and appreciate life. This is always true for everyone and particularly for those who are being given the gifts of opportunity this aspect often brings.

March 29th Saturday

Moon enters Pisces   1:26 a.m. PST   4:26 a.m. EST

Overnight, the Moon enters Pisces and the general course of our moods focuses on emotional or spiritual issues, but most of our concerns will be nebulous and vague. People tend to be dream oriented and somewhat withdrawn during a waning Pisces Moon. There is a tendency towards escapism and the need to be distracted from mundane activities. Art, music, and dance serve as good outlets for pent up emotional energy.

March 30th Sunday

Moon in Pisces goes V/C   10:59 p.m. PST   1:59 a.m. (3/31) EST
Sun square Mars begins (see 4/17)

Moon in Pisces, as ever, brings strong intuitive impressions and many folks are more easily inclined towards psychic awareness. Imaginative, artistic and spiritual moods set the stage. For some folks the waning Pisces Moon brings the need to face up to feelings of depression. Release self-deceptions and learn to recognize delusions and those ever popular illusions of grandeur. Keeping it all in perspective helps to minimize the gloom. Meanwhile, a little escapism and creative fantasizing may be just the way to liven up this early spring day.

March 31st Monday

Moon enters Aries   12:04 p.m. PST   3:04 p.m. EST
Mercury trine Pluto   1:12 a.m. PST   4:12 a.m. EST
Mercury sextile Saturn begins (see 4/1)

This morning the void-of-course Pisces Moon tends to make it very difficult for many to get motivated. Moods start out spacey, and many folks tend to be more easily distracted. By noon on the west coast and 3:00 p.m. on the east coast, the Moon enters Aries and the spirit of spring lunges forward. We are now at the very dark phase of the Moon. A strong internal process is brewing. Hot emotional energy is putting us in touch with spring restlessness. Newly emerging hope is about to be initiated. Old anxieties and pressures are best dealt with now so that we can approach the new month with a fresh start.

Mercury trine Pluto (occurring March 28 – April 3.) This aspect brings favorable news and optimistic discussion around issues of control and power. This is a favorable aspect for attempting communications with those of another generation, and to put the message out there wherever the gap exists. Mercury is the communications tower that transmits information concerning those lively issues that deeply concern us. Pluto's disruptive energy is focusing our attention on such issues as contagious diseases, senseless crime, misunderstandings between cultures, facing up to addiction, and many other painful realities. This is a good time to express encouraging words and reinforce the troubled people of our world with a sense of hope. This aspect brings hope like a gift, and although the myth of Pandora's box shows hope as an illusion and one of the dark mysteries of our souls, at times like the present hope regenerates our senses and fills us with the potential for triumph. This would be a good time to share stories of triumph, spreading those miraculous stories that remind us of the great potential of winning: winning against all odds. When this aspect happens there is a gift being bestowed in some way. We are gifted in the receiving and relaying of informative discussions, especially concerning power issues that help our understanding of the destructive forces at work on the planet.

April 1st Tuesday
April Fools' Day
New Moon in Aries
Moon conjunct Sun	11:19 a.m. PST	2:19 p.m. EST
Mercury sextile Saturn	8:29 p.m. PST	11:29 p.m. EST

Today's **New Moon in Aries** (Moon conjunct Sun) comes to us on the first day of April, classically known as April Fools' Day. The fool is divinely inspired, happy-go-lucky, and fearlessly ready to face the challenges of life. He is also ready to start something new! This is appropriate for the New Aries Moon. It's a good time to start anew, not only because the Moon has reached the new mark and our moods are geared in this way, but especially so because the Aries Moon invokes the powers of initiation and newness as an essential part of the regenerative force. This is a time to generate and promote inspiration and happiness. Aries is the sign of the warrior. The fight to sustain love on planet Earth calls for many courageous battles, and now is an excellent time to actively initiate new projects and endeavours that will help serve one's sense of well being. Spring is truly here and new projects abound. Activate now!

Mercury sextile Saturn (occurring March 31 – April 3.) For a short space in time, this aspect gives people an opportunity to learn vital lessons concerning boundaries, limitations and responsibilities. This is a good time to teach people about handling responsibilities and disciplines. Mercury sextile Saturn emphasizes favorable news and communications concerning matters of restriction and timely completion. Mercury sextile Saturn holds the potential to bring out very important news, so long as we are paying attention and listening. This tends to be a time when struggles and difficulties are frequently discussed, and people collectively draw conclusions concerning how to best handle their problems or responsibilities. This is a good time to discuss where to set up boundaries and how to implement security systems. This is also an opportunistic aspect for setting up guidelines and communicating work skills. Make use of it while the opportunity is here; this aspect is only happening for a couple of more days.

April 2nd Wednesday
Moon in Aries goes V/C	2:05 p.m. PST	5:05 p.m. EST
Sun sextile Neptune	12:34 p.m. PST	3:34 p.m. EST

Now the newly waxing crescent of lunar light awakens our moods to the spirit of the pending spring season and the integrity of renewed selfhood. Moon in Aries focuses our moods on the need to do things for the self. Aries Moon always has a tendency to stir up and activate events and emotional reactions. The things about our life that must come first seem to have the loudest voices of the day. All of this becomes particularly true as the afternoon/early evening brings a void-of-course Moon, and there is a tendency towards a slowing of progress due to short tempers.

Sun sextile Neptune (occurring March 28 – April 7.) Sun sextile Neptune creates a particularly opportunistic aspect for those Aries people celebrating birthdays this year from March 28th through April 7th. These Aries folks are experiencing an opportunity to awaken in the realm of spirituality and creativity. There is an awareness of the self that goes deep here, and these birthday people are likely to be particularly spacey and difficult to reach while this phenomenon of great depth is occurring. This will be your year, birthday folks, to explore personal opportunities of spiritual growth. This serves as a good time for these folks to get away from it all, and find a sanctuary to meditate and open up to some valuable answers with regard to old questions that are haunting them. These folks are in a place that gives them an opportunity to better understand the work of their path, but this is probably only true if they act on their intuitive sensibilities on their own, without the influences of others. That shouldn't be too hard for these enterprising and self-motivated Aries natured people among us. This will be your year (Aries birthday people) to enhance your intuition and primal instincts by tapping into them while they are easily available.

April 3rd Thursday

Moon V/C in Aries
Moon enters Taurus   12:20 a.m. PST   3:20 a.m. EST
Jupiter goes direct   7:03 p.m. PST   10:03 p.m. EST

The newly waning Moon is in Taurus today, giving us a fond appreciation for the bountiful beauties of spring. We are now more geared towards handling money matters, and how very appropriate that is on this Taurus Moon day when Jupiter (representing expansion of wealth) goes direct!

Jupiter goes direct (Jupiter direct April 3, '03 – Jan. 4, '04.) Let us celebrate as the planet Jupiter moves forward at the eight degree mark in the sign of Leo. Jupiter is associated with advancement, prosperity, opportunity, fulfillment, and inheritance. Jupiter has been retrograde for the past four months, since December 4th, 2002. The process of Jupiter retrograde is always difficult for systems such as business and market control. The predictability of economic growth is often challenging when this retrograde process happens. Jupiter represents skill, fortune, luck, wealth, expansion, well being, and joviality. Jupiter engages one with a sense of happiness and fulfillment. Jupiter completes its orbit around the Sun in a little under 12 years, and since this planet will go retrograde at times (appear to orbit backwards from our geocentric view), it can go through as many as four signs or as few as one sign in one year. We started off this year with Jupiter retrograde in Leo. Now as Jupiter moves forward with no more retrograde periods in the year 2003, it will end up this year at the 18 degree mark of Virgo, only having gone through two zodiac signs all year. Blessed are the Leo and Virgo people, as this prosperity planet has been and will be sweeping through their personal realms, giving them the opportunities and growing tools needed to advance. This will be the first time in several years that Jupiter won't be retrograde through the summer and autumn months. This means that with this influential social planet, we can proceed forward in our aspirations and efforts towards economic growth. In the past, Jupiter retrograde through the summer months has challenged the survival of summertime businesses, tourist related retail shops and many smaller businesses. As for steady improvement of business in general, the forward moving Jupiter may now bring some relief to those who have notably suffered in the past four months. This will be the time to correct business related setbacks and mistakes. Owners of summer related businesses can now breathe a greatly needed sign of relief, as the setbacks of the past decade of Jupiter retrograde through those long summer days won't be happening this year!

April 4th Friday

Moon in Taurus goes V/C	4:15 p.m. PST	7:15 p.m. EST
Sun sextile Neptune	12:34 p.m. PST	3:34 p.m. EST
Mercury sextile Uranus begins (see 4/6)		

Taurus Moon shifts our moods towards a preoccupation with earth related matters. Waxing Taurus Moon in the spring often puts the focus on spring cleaning and yard sales. This is the time to tend to the physical things of our life and clean, shine, wax, polish and upgrade the value of those things. Moon in Taurus puts us in touch with the value of not only "things", but also the soothing aesthetic value of comfort, atmosphere, and beauty that enchants us all. By afternoon PST / evening EST the Moon goes void-of-course and a lazy, indulgent sort of mood slows progress. Don't expect to be accomplishing much in the way of physical work come evening.

April 5th Saturday

Moon enters Gemini	1:24 p.m. PST	4:24 p.m. EST
Mercury enters Taurus	6:38 a.m. PST	9:38 a.m. EST

Although there is a tendency to want to do so many things on a physical level, there is also a tendency to fall short of completing physical tasks this morning with the Moon still void-of-course in Taurus. By 1:24 p.m. PST / 4:24 p.m. EST, the Moon enters Gemini and the mood picks up with a lot more chatter and talk. Gemini Moon brings curious moods and a more lively level of focus and interest in the world of unending trivia.

Mercury enters Taurus (occurring April 5 – June 12.) Mercury now moves into the sign of Taurus, and communications will focus on manifesting sales and generating economic growth. All of this is especially emphasized now that Jupiter is moving forward (see April 3rd) throughout the rest of the year. Mercury will go retrograde (April 26th – May 20th) and will remain in Taurus for an extended period of time, until June 12th. While Mercury currently moves forward through Taurus, it is a good time to clean up concerns around valuables, and to deal with issues concerning documents, contracts, speeches, and business procedures. While Mercury is retrograde in Taurus at the close of this month, we are likely to run into numerous contingencies and misunderstandings concerning our valuables and business related matters. For now, Mercury in Taurus brings on a new wave of discussion concerning the natural beauties and luxuries that surround us. Mercury is the messenger, the speaker and the director of the topic and the subject matter at hand. Mercury is also classically known as "The Merchant," "The Trickster," and "The Thief." In the fixed earth sign of Taurus, Mercury inspires the inclination to buy, sell, trade, barter, and negotiate terms of sale. Conversations are drawn to the physical world as we are more naturally inclined to discuss the fascination we have with the digitized billboard of life, showing us what there is out there to buy, possess, and own. From now until May 20th, Mercury will be in Taurus, stirring up our communications around issues of ownership, and will no doubt be presenting a "steal of a deal" in barter land. Spring cleaning events lead to many garage and lawn sales. Resourceful thinking and information processing leads to the extra buck.

Don't forget to turn all time pieces ahead one hour this evening before going to sleep. Tomorrow is the first day of Daylight Savings Time.

April 6th Sunday
Daylight Savings Time begins
Turn clocks ahead 1 hour at   2:00 a.m. PDT   2:00 a.m. EDT
Moon in Gemini
Mercury sextile Uranus   12:26 a.m. PST   4:26 a.m. EDT
Mercury square Jupiter begins (see 4/10)

If you didn't remember to turn your North American time clock AHEAD one hour last night, do so this morning; we are now officially on *Daylight Savings Time*. The waxing Moon is in Gemini and opens up our moods to the need to communicate and talk about what has been on our minds. Talking about our feelings is just another way of letting our feelings out. Gemini Moon often focuses our attention on issues which involve mixed-feelings, and this often requires additional thought and contemplation.

Mercury sextile Uranus (occurring April 4 – 8.) This represents an opportunistic position for the voices of rebels and revolutionaries to be heard. Those who are born at the Aries / Taurus cusp (April 15 – 25), may very well find themselves speaking out on their need for freedom at this time. Here is an opportunity for brilliance to be enhanced. This aspect brings news of change - radical change - and is a good time to exercise the more radical side of our beings with a message that holds the potential to free others. Some may act on this aspect with wild abandon, creating an affect of repelling and offending, while for others this radical communication will represent freedom from a particular kind of slavery that has held them back.

April 7th Monday

Moon in Gemini goes V/C   2:34 p.m. PDT   5:34 p.m. EDT

Questions, details, ideas, discussions. Where there are matters of concern, there is talk. When going through the process of shifting through the details of trying ideas on for size, take not so lightly - and yet ever so lightly - to the power of thought and the power of discussion. Learn to flip the coin of duality by taking in, hearing and witnessing both sides of the equation. Choose your thoughts with integrity and wisely, and on the flip side of the coin, learn to laugh at the comedy of spontaneous confusion in a knowledge-driven society full of layered ignorance and unsorted data. This is a time to play around with new data and allow for new ideas, but not to get caught or completely hypnotized by the viewpoint of any one particular source of research such as a website. Get to know your wiser self by choosing your references well. Avoid idle chatter and gossip. New feelings and moods arise because the Gemini Moon thoughts have stirred the cauldron of our emotions. Afternoon brings a void-of-course Gemini Moon; expect a scattered slowing of progress later in the day and into the evening.

April 8th Tuesday
Holy Day of Thelema (Nuit)

Moon enters Cancer   2:36 a.m. PDT   5:36 a.m. EDT
Venus square Pluto begins (see 4/12)

Feelings run strong throughout the day today. This will be good if feelings are focused on optimistic and more positive outlooks. Waxing Cancer Moon brings out some quality of Mother, and mother related focuses are strongly at work. This is a good time to remember not to be so hard on oneself for feeling the way one truly feels. It is equally important to consider the feelings of others, as moods do tend to be rather sensitive on Cancer Moon days. Emotions are meant to flow and Cancer Moon always puts us in touch with this fact.

April 9th Wednesday
Holy Day of Thelema (Hadit)

First Quarter Moon in Cancer
Moon square Sun   4:40 p.m. PDT   7:40 p.m. EDT
Moon in Cancer goes V/C   10:34 p.m. PDT   1:34 a.m. (4/10) EDT
Sun trine Pluto   8:28 p.m. PDT   11:28 p.m. EDT

The **First Quarter Moon in Cancer** (Moon square Sun) urges us to share our feelings and take care of our emotional needs, particularly in the light of our own home. Home focused activities bring warm expressions of contentment. Whatever else is going on at this time, with First Quarter Cancer Moon the emotional current tends to be magnified. Nurturing foods and trustworthy company are important components of today's activities. Treating ourselves and others in a nurturing way becomes the key to enhancing or cleansing our emotional perspective. Be careful not to push the buttons of sensitive people and use words wisely while considering the feelings of yourself and others.

Sun trine Pluto (occurring April 3 – 16.) The Sun trine Pluto creates positive, life altering changes, particularly in the lives of those Aries people celebrating birthdays this year from April 3rd through the 16th. These Aries born folks are currently undergoing the favorable trine aspect of Pluto to their natal sun, bringing out experiences that involve transformation, encounters with greater powers and fate. It is always difficult to speculate just how the Pluto experience will manifest. For these birthday folks, the concept of being gifted with fate may seem rocky and not particularly advantageous. Have no fear; this is a time to get in touch with your power, birthday Aries! It is wise to remember Pluto moves slowly in our cosmos, and powerful encounters that seem deadly or harsh are actually a necessary process. Though unavoidable, matters involving fate can be positive, and the trine aspect does represent a gift being bestowed, however unlikely this may seem. Be grateful that this is the trine aspect that brings power issues into your life in a more positive fashion with Pluto. Observe the events of this time in the life of these birthday folks - it represents a celebration of the newly transformed self. Finding out how to benefit from this power is a big part of discovering this fateful gift of Pluto. For Aries birthday people, the work of destiny bestows untold gifts this year. For everyone, this is a time of positive transformation.

April 10th Thursday
Holy Day of Thelema (Ra-Hoor-Khuit)

Moon enters Leo 11:54 a.m. PDT 2:54 p.m. EDT
Mercury square Jupiter 4:08 a.m. PDT 7:08 a.m. EDT

The void-of-course Cancer Moon may be the cause of morning moodiness. By noon PDT / just before 3:00 p.m. EDT, the Moon enters Leo and our moods shift into a more energetic, upbeat and playful mode. The Moon is waxing, and many folks are looking to be entertained. *Never underestimate the value of cheap theatrics!*

Mercury square Jupiter (occurring April 6 – 14.) This aspect creates a difficult block between the media, or communications industry, and the sponsors and producers of consumer goods. Another way of putting this may be to note that this block of energy flow occurs between Mercury, represented as the salesman, informant, and negotiator, and Jupiter, represented as the source that allows wealth to flow: manufacturer, banker, fund raiser, etc. This is the place where one's value is realized and assessed, and potential for growth is emphasized through the tedious process of trial and error. This is a time to be particularly cautious when looking for a job or changing jobs, asking for a raise, or signing any binding contracts concerning long-term investment and payment schedules. This aspect has a tendency to create expensive misunderstandings concerning real estate and other large-scale investments. Bank loans are most likely a large hassle at this time. Dig harder to clarify the details of investigating a long term investment.

April 11th Friday
Moon in Leo

Today the Moon is in Leo and the general course of our mood is energetic and openly focused on our own identity. The Sun and Moon are both in fire signs, and archetypes abound with tales of the self, bursting with character and ego. A waxing Moon in Leo uplifts our moods with entertainment, magnetism and stimulating energy. This is a good time to be sure to do something special for oneself, and to reinforce one's own integral outlook on the importance of living life according to will power. Get in touch with your sense of personal vitality and make it shine!

April 12th Saturday

Moon in Leo goes V/C	7:18 a.m. PDT	10:18 a.m. EDT
Moon enters Virgo	5:07 p.m. PDT	8:07 p.m. EDT
Venus square Pluto	11:00 p.m. PDT	2:00 a.m. (4/13) EDT

No matter at which end of the continent you find yourself, early today the Moon in Leo goes void-of-course for the entire day. Any number of possibilities can take place today: forgetfulness, clashing egos, trouble being patient in slow moving lines. All this aside, there is an air of celebration in the wings. A Saturday Leo Moon is a great time to take the family to a park or enjoy some form of entertainment with friends. Laziness is another common symptom of a void Leo Moon. Nothing much wrong with that if you don't have to worry about doing the job with precision. In the evening when the Moon enters Virgo, our moods shift over towards perfectionism, and an emphasis on cleanliness and order.

Venus square Pluto (occurring April 8 – 17.) This week may seem hard on the heartstrings since this is a difficult aspect for many people. Venus square Pluto usually involves difficulties such as, loss or death of a loved one, and the obstacles of rejection, slavery and general oppression concerning those aspects of life to which we are undeniably attached and we hold dear. If something of this nature is occurring for you at this time, it is best to recognize that love will triumph in every dimension despite the pain of separation, or the disease and strife of the beloved. To make matters worse by denying this process of life (rejection, death, disease and loss) is to prolong the pain and make worse the necessary transformation that must occur. As with any hardship, acceptance comes with time but denial can create madness. Let the obstacles of love's pain become building blocks towards a better outlook, and a stronger love will supersede the current trials of the heart. Venus is now in Pisces while Pluto is in Sagittarius. The intuitive, instinctual and hypersensitive side of our affections is likely to take a pretty good beating. Be strong yet gentle in matters of love at this time. This aspect repeats on Sept. 5th, 2003 when Venus is in Virgo.

April 13th Sunday
Palm Sunday
Moon in Virgo
Mercury square Neptune   4:32 p.m. PDT   7:32 p.m. EDT

The waxing Virgo Moon impresses us with the need to get back to more practical concerns and set some order into our universe. This is a good time to do some spring cleaning and organizing. Purifying and cleansing the body and getting back to basic health practices also becomes a focus today. Virgo Moon stresses prudence and moderation overall.

Mercury square Neptune (occurring April 9 – 27.) This aspect commonly brings about difficulty with communications concerning the challenges and obstacles of the spirit world and human spirituality. This may seem like a time when it is difficult for spirit travelers and channelers to make a connection with the spirit world; for certain, there will be obstacles along the way. Prayers to our ancestors and spirit connections may seem thwarted by novel distractions. Mercury applies to the act of communicating, while Neptune encompasses the Great Mystery and the evasive, hypersensitive realms of divinity. Neptune's hypnotic and drug-like force of an overpowering passive resignation leads to a state that goes beyond the everyday human experience, and which cannot fully be described or communicated with a media such as words. Neptune is in Aquarius stirring up issues around human divinity and the science of humanity's beliefs in this confusing and changing shift towards the New Age. While Mercury is squaring to Neptune, our minds are a lot more challenged regarding issues of divine experience, and relaying all this information may seem all the more difficult with this aspect. Anticipate religion related arguments and disputes, and resistance to spiritual teachings.

April 14th Monday
Moon in Virgo goes V/C   11:38 a.m. PDT   2:38 p.m. EDT
Moon enters Libra   6:42 p.m. PDT   9:42 p.m. EDT
Sun sextile Saturn   1:37 p.m. PDT   4:37 p.m. EDT

Throughout morning, the waxing Virgo Moon impresses our moods with the need to get things just right, to get our accounting in order, and to get organized wherever necessary. By 11:38 a.m. PDT / 2:38 p.m. EDT, the Moon goes void-of-course, and the remainder of the day brings a tendency for some folks to be a bit critical, to point out all the obvious mistakes in a somewhat ridiculing fashion. Such fastidious nitpicking can cause a real slowing down of progress, and it is important to be aware of the tendency to argue over how things should be done to the point of not getting anything done. Papers and important documents are commonly misplaced on void Virgo Moon days. Resolve now to keep an eye on things, and this may assist in avoiding that potential problem.

Later in the evening, Moon in Libra brings an emphasis on putting some balance back into relationships. Working partners will need to take some time to smooth over the events of the day with encouraging words.

Sun sextile Saturn (occurring April 9 – 20.) This aspect particularly affects those Aries people celebrating birthdays this year from April 9th through the 20th. This aspect helps these birthday Aries focus their energy and disciplines throughout this year with greater clarity, and the timeliness of events holds the promise of opportunity. As Saturn goes sextile over these birthday people's natal sun, there is a greater sense of making progress through discipline, and these people may very well actually begin to see the rewards of their diligent labor in the coming year. This is only true so long as they apply themselves to their work, and keep an open eye for opportunities as they arise. That can't be too difficult for an Aries!

April 15th Tuesday
Moon in Libra
Full Moon Eve

The **Full Moon Eve** is upon us. Tonight it will be full in Libra; tomorrow afternoon the Moon reaches it peak of fullness opposite the Sun. This is the time to make connections with friends, loved ones and family. The fullness of change occurs during this season when the first full moon of spring brings us outdoors and connects us with those associates we haven't seen much over the winter months. Libra Moon is a time of making lots of decisions and adjustments as this new spring season activates us. Our moods focus on balancing and harmonizing partnerships, marriage, and friendships. Enduring the hardship of relationships is a process of the balancing act. Friends will share their strengths as well as their weakness. Troubled times strengthen even the weakest links in friendships. Refuse to contribute to the weakness of your friend; in turn, nurture your friendship with patience and understanding. Use this full Libra Moon energy to empower your relationships. Apply diplomacy and discretion where necessary; peace and goodwill can be achieved among loved ones, but a definite effort is required.

Athena is an appropriate mythical goddess for this Full Libra Moon. She stands for truth and justice. Her totem is the owl, a symbol of wisdom. Apply wisdom, and balance the scales of your bonds of friendship with truth. (See frontispiece.)

April 16th Wednesday
Full Moon in Libra
Moon opposite Sun	12:36 p.m. PDT	3:36 p.m. EDT
Moon in Libra goes V/C	1:22 p.m. PDT	4:22 p.m. EDT
Moon enters Scorpio	6:16 p.m. PDT	9:16 p.m. EDT
Venus square Saturn	11:51 p.m. PDT	2:51 a.m. (4/17) EDT

The **Full Moon in Libra** (Moon opposite Sun) reaches its peak of opposition today. This is an important time to just let go of those unsettled feelings about your friendships. At 12:36 p.m. PDT / 3:36 p.m. EDT, the Moon reaches its full mark. Energy runs high at this point, and as the night wears on, the Moon still appears to be full. Some say the Moon is considered to be full on the day before as well as the day after it opposes the Sun. If this is so, then technically it could be said that later tonight the Moon is on the waning side of full. Come afternoon, decision making may seem nearly impossible as a number of adjustments are needed to be made with the Moon void-of-course. This evening's Scorpio Moon brings the need to release emotional energy that has built up through this high energy interim of Full Moon expressions.

Venus square Saturn (occurring April 12 – 22.) Venus square Saturn creates obstacles and restrictions concerning the timely expression of love. This aspect sometimes creates blocks in the flow of care and love due to external responsibilities and restrictions that cause and create separation. It may be difficult to engage in some romance, as there may seem to be something always getting in the way. Sometimes people are distracted from properly providing care and concern where it is most needed due to the high demands of the world at large. No matter how much one prioritizes their focuses of love, it is still likely to be misinterpreted on some level during Venus square Saturn. While this aspect is occurring, it is wisest to work a little harder at love related matters. Perhaps it is best not to get bent out of shape over some people's need to create restrictions and limitations which, for the time being, allows these folks to protect and guard their sense of harmony and peace while the trouble behind these love related matters is being worked out.

April 17th Thursday
Passover
Moon in Scorpio
Sun square Mars   6:55 p.m. PDT   9:55 p.m. EDT

The weirdoes appear to be out in droves as the Moon now wanes in Scorpio throughout the day. Self-destructive tendencies may run strongly in some folks. There is a creative drive and thrust in the air that may seem very exciting. Violent outbreaks are sometimes triggered by a simple lack of consideration or by an inability to perceive someone's overly sensitive moods.

Sun square Mars (occurring March 30 – May 5.) This aspect particularly affects those Aries and Taurus born people celebrating birthdays this year March 30th through May 5th. This aspect creates the illusion that obstacles are constantly getting in the way of the actions (and will) of these people. Everywhere they turn there is another obstacle getting in the way of their actions. This may serve as a good time for these people to lighten up on their expectations of themselves and of life for awhile, and not let such setbacks get in the way of their enjoyment of life. There may easily be a lot of anger happening in the lives of some of these Aries/Taurus birthday folks, causing them to be more prone to accidents or spats with others. These folks are likely to run across more difficulty in identifying with various activities as they occur; this is not unusual after all, given the times. Relax, birthday people! In time it will be easier once again to get your personal goals and your willpower into a state of action.

April 18th Friday
Good Friday
Moon in Scorpio goes V/C	2:52 p.m. PDT	5:52 p.m. EDT
Moon enters Sagittarius	5:51 p.m. PDT	8:51 p.m. EDT

Waning Scorpio Moon is an especially important time for merchants, sales people and the general public to be aware of pickpockets, thieves and deceivers. Stay alert and sharp! Desperate people have a way of coming out and being noticed on a waning Scorpio Moon. This is a time when much of our own internal desperation is reminding us of the importance of addressing the personal issues that are surfacing. Sexual release, therapy, emotional purging, and working with pleasing hobbies that help relieve stress are good practices for this time. By evening, the Moon enters Sagittarius and our moods are more subdued; there is a little less of a reactionary response taking place and more of a philosophical outlook on the dramas of the day.

April 19th Saturday
Moon in Sagittarius

The final day of Sun in Aries is upon us. As the Sun travels through the cardinal fire to merge into the fixed earth sign of the zodiac, the bloom of spring now opens the way to its beauties. Throughout the day, our Sagittarius Moon moods are swayed by the ever popular need to explore and look out into the universe, and to see something about the whole picture that makes our journey worthwhile. The Sagittarius Moon wanes, creating the need to vent pent up feelings, and the spirit of the day is all aflame with strong imagination at work. The Sun and Moon are in fire signs, awakening life and spurring our insights. Physical activity or indulging in a favorite sport is an excellent outlet on a Sagittarius Moon day.

TAURUS

Key phrase "I Have"
Fixed Earth Sign
Symbol: The Bull

April 20th through May 21st

April 20th Sunday
Easter Sunday

Sun enters Taurus	5:03 a.m. PDT	8:03 p.m. EDT
Moon in Sagittarius goes V/C	6:02 p.m. PDT	9:02 p.m. EDT
Moon enters Capricorn	7:20 p.m. PDT	10:20 p.m. EDT

Throughout today, waning Moon in Sagittarius impresses upon our moods the need to put what is going on around us into some kind of cohesive and proper perspective. Sagittarius Moon invites us to apply vision and creative awareness in order to make sense of it all. By evening the Moon enters Capricorn and enterprising desires lead to an industrial plan. The Sun and Moon shift from fire signs yesterday to earth signs by nightfall this evening. A real sense of down-to-earth indulgence has overtaken our senses.

Sun enters Taurus (occurring April 20 – May 21.) Happy Birthday to our Taurus friends! The constellation of Taurus has within it the bright vision known as the Pleiades, a stellar constellation with seven very bright stars, also often referred to as The Seven Sisters. These stars, mostly visible in autumn and winter, shine in the night sky like a string of diamonds, and the Pleiades is a constellation cherished by many stargazers. Taurus represents love of earth, and is known for qualities such as beauty, simplicity, practicality and sensuality. The bull represents the most practical symbol for the birth of agricultural awareness. Taurus has an obstinate and bullish side that brings out the fixed qualities of this possessive and unwavering sign. The key phrase for Taurus is "I have ," which also translates to "I own " or "Mine!" In fact, owning and sporting bulls has for many centuries been a symbol of prosperity and prestige. The horned god is a symbol of fertility, and the season of Taurus brings out the fruition of blossoming and the beauty of earth's bounty. Taurus is ruled by Venus and is filled with attraction to and appreciation for valuable and precious materials, particularly rare valuables. Taurus folks have a knack for smelling money and for finding the most valuable item at every sales counter. No matter how old, battered and antique the item may seem, Taurus will recognize the inherent value. As a general rule, Taurus energy promotes a strong desire to keep the physical world fit, and keep possessions and personal effects shining and looking good. Taurus has a very matter-of-fact way of looking at life, and likes to keep the surroundings neat and functional as well as aesthetically pleasing and acceptable. This is not to say all Taurus folks are orderly according to the rest of the world! Taurus folks have a very sensitive and often sentimental side and find it difficult to change and adapt swiftly when their life seems to be in perfect order. When Taurus folks become attached, it is very hard for them to let go. This is perhaps the most difficult sign to accept death, since this is the polar opposite to Scorpio which in one regard represents death. Taurus is more bound to preserving and enhancing life and life focuses. When it comes to giving up the body, or giving up anything, Taurus has a hard time justifying letting go after all the hard work of preserving. Taurus is attracted to beauty, wealth and material gain, and ah, yes, the scent of fresh dirt. It makes perfect sense that this sign would find it hardest of all to give up these accomplishments at the end of their sojourn here on the planet. Entropy is therefore one of Taurus' worst enemies. Sun in Taurus represents a regenerative time for many folks. A few years ago, we experienced an advantageous time for Taurians as we observed the phenomenon of the planetary stampede of SEVEN out of the TEN planets of our solar system being in the sign of Taurus on May 3rd, 2000. Many astrologers spoke about this occurrence, and some said there would be earthquakes since Taurus is the fixed earth sign, while others speculated there would be extreme economic havoc. Over the past few years the world has been affected by numerous earthquakes, wars, and economic unrest. The trading market was expected to be volatile and unpredictable, and for many folks, finances and money issues would run rampant. Those whose positions were enhanced by this occurrence are the earth signs of the zodiac (Taurus, Virgo and Capricorn), as well as Cancer and Pisces people. Those who are most likely to have been affronted and challenged by the energies of all those planets in Taurus were the Scorpios, Aquarians, and Leos. This year there are not as many upsets occurring with the Taurian life issues, although much of that Taurus alignment event kicked off big economic change. Even three years later it all continues to erupt, creating an astonishing picture of our economic process.

April 21st Monday

Moon in Capricorn
Venus sextile Mars	1:50 a.m. PDT	4:50 a.m. EDT
Venus enter Aries	9:18 a.m. PDT	12:18 p.m. EDT
Mars enters Aquarius	4:48 p.m. PDT	7:48 p.m. EDT

A waning Capricorn Moon brings a growing concern around getting the important jobs focused on and completed. A strong sense of work and duty yields concentrated efforts.

Venus sextile Mars (occurring April 14 – 27.) This aspect is favorable, and brings opportunities to situations involving love and beauty. Venus emphasizes the vibrations of love, magnetism, beauty and sensuality. The Mars influence emphasizes the awareness and application of action, movement, involvement, and also harnesses focuses of strength and energy. This week many love matters are being stirred; Venus reminds us to draw towards ourselves the pleasures we desire. Mars is reminding us to apply action with love.

Venus enters Aries (occurring April 21 – May 16.) Today Venus enters Aries, and the expression of beauty, love and attraction takes on a fascination for the warrior spirit. While Venus is in the sign of Aries the expression of love and beauty becomes a reflection of the self. Attraction is often impulsive and unpremeditated. Venus represents magnetic draw and attraction, and at this time the planet of love and beauty focuses our attention on the force and fire of Aries related interests. Hot, seductive, impulsive love abounds. This brings sheer love of and appreciation for such activities as competition, rights of selfhood, and initiation into new endeavours. For many, a new image will emerge as a result of new haircuts, new spring fashions and new means of approaching old business. Venus in Aries brings out the warrior and conqueror quality in many people, and a new sense of life and vitality is brought to the surface. Venus in Aries emphasizes ardent, open and forthright expressions and proposals of love, especially from our Aries friends who may be blinded by the lust for beauty at this time. Love expressions are more easily and readily declared. Naive expressions of love are aggressive in their demands. Venus in Aries focuses our attractions on the emergence of the spring season and the desire to take action on spring related events. New hobbies, crafts and talents will spring forth at this time. Remember, Aries rules the head; there are numerous ways you can use your head before plunging head first into love matters. At the same time, it is wise not to be so militant in the display of personal defences and in the expression of one's true feelings of affection.

Mars enters Aquarius (occurring April 21 – June 16.) Today the red warrior planet Mars, enters the sign of Aquarius. As Mars moves through Aquarius over the next eight weeks, a surge of energy and vitality takes place in the lives of Aquarius people. Now the fixed signs of the zodiac go into an activity mode, for as Mars goes through Aquarius, the Scorpio and Taurus people will experience Mars squaring with their natal sun signs, causing their lives to be more prone towards accidents, fights, fevers, and unyielding activities of great challenge. Mars in Aquarius will be opposing the fixed sign of Leo, creating a more acute awareness on the part of our Leo friends that the activities in their lives are a challenge to keep up with; occasional bouts of exhaustion will be common in these months to come for Leos. Simultaneously, Mars in the air sign of Aquarius will trine with the other air signs of the zodiac, Gemini and Libra, to activate and stimulate these folks' need for mental order, and their need to apply intelligence in order to persist through the puzzling events ahead. Mars in Aquarius emphasizes activities concerning science, technology and computer data banks, as well as humanitarian endeavors. Watch out for the tendency of electrical equipment to overheat and fry during these months.

April 22nd Tuesday

Moon in Capricorn goes V/C	5:40 a.m. PDT	8:40 a.m. EDT
Moon enters Aquarius	11:58 p.m. PDT	2:58 a.m. (4/23) EDT
Sun sextile Uranus	5:55 a.m. PDT	8:55 a.m. EDT

Practical desires are evident today, nonetheless the waning Capricorn Moon is void-of-course all day and all evening. What this means is although there is a need to get things done on the physical plane, contingencies and minor setbacks will certainly slow the process. The Capricorn goat must take the long way around the cliff: one step forward, two steps back. It is a good time to be aware of your tendency to take it all too seriously. Attempt to shrug off the setbacks, push ever onward, and try again tomorrow.

Sun sextile Uranus (occurring April 17 – 27.) Sun sextile Uranus particularly affects those Aries and Taurus folks celebrating birthdays this year from April 17th through the 27th. These birthday people are under the direct influence of Uranus in a sextile position to their natal sun. They are being given an obvious opportunity to blow off some chaotic steam, and to reach for qualities of freedom that have been absent in the recent past. This will be your year to make radical breakthroughs, birthday Aries and Taurus people! There is *no* holding back so…Go for it! The victory of creative change brings a better outlook on life.

April 23rd Wednesday
Secretary's Day

Last Quarter Moon in Aquarius
Moon square Sun   5:18 a.m. PDT   8:18 a.m. EDT

The Moon has now waned down to the **Last Quarter mark in the sign of Aquarius** (Moon square Sun.) Aquarius Moon encourages our conscience to have compassion for our kinfolk, to sort out what it means to assist and guide others. This is often a questionable sport, given that most folks don't always know what's good for them. A kind word or a sympathetic ear has great healing power and oftentimes this promotes greater peace. Aquarius Moon has a way of bringing out the strangest of strangers who bear the boldest commentary. Unusual occurrences seem to be a wee bit stranger than the last observed standard of what's out-of-the-ordinary. Don't let today's little surprises confuse your sense of right and wrong. We are slowly integrating the thoughts and ideas of this troubled world, and the closer we get to looking the problems in the face, the more motivated we will be to find solutions that feel right.

April 24th Thursday

Moon in Aquarius goes V/C   11:18 p.m. PDT   2:18 a.m. (4/25) EDT
Venus trine Jupiter begins (see 4/28)

The Moon wanes in Aquarius, bringing feelings concerned with the human condition, and the knowledge - or lack of knowledge – that envelopes us. The systems by which we operate are a statement of our being. Every stage of our technological development brings more complexity to our questionable economic structure. As we begin to develop a greater picture of the operations of our local environment, we can access things more effectively and adapt more easily to the computerized society in which we find ourselves. Some systems work and some systems don't, and we are now required to be more clear about how to restructure our databases to fit the working systems. Applying our fixed knowledge with focus, determining what we need and working with what we have are the keys to producing breakthroughs in the systems.

April 25th Friday
Moon enters Pisces	8:02 a.m. PDT	11:02 a.m. EDT

The waning Pisces Moon is a time to be aware of people's tendencies towards escapism and overindulgence. Dreamy, somewhat spacey and artistic moods ebb and flow like the sea. This is a time when our moods are drawn towards evaluating of our beliefs. Physical changes are actively taking place around us as the young Taurus Sun energy busily conjures spring activity. Imaginative reflection is touched within us as we observe the beauty in nature.

April 26th Saturday
Moon in Pisces
Mercury goes retrograde	4:59 a.m. PDT	7:59 a.m. EDT
Saturn opposite Pluto ends
Mars opposite Jupiter begins (see 5/8)
Sun square Neptune begins (see 5/3)

The world is full of subliminal messages working to capture our mood. This is why the waning Pisces Moon sometimes causes the desire to block it all out and let the imagination wander elsewhere. This is all fine when one has the luxury of doing so. While some of us are striving to keep it together, others are allowing themselves to be carefree and let loose, and others might only find comfort in a hidden sanctuary. For the most part the waning Pisces Moon leads our moods into all kinds of complexity and overwhelmed feelings. At least it teaches us how to adapt to a wide range of emotions.

Saturn opposite Pluto – Ends today (occurring January 2 – April 26, 2003.) GREAT NEWS – READ ALL ABOUT IT! This day brings to a close the notorious aspect of Saturn opposite Pluto, a long winded aspect that first came into play (in the 21st century) back in August 2001, then repeated in November 2001 and again in May 2002. Saturn and Pluto never actually reached an exact opposition this year due to the end of Saturn's retrograde period on February 21st. Nonetheless, Saturn and Pluto have indeed been doing this opposing dance since January 2nd. Today we can take comfort in the fact that the Saturn-opposite-Pluto dance has ended. Before and certainly after the events of

September 11th, 2001, a slew of reputable astrologers all pointed their fingers at this aspect, and claimed it was a major catalyst for catastrophic events. Saturn represents our guard or defence, which is being placed in a challenged state of awareness (the opposition) over the sometimes devastating powers of fateful transformation, fate being Pluto's work. Death and destruction are just two small facets of an elaborately cut diamond. There is no going back once history is made. We are transformed by the immensity of North American and global changes that have affected us all. How do we go forward in response to this phenomenon? It never is really over, it's always just a question of how we choose to respond to each layer of hardship as we step on to new plateaus of evolution. The security guidelines we've created for ourselves and to which we've adhered as a result of this new century's events has created a new foundation to sustain us for now. It is up to us to determine how we redefine our responsibilities the next time Saturn and Pluto do their dance. The opposition of Saturn and Pluto will happen again in 2009 and 2010.

Mercury goes retrograde (Mercury retrograde April 26 – May 20.) Hang on to your thinking caps as the planet Mercury goes retrograde in Taurus today through May 20th. Mercury retrograde in Taurus will bring communication breakdowns for issues around business, salesmanship, the practical feasibility of investments, and keeping track of shipments and goods. A poor sense of timing in communications is always evident with Mercury retrograde, and important connections, often business related, are likely to be missed by minutes. This all happens for the course of a three-week period in which the overall purpose of communications will be disrupted, particularly for those people who don't pay careful attention to or double check their schedules (as well as everyone else's schedules.) The key to getting through the Mercury retrograde period is to anticipate trouble in relaying information. This is the time to pay careful attention to messages, and to not get bent out of shape when misunderstandings and setbacks occur. While writing, speaking, talking and making plans, one has to be extra cautious when relaying and deciphering messages. Business contracts will probably be loaded with glitches, so be sure to scan through them with persistent care. Beware of trickster salespeople. In general, while Mercury is retrograde in Taurus, people have a tendency to frequently misplace things. Since Mercury represents memory, it is wise to be particularly aware when you, and those around you, set things down or file them away somewhere. A good mantra at this time is, "Watch what you're doing (or saying!)" Those who pay attention to what they're doing, as well as what other people are doing, will come out on top. The good news is that introspective thinking and meditation can be enhanced at this time.

April 27th Sunday

Moon in Pisces goes V/C	10:18 a.m. PDT	1:18 p.m. EDT
Moon enters Aries	6:54 p.m. PDT	9:54 p.m. EDT

This morning the Moon in Pisces goes void-of-course and will remain void in Pisces throughout the entire day. This is a day when most of us will be somewhat spaced out and unable to pay attention to very much for very long. The waning and void Pisces Moon brings out a dreamscape effect, and there is a tendency towards escapism. Drug and alcohol use is probably up at this time, and many people may choose to escape from their pain by whatever means they can. This is not a good day to have high expectations for the performances of others, and it may be particularly difficult to concentrate on one's own efforts for very long. Let intuition be your guide and be patient today. This evening the waning Moon enters Aries, and may bring a display of short temper or impatience with oneself or others.

April 28th Monday
Moon in Aries
Venus trine Jupiter   8:19 p.m. PDT   11:19 p.m. EDT

Waning Aries Moon encourages our hearts to let go of grudges and all of those minor and irritating defense modes that have held us back from applying our more positive and constructive capabilities. This is the time to reincorporate personal confidence through self assurance.

Venus trine Jupiter (occurring April 24 – May 5.) Venus trine Jupiter brings gifts of love. Love (Venus) is harmoniously placed with prosperity and opportunity (Jupiter.) This is a great time to give gifts of love, and for many folks, it is a time of expansive outlook. Getting ahead, in this case, has everything to do with appreciating and loving those areas of life that we wish to expand and prosper. A relentless positive outlook can indeed make this happen. Those who are in tight financial situations must look beyond what holds them back, and realize that what they love and appreciate in life does not have to be all about wealth and riches. Without love in your life and a love for what you are doing, an expanding empire will eventually lose its luster. Expansion can happen in the places we find love. Venus trine Jupiter reminds us that fortune can be realized with simple aesthetics and quality moments. Innovative gifts of love have a strong affect on loved ones at this time.

April 29th Tuesday
Moon in Aries goes V/C   11:12 p.m. PDT   2:12 a.m. (4/30) EDT
Sun square Jupiter   12:32 p.m. PDT   3:32 p.m. EDT
Venus sextile Neptune begins (see 5/2)

It's a Mars day: Tuesday with a waning Moon in Aries. Moods are driven by force and energy on this busy day. Self-awareness activates our sense of being. Masculine energy needs a place to vent. The tendency to act on impulse is strong.

Sun square Jupiter (occurring April 22 – May 6.) Sun square Jupiter is particularly affecting those Taurus people celebrating birthdays this year from April 22nd through May 6th. This aspect is creating difficulties and obstacles with regard to the prosperous welfare of these folks. The act of getting ahead financially or just staying on top of current financial shifts may be difficult for these Taurus people. This aspect may also be affecting many others who are experiencing money or career obstacles through personal shifts. Persistence to stay on top of financial matters is essential. Apply practicality and diligence (Taurus folks), as these traits are the stronghold that exists within your Taurus nature. Although you are not living as prosperously as you may desire, you do have it in you to come through this. Obstacles create challenges but do not necessarily dictate endings to the work of improving one's welfare. It is your Taurus personality (Sun) that is being challenged (square aspect) concerning matters of advancement (Jupiter), and challenging you to make do with less than you were anticipating having at this time. This may be a time to define and redirect personal goals. Taurus birthday folks at this time must reexamine what truly brings prosperity for them in their lives, especially in this year to come.

April 30th Wednesday
Moon enters Taurus   7:26 a.m. PDT   10:26 a.m. EDT

Last night the Aries Moon went void-of-course, and the very early morning risers begin the day like the act of accidentally bumping into a beehive nest. Early a.m. (7:26) on the west coast and later in the morning (10:26) on the east coast, the Moon enters Taurus, and the stubborn stampeding attitude of the bull sets all matters strait with less than subtle tactics. Now that the Moon wanes darkly before it settles into newness, stubbornness abounds. The wise old soul within puts us in touch with a sense of value. As the month now comes to a close, Taurus Moon calls to us to put our finances in order for the new month ahead. This is the eve of May Day celebration. A restless sort of energy fills the young bull's beastly spirit.

May 1st Thursday
Beltane / May Day
New Moon in Taurus
Moon conjunct Sun   5:15 a.m. PDT   8:15 a.m. EDT
Moon in Taurus goes V/C   10:27 p.m. PDT   1:27 a.m. (5/2) EDT

The first morning of this new month is a **New Moon in Taurus** (Moon opposite Sun.) New Moon in Taurus emphasizes the acquisition of new possessions, or it could mean there is a need to restore, replenish, and maintain the old ones. Personal contentment can be found in possessions. Search for the value of what you need and want. This serves as a good time to clean the bad energy off misguided objects of power. The Moon is exalted in Taurus and calls to us to enjoy the beauty that surrounds us, turn down the noise and go enjoy nature! Today is a traditional old-world holiday known as **Beltane** or **May Day**. This holiday celebrates fertility, and the festivity most widely known is the Maypole dance. The Maypole stands vertical and a hawthorn wreath is hung from the top to signify the cycle of life returning to its fruition. Persephone, who has finally returned from Hades, now stands before us in all her beauty and fertility. The circular wreath also signifies the feminine counterpart to the phallic symbol of the maypole. Long, brightly colored ribbons also hang from the top of the pole. Each Maypole dancer holds a ribbon, and some dancers move clockwise while other dancers move counter clockwise. As the dancers spiral around the pole leaping up-and-down, the ribbons are woven around the Maypole in a braided pattern. They are awakening the spirit of the Green Man. Throughout Europe, gardens and buildings are adorned with statues and carvings of the famous Green Man who bears a mask of leaves. The Green Man delights in the chase of the fair maiden. The Islamic version of this archetype is called "Khidr", and represents the ancient green one whose inner dimension transcends form. He appears to men in those moments when their own souls bear witness to an awareness of that dimension. In those moments, there is a spontaneous realization of spiritual truth. He is the King's fool, and the king of all fools. In his passionate frolic, the Green Man's tradition calls to us all to take joy in the fertilizing of those parts of ourselves and our lives that need to be brought to fruition. Many small towns and suburbs in North America still acknowledge today as May Day with old traditions; a day when flower baskets are put on display in front of the home to be judged and prized or just appreciated as an acknowledgment of the fruitful blossoming of spring season.

May 2nd Friday

Moon V/C in Taurus all day
Moon enters Gemini   8:27 p.m. PDT   11:27 p.m. EDT
Venus sextile Neptune   6:02 a.m. PDT   9:02 a.m. EDT
Mercury square Neptune begins (see 5/12)
Sun conjunct Mercury begins (see 5/7)

Spring is thoroughly upon us. It is difficult to get motivated on this void-of-course Moon in Taurus day. Some might argue that it is downright impossible to get motivated. Beauty abounds, the spirit is lazy and just wants to watch the scenery. That is the basic gist of a lazy void Taurus Moon. It is easy to become preoccupied with passing butterflies and most difficult to keep one's mind on mundane work. This evening the Moon shifts over into Gemini and our moods are sparked by a talkative spirit.

Venus sextile Neptune (occurring April 29 – May 5.) This is an excellent aspect to reach out spiritually to those we love as well as our spirit guides. This aspect also holds the potential for us to realize the profound beauty and the depths of which true love is capable of. Persist with loving expression and devotion towards your beliefs. See January 17 for more on Venus sextile Neptune.

May 3rd Saturday
Moon in Gemini
Sun square Neptune   5:19 p.m. PDT   8:19 p.m. EDT
Venus trine Pluto begins (see 5/7)

How playful we are today. This time invites us to apply the good medicine of laughter and joy. Gemini Moon waxes and puts many people into curious, talkative and interactive moods.

Sun square Neptune (occurring April 26 – May 10.) This aspect especially affects those Taurus born people that are celebrating birthdays this year from April 26th through May 10th. Neptune in the square position to these folk's natal sun brings a sense that there are obstacles getting in the way of spirit, the spiritual path, or the acknowledgment of one's beliefs. The challenge for these Taurus birthday folks is to overcome the doubts and confrontations that interfere with the practice of believing. Over the next year, there will undoubtedly be some spiritual adjustments, and perhaps a change of belief is required for those Taurus folks encountering birthdays at this time. Taurus change? Never! Well, unless it suits them...

May 4th Sunday
Moon in Gemini
Mars conjunct Neptune begins (see (5/14)
Saturn trine Uranus begins (see 6/24)

Suddenly it all seems to get a little too busy in this earthy Taurus Sunday setting. The youthfully waxing Moon in Gemini fills our moods with an intrusion of mutable thoughts and busy concerns. The unseen celestial aspects at work are building up various degrees of intensity. Springtime frenzy is changing the rate at which we are able to plan and keep track of matters. Getting an earful of everyone else's affairs can seem tedious, but it's just a way for folks to vent that extra nervous energy. Gemini Moon reminds us to filter through all the trivia and take it in stride. Prioritize the important stuff. Learn to enjoy setting straight all the minor details.

May 5th Monday
Cinco de Mayo
Moon in Gemini goes V/C   1:43 a.m. PDT   4:43 a.m. EDT
Moon enters Cancer   8:42 a.m. PDT   11:42 a.m. EDT

Throughout most of the morning on the east coast and some of the morning on the west, the Moon in Gemini is void-of-course, creating a little bit of a scattered environment for getting details in order. By afternoon, the Moon has settled nicely into Cancer, and the proper method of tending to our moods is to pamper them. A little extra nurturing and caring becomes an essential part of Cancer Moon moods. Setting one's perimeters and creating a comfortable environment makes for a productive day. Less ideal circumstances may invite a bit of moodiness and perhaps a bit of a crabby attitude towards handling the affairs of the day. It is important to take care of oneself, and to recognize that a nourishing meal and a quality break can help ease any emotional disruption that comes up during the day.

May 6th Tuesday
Moon in Cancer goes V/C   9:21 p.m. PDT   12:21 a.m. (5/7) EDT

Waxing Moon in Cancer makes us more aware of our home life and the desire for motherly affection. The need to nurture and build on the emotional centers calls to many folks. Cancer Moon is a good time to indulge in a warm bubble bath or enjoy a good home cooked meal. This is a time when many will be prone to sharing their feelings as well as getting in touch with their feelings. A day of the waxing Cancer Moon brings rich expressions of emotion and depth of perception and understanding. Psychic qualities are clearly at work. Not everyone abides by this positive picture of the Cancer Moon experience, but either way, you can bet there will be emotional outpouring of all kinds as the Taurus Sun continues to keep us smelling the flowers. This is a time to connect with your heart's desire, to nurture the weak parts of your heart, and to reinforce love affirmations. Tomorrow brings a long day of slow progress with the void Moon. It is best to enjoy getting as much work done as possible today.

May 7th Wednesday
Moon V/C in Cancer all day
Moon enters Leo   6:46 p.m. PDT   9:46 p.m. EDT
Sun conjunct Mercury   12:21 a.m. PDT   3:21 a.m. EDT
Venus trine Pluto   10:33 a.m. PDT   1:33 p.m. EDT

Disoriented feelings are a common symptom of a long void-of-course Cancer Moon day. This is a busy time, and for some the pressure comes out today in an emotional release. Tonight the evening closes with the Moon in Leo. Animal instincts are strong.

Sun conjunct Mercury (occurring May 2 – 11.) This aspect creates a much more thoughtful, communicative, and expressive year ahead for those Taurus people celebrating their birthdays from May 2nd through the 11th this year. This is your time (birthday Taurians) to record ideas and relay important messages. Pay close attention to your imaginative thoughts as they are touched by Mercury, creating the urge to speak and be heard. Your thoughts will reveal a great deal about who you are at this time and in the year to come.

Venus trine Pluto (occurring May 3 – 11.) Fate, power, love, intensity. Venus trine Pluto is certainly exciting. This aspect often allows a breakthrough to occur for those who fear accepting the work of fate. Adoration and loving energy flows more easily between generations. Venus trine Pluto can often help us to overcome the pain of separation concerning love. It is the place where love triumphs over death. Replace what is lost with the act of love itself. In this there is great power.

May 8th Thursday

Moon in Leo
Mars opposite Jupiter   10:35 a.m. PDT   1:35 p.m. EDT
Mercury square Mars begins (see 5/13)
Mercury square Jupiter begins (see 5/19)

Waxing Leo Moon brings playfulness and the need on the part of many people to be self absorbed or independent. Others may display their sense of importance by being entertaining and attention grabbing. Many will be focusing on building up their talents and willpower.

Mars opposite Jupiter (occurring April 26 – May 21.) This aspect may bring an acute awareness of those places where there is economic oppression or shortcomings. Active forces are diametrically opposed to expansive fortitude. Various philosophies at work may be backfiring. Mars in Aquarius creates activities around humanitarian and moral issues. Jupiter is in Leo, setting off a focus on the growing needs of the individual and the self-made image that is sustaining a personal sense of well-being during our changing economy. Mars opposite Jupiter may be causing many unexpected expenses, which could lead some folks to anger and protest. This is a very busy and sometimes difficult time to excel in business endeavors, especially in active trade markets. This aspect suggests that it would **not** be advisable to approach the job market with an aggressive level of output. Contrary to the popular belief that we must sell ourselves, trying to get ahead is not easily attainable with headstrong attitudes and unwarranted self-confidence. Mars in Aquarius demands that we be confident in what we do know, and not doctor the ego with unrealistic claims of expertise. Such confidence is best when it is backed by a strong foundation of research and development and a well founded awareness of the field in which one is trying to excel. While Mars is opposing Jupiter, it is wise to remember that when one is spurred to angry levels, take heed not to bite the hand that feeds you.

May 9th Friday

First Quarter Moon in Leo
Moon square Sun   4:53 a.m. PDT   7:53 a.m. EDT
Moon in Leo goes V/C   8:13 p.m. PDT   11:13 p.m. EDT

Energy levels are up and the expression of a **First Quarter Moon in Leo** (Moon square Sun) places our moods in states of playfulness, indulgence, and the need for self-expression and adoration. Today's attractions tend to be towards those areas of life with which we identify with the most. With the Sun in Taurus, the Moon in Leo is most likely expressed by the act of flashing around our best toys. Moods reflect on the competition of who has the best, the biggest, the shiniest, and the most expensive toys, cars, clothes, house and garden. Entertainment value and quality of presentation are just as important. Bonus points go out to those who not only have the finest trimmings, but know how to use what they have in an imaginative, original, and creative manner. Cool is always "in," and requires the assurance of the proper attitude. Later this evening, the Leo Moon goes void-of-course; as for the rest of the evening, don't get caught up in an identity crisis.

May 10th Saturday
Moon enters Virgo   1:31 a.m. PDT   4:31 a.m. EDT
Venus sextile Saturn begins (see 5/14)

Overnight the Moon enters Virgo and our moods lean towards the urge to push past all the clutter and put the immediate universe at hand into some form of order in keeping with the earthy emphasis of this time. Sun in Taurus and Moon in Virgo bring out definite spring cleaning urges for those who are ever inclined in this fashion. The need to account for what we have and what we need is an essential part of this mood-set. This is an especially good time to ground out and apply important physical health practices.

May 11th Sunday
Mother's Day
Moon in Virgo

The Moon now waxes strongly in Virgo and a sense of needing to be more resourceful and prudent overcomes many. Moon in Virgo places an emphasis on accounting for what's around us and cleaning up the physical disruption in our midst. This really is a good time to tidy up the home and apply health practices such as dental hygiene, etc. This Moon emphasizes a great deal of commotion around issues of money, wealth and resources.

Regarding Mother's Day

See the special supplement included at the end of this book for a set of special commentaries on Mom. This is Mother's day after all, and the Moon speaks to us about our Mother in valuable ways. She who gives and she who nourishes, she who toils to give life and preserve it, she who instinctively knows how to reach the core of our feelings. She is Mother, the door of life and the first one there for us. Nature and Earth are connected with the feminine archetype of Mother and so is the Moon, whose influence affects our moods and our emotional shifts and changes throughout life. Her art is the science of reflection, the reflection of the heart. She has a dark side and a bright side and she recognizes that very thing in us. She nourishes a part of herself by nourishing her child. She also sacrifices a great part of herself in this act of love and heartfelt generosity. She gives for the sake of giving and not for reward or approval. Not everyone has the purity of this archetypal picture of their own mother, or their own experience of nurturing. The dark side of the emotions can run just as deep. Want to find out more about the Moon's influence on your relationship with your mother? Flip to the **Special Supplement** at the back of this book, and find out more about your relationship with your mother in the **MOTHER'S DAY MOON GUIDE!** Look up the Moon sign that you were born under and read about how Mom related to you personally in your tender youth as the bonds of motherhood unfolded.

May 12th Monday

Moon in Virgo goes V/C	12:09 a.m. PDT	3:09 a.m. EDT
Moon enters Libra	4:42 a.m. PDT	7:42 a.m. EDT
Mercury square Neptune	9:31 a.m. PDT	12:31 p.m. EDT

Waxing Moon in Libra brings about the spirit of friendship, and the need to harmonize our relationships becomes the focus of the day.

Mercury square Neptune (occurring May 5 – June 3.) This aspect often brings difficulty in communications concerning the challenges and obstacles of the spirit world and human spirituality. Talk and discussion concerning our beliefs may be greatly misunderstood, especially now that Mercury is retrograde. This aspect last happened on April 13th and now repeats due to Mercury retrograde. Neptune is in Aquarius, stirring up issues around human divinity and the science of humanity's beliefs in this confusing and changing shift of the dawning age. While Mercury is squaring to Neptune, our minds are a lot more challenged with regard to issues concerning divine experience, and relaying all this information may seem all the more difficult with this aspect. Anticipate religion related arguments and disputes, especially now that Mercury is also squaring to Mars (see May 13th), causing the potential for violence. Avoid tabloid injustice by guarding your beliefs from the indiscretions of the profane. Deep subjects must not be treated lightly while Mercury squares Neptune. This aspect last happened on April 13th, and will repeat again on May 27th and October 30th of this year.

MAY 13th Tuesday

Eta Aquarids Meteors
Moon in Libra

Mercury square Mars	10:20 a.m. PDT	1:20 p.m. EDT

As we continue onward with the Moon in Libra, this is a time to enjoy good foods and the company of people and relations that enhance one's joy of life.

Mercury square Mars (occurring May 5 – 21.) This is not a time to lose one's temper, but it is likely that many people will tend to do so while Mercury squares with Mars. Mercury is retrograde; be especially careful to watch what you say. Think before you speak, as words can be easily taken the wrong way. This aspect is prone to rousing arguments and mental blocks concerning the actions of others. Mercury square Mars makes it difficult for some to justify their actions or explain why they take a certain stand in life. Communications may become easily blocked or misunderstood if one is too caught up in the action of what is going on. This serves as a good time to hold off on making risky comments, particularly around associates, customers, and strangers, and to be careful not to misinterpret information as being hostile or personal. For many this may just be a time of letting off some steam and complaining a bit.

May 14th Wednesday

Moon in Libra goes V/C	1:13 a.m. PDT	4:13 a.m. EDT
Moon enters Scorpio	5:14 a.m. PDT	8:14 a.m. EDT
Venus sextile Saturn	2:15 a.m. PDT	5:15 a.m. EDT
Mars conjunct Neptune	7:37 a.m. PDT	10:37 a.m. EDT

The waxing Scorpio Moon is now working its way towards the full stage. Energy builds and intensifies. Emotional currents are strong and particularly intense, as this upcoming Full Moon is going to be eclipsed.

Venus sextile Saturn (occurring May 10 – 17.) Venus emphasizes the vibrations of love, magnetism, beauty and also sensuality. This aspect often provides an opportunity to attain desired objects. Saturn's influence emphasizes the awareness of time, limitations, and restrictions. It also harnesses our dedication to responsibility and discipline. There is a passionate drive at this time to protect loved ones and limit their exposure to whatever creates the protective one's concern. The sextile aspect allows for greater opportunity to stand on guard favorably and be protective in a way that will be easily understood. Perfect timing brings pleasure. While hot and heavy aspects stir up activities this month, this is the time to take the opportunity to protect what we love with guidance and nurturing.

Mars conjunct Neptune (occurring May 4 – 24.) Mars, the planet of activity and action is in the same degree in the sky (13 degrees in Aquarius) as Neptune, the planet of mysticism and spiritual bounty. This aspect generally brings about an active fondness for the arts, and magnifies generosity, spiritual activity, and enthusiasm. There is mysticism, romance, and adventure in the air with this conjunction. This will add a special and very spiritual quality to the activities of spring. Mars comes on very strong, directing the forces of our actions while Neptune enhances a deeper, more dramatic spiritual awareness. This is a time to be especially careful not to overindulge in strong beverages, rich fatty foods, drugs, chemicals, anesthetics, etc. It's an important time to ensure one has the proper nutrients. Mars conjunct Neptune can also create busy activity in temples and churches or any kind of spiritual retreat. On the downside, there may be a militant flare of energy brewing in the sanctuaries of holy places. On a more positive note, it is an active time for folks on spiritual quests as well as artists, musicians, choreographers and designers. Mars conjunct Neptune in Aquarius brings an active openness to rise above the unimportant mundane concerns with heightened awareness.

May 15th Thursday

Full Moon in Scorpio - Lunar Eclipse
Moon opposite Sun   8:36 p.m. PDT   11:36 p.m. EDT
Moon in Scorpio goes V/C   8:36 p.m. PDT   11:36 p.m. EDT
Neptune goes retrograde   5:50 p.m. PDT   8:50 p.m. EDT

There is one big bad moon on the rise tonight! The **Moon is Full in Scorpio** (Moon opposite Sun) and this brings about very intense and vibrant feelings in the air. Density and matter shadow personal awareness and intuition. Few sources of information regarding the significance of a Lunar Eclipse have ever agreed, and for the most part the mystery behind the psychological effects remains, and the entire event is strictly speculative. Most do agree that just as strange occurrences happen around the event of the Full Moon, dark and eerie phenomenon that is highly unpredictable affect the psyche during Lunar Eclipses. Lunar Eclipse in Scorpio may therefore bring about some tension concerning the need for emotional security, and it is best to acknowledge that behavioural patterns among friends and loved ones may seem unusual at this time. Be aware of the tendency towards abuse, violation of personal space, crime, drama, and troublesome disturbances. The struggle for life and death is intense on a Full ecliptic Moon in Scorpio Night.

Neptune goes retrograde (Neptune retrograde May 14 – Oct. 23.) Like clockwork, every year the planet Neptune goes retrograde for about five months then continues in a forward moving fashion. Today Neptune goes retrograde and remains in this celestial pattern through October 23rd this year. Neptune, the planet of the spirit world which governs the interaction of all spiritual beings, will be backtracking through the sign of Aquarius. Neptune is one of the three outer planets famous for moving very slowly through the zodiac signs. How slowly? Neptune was in the sign of Capricorn from November, 1984, through January, 1998, when it entered Aquarius. Now this highly evolved celestial influence is 13 degrees into the sign of Aquarius, and will be moving back to the 10th degree of Aquarius when it goes direct this year. Neptune will not enter the next sign of the zodiac, Pisces, until April, 2011. Neptune in the sign of Aquarius brings on a special interest in the spiritual development of humanity. While Neptune is retrograde, many of the spiritual issues that have come up in the last five to six months will reoccur for those who have been strongly tied into Neptune related activities. Neptune harmonizes spiritual vibrations and brings on a very strong sense of intuition and higher feminine wisdom. For the next five months, be aware of the frequency of escapism and the tendency towards internalizing deep rooted spiritual matters. Being firm within one's own spiritual center will allow for progressive spiritual growth. Be careful not to blindly disrupt the core of someone else's belief system. Also take caution not to become ensnared by someone else's blindness concerning your own belief system during Neptune's retrograde months.

May 16th Friday

Moon enters Sagittarius   4:43 a.m. PDT   7:43 a.m. EDT
Venus enters Taurus   3:58 a.m. PDT   6:58 a.m. EDT

Although the intensity of the Full Moon already reached its peak last night, the lunar energy now in the sign of Sagittarius is basking in strength and the urge to break out of the usual routine. The philosophical clarity of Sagittarius allows us to look at the bigger picture of where energy goes and how to make the most of our situation. Though all of this energy is still strong, it is now beginning to dissipate, and this is a good time to reflect and push past all the intensity with a clearer and calmer vision.

Venus enters Taurus (occurring May 16 – June 9.) Venus in Taurus is the time for an extraordinary attraction to beauty. Here in the sign of Taurus, Venus is at home nurturing our sense of sensual pleasure and enhancing our appreciation of this beautiful spring season's peak performance. Venus in Taurus brings out aesthetic awareness, as well as a greater emphasis on the love of having valuable items, wealth, and riches. Sensual pleasures are enhanced with Venus being at home in the territory of Taurus. Venus draws and attracts, and Taurus represents material acquisition and containment. Now is the time to acquire, polish, clean, and beautify the things that give us a sense of truly having something. To create beauty around oneself is to enhance a sense of well being; it's a human nature thing. Beauty, of course, varies in the eyes of different beholders. Simple pleasures are the best; an effort to enjoy the beauties of life is not necessarily expensive!

May 17th Saturday

Moon in Sagittarius
Sun square Uranus begins (see 5/24)

The Moon wanes in Sagittarius and the course of moods focus on the wider picture of life and global happenings, while the need to shake off some restless energy persists to affect our senses. This may be a good time to think about what kind of travel will take place in the coming season. Waning Sagittarius Moon is also a time to focus on introspective visionary awareness.

May 18th Sunday

Moon in Sagittarius goes V/C   1:41 a.m. PDT   4:41 a.m. EDT
Moon enters Capricorn   5:03 a.m. PDT   8:03 a.m. EDT
Venus sextile Uranus   8:38 a.m. PDT   11:38 a.m. EDT
Mars sextile Pluto begins (see 5/24)

The dry, stoic, serious and determined moods of a waning Capricorn Moon unfold today as the general desire to push superfluous concerns aside leads many of us to the workplace and attainment of goals. Manipulative leaders are on the move. The stubborn Capricorn goat strives to get ahead, and will use whatever resources abound to make it up the rough steps of its ascension.

Sun in Taurus, Moon in Capricorn makes for a practical, ambitious and highly physical and material-oriented day of events. Light and airy distraction and mindless babble have no room where serious intent and the need to physically surpass objectives is foremost in our minds. If there is at least one good objective to achieve in your own world, this is a splendid time to complete it.

Venus sextile Uranus (occurring May 15 – 21.) Here is opportunity for eccentric love to erupt. This aspect brings an attraction to the act of breaking out of useless tendencies and habits and also brings an opportunity for love related matters to break through the imprisonment of the soul caused by not having personal needs met. This is the time to work out pent-up frustrations with loved ones, and to reconcile differences by applying love and accepting divergence. Give freedom and slack to your loved ones without letting yourself be oppressed. For more information on Venus sextile Uranus, see February 2, when this aspect last occurred.

May 19th Monday
Victoria Day
Moon in Capricorn
Mercury square Jupiter   4:47 p.m. PDT   7:47 p.m. EDT

Once again the intense mood set of Capricorn Moon keeps the serious and the diligent on the prowl to push aside all weakness and absorb all strength for use.

Mercury square Jupiter (occurring May 8 – June 3.) This aspect creates a difficult block when it comes to advertising and broadcasting. This block of energy flow occurs between the powers of Mercury, represented as the salesman, informant, and negotiator, and the powers of Jupiter, represented as the source that allows wealth to flow: manufacturer, banker, fund raiser etc.. While this aspect is occurring, it may be best to be cautious when seeking employment, requesting promotions, asking for a raise, or signing any binding contracts concerning long term investment and payment schedules. All of this is especially true while Mercury is now retrograde and is currently repeating this same aspect of April 10th. Mercury square Jupiter events have a tendency to create expensive misunderstandings with regard to real estate and other large scale investments. Perhaps these expensive misunderstandings happen when the mindless among us open their mouths when they shouldn't. A common mistake is trying to sell someone on something they have already agreed to buy. Don't lose the sale by overselling. Disruptions may occur, with people caught up in having to explain to everyone why they can't or won't afford something. Mercury square Jupiter tends to stretch out the truth, and the wrong things said may travel out beyond the usual bounds. Bank loans are most likely a large hassle at this time. Dig harder concerning the details of long term investments. Fortunately, Mercury will go direct tomorrow; even so, while Mercury squares to Jupiter for this prolonged period of time, it is wise to carefully consider the source of our information before investing.

May 20th Tuesday

Moon in Capricorn goes V/C	6:29 a.m. PDT	9:29 a.m. EDT
Moon enters Aquarius	8:01 a.m. PDT	11:01 a.m. EDT
Mercury goes direct	12:33 a.m. PDT	3:33 a.m. EDT
Mercury conjunct Venus begins (see 5/26)		
Venus square Jupiter begins (see 5/26)		

The final day of Sun in Taurus is upon us, and this morning the Moon enters Aquarius. This is the time when many will be making social connections. The signs of the times are all around us, applying some very interesting twists and turns in the ventures and knowledge of humankind.

Mercury goes direct (Mercury direct: May 20 – Aug. 28) If the past three weeks (since April 26th) have seemed very difficult in regard to relaying simple messages, Mercury retrograde in Taurus is the likely culprit who has put a damper on communicating. Mercury retrograde in Taurus has no doubt caused a disruption in banking affairs, business transactions, and particularly in communications concerning keeping track of goods. As a general rule, communications are often set back during Mercury retrograde and it's all due to the fact that many of us aren't being smart enough to interpret properly or review the facts carefully. Now that Mercury is going direct in Taurus, this is a good time to make up for misunderstandings and postponements concerning unsettled property disputes. With Mercury moving forward, this will be a better time to settle hot tempered arguments that have cropped up in recent past. Unsettled contracts can be corrected and negotiated more clearly and swiftly now, and there is likely to be much less difficulty interpreting and translating. Mercury is the planet that carries the message, and for the past few weeks, this retrograde planet has been leaving us without a clue as to how communications have been so mixed up. Now at least the majority of us who are so strongly affected by Mercury retrograde can move forward in our thinking and our way of presenting our thoughts. We can interpret others better and get on with business. For now, it's down to the business of celebrating that Mercury has gone direct! Give it a couple of days for Mercury to proceed forward and you'll notice the change in the efficiency of communications. This is all very good timing for Gemini folks, ruled by the quicksilver swiftness of Mercury, now that the solar days of Gemini are about to unfold.

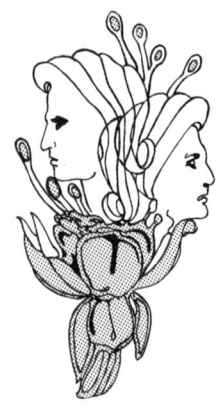

GEMINI

Key phrase "I Think"
Mutable Air Sign
Symbol: The Twins

May 21st through June 21st

May 21st Wednesday

Sun enters Gemini   4:12 a.m. PDT   7:12 a.m. EDT
Moon in Aquarius

On some level, the desire for freedom or the personal breakthrough calls out to folks. The restlessness of the spring season stirs our hearts. People we haven't seen in some time are coming out in droves. Untested theories and certain types of knowledge can sometimes be an illusion; this is an important time to banish fear and test the realms with one's own sensibilities. With the Moon and Sun both now in air signs, there will be a lot on our minds and much to talk about.

Sun enters Gemini (Sun in Gemini: May 21 – June 21.) Happy Birthday, Gemini Twin, Happy Birthday, Gemini Twin, indeed! Sometimes we Gemini folks need to be told twice: there are two of us after all! The final lap of springtime now commences! Discussions, writings, speeches, and investigations are all Gemini related events unfolding at this time. Gemini people love to think. They're often thinking of ways to change the picture and to make it brighter and more detailed. The mutable, adaptable mind must be free to roam with different concepts and ideas that haven't been fully integrated into the big picture. Gemini is a tapestry weaver of thoughts, a fine storyteller, an articulate and eloquent speaker. The Gemini mind captivates audiences with details. Gemini has a way with words. Gemini is a mutable air sign; this Mercury ruled sign works hard to get the message across. Gemini folk are generally good thinkers, but the down side is that there is an endless curiosity which can sometimes drive the Gemini personality (or people around them) to restlessness or nervousness. Duality is the key factor that shapes the Gemini perspective, and there is always a need to explore the two sides of life, as well as act out the two sides or viewpoints of themselves. They often identify with both male and female perspectives on life, along with a detailed refinement. Gemini *needs* to keep thinking and paying attention to the details of life. The Gemini days are the days in which we can become easily distracted, scattered, or spread too thin on our mental plane. Stay focused, and have fun!

May 22nd Thursday
First Quarter Moon in Pisces
Moon square Sun	5:31 p.m. PDT	8:31 p.m. EDT
Moon in Aquarius goes V/C	11:49 a.m. PDT	2:49 p.m. PDT
Moon enters Pisces	2:41 p.m. PDT	5:41 p.m. EDT

For much of the day the Aquarius Moon keeps us busy applying our finest knowledge to each situation. By 11:49 a.m. PDT / 2:49 p.m. EDT, the Moon goes void-of-course, and for a few hours in the day, there is a tendency for people to question each other's knowledge on certain subjects. Minor delays and setbacks are common for a time, but by 2:41 p.m. PDT / 5:41 p.m. EDT, the Moon enters Pisces. This is the **Last Quarter Moon in Pisces** (Moon square Sun.) Entranced… There is a dreamy, mysterious, enchanting, and as some might perceive, fearful depth to the word "entranced." This is the place where the imagination roams with on weight accuracy and one's belief system is profoundly touched. Waning Pisces Moon tends to keep us entranced by an endless number of things. Those areas of our life that bring depth and meaning are often brought out on a Pisces Moon. At times like this, many may choose to be intoxicated on substances that block pain and fear in an effort to escape. Emotional, spiritual, and artistic moods set the tone of the day as the season of spring progresses. The Moon is always at work on some level of the subconscious. Our Moon creates the most frequent aspects to other planets, often on a daily basis. These aspects reflect on our subconscious, constantly altering our moods. Churches, temples, and sacred spaces all undergo a spiritual cleansing process on waning Pisces Moon. This serves as a good time to cleanse the spiritual cobwebs of our own lives, and to reinforce personal fortitude with the strength to overcome addictions using sheer willpower and belief in oneself.

May 23rd Friday
Moon in Pisces
Mercury square Jupiter	6:26 p.m. PDT	9:26 p.m. EDT

Inspiration or depression? You never know quite which way the tides will turn with a waning Pisces Moon. Moods are blanketed with shifting, dissolving impressions which are not likely to be understood through logic. It is here that many are inclined towards crisp psychic impressions that have no merit through reason. Go with the flow is the name of the game. If people seem vague and appear to be spacing out somewhere, pay no mind; it is not likely that your company is the cause. Pisces Moon encourages us to drift elsewhere for the sake of accessing an entirely separate part of ourselves that is very private and quite spiritual. Genius is inspired in these places, as is depression - the counter charge of such revelations. Using creative methods of release is a splendid way to equilibrate the forces of the heart and the imagination. Escapism is available in many forms. It's up to you to know the difference between what is abuse and what is enhancement of your state of being. Learn the facts!

Mercury square Jupiter (occurring May 8 – June 3.) Now that Mercury has gone direct, the planet of communications is repeating a number of aspects. Now Mercury is no longer retrograde, and though it is still not a great time to ask for a raise or a handout, some of the misunderstandings of the past few weeks will be worked out through this aspect. See May 19th for more details on this aspect which continues to affect us.

May 24th Saturday

Moon in Pisces goes V/C	10:33 p.m. PDT	1:33 a.m. (5/25) EDT
Sun square Uranus	12:35 a.m. PDT	3:35 a.m. PDT
Mars sextile Pluto	11:52 p.m. PDT	2:52 a.m. (5/25) EDT

Throughout the course of the day the Pisces Moon wanes as our moods are caught up in the reverie of the dream world. Spacey moods are a reflection of the internal process of working out personal beliefs.

Sun square Uranus (occurring May 17 – 30.) This aspect affects those Taurus and Gemini people (in particular) celebrating birthdays this year from May 17th through the 30th. The square of Uranus to these Taurus and Gemini folk's natal sun brings about a strong dose of unrestrained chaos and challenging events. This may be the year for you Taurus/Gemini birthday folks to surrender to those aspects of life that are truly out of your control, and concentrate more rationally on those facets of life over which you do have control. Sometimes the aftermath of Uranus influence is an improvement, but with the square aspect at work, it is likely that these people will feel personally challenged. It is important to understand that some kinds of personal challenges are best left alone, while other challenges must be confronted directly without causing destructive damage, particularly to the self. On the other hand, birthday Taurus/Gemini folks, if your life has no foundation, there is no point in holding on to the illusion of stability at this conjuncture of your sojourn. This aspect will pass, and it is vital not to give this rapid change too much resistance, lest you be bound to the reversals of trying to fight chaos with logic at a time when it is futile. Matters will settle down in due time; try not to be so attached to the chaotic events as they occur, and the outcome will seem less costly to your sensitive Taurus and overwhelmed Gemini outlook. If you need it, project the picture of peace and it will be there for you at the other end.

Mars sextile Pluto (occurring May 18 – 31.) Mars, the planet of action is in a favorable position to Pluto, the planet of the generations. This is a superb time to take up activities with people who are older or younger. This is also potentially a very good time to reconcile differences. Those that are not in accord with others at this time are likely to stand out quite obviously. This may be a good aspect for allowing a fever to break, and for those who have been ill, a time for confronting the battle of attempting to get better. Mars sextile Pluto is busy stirring up action around heavy issues that create fateful transformation. Mars represents the masculine push of our personal lives and those areas of our lives where we activate our will and our vitality and energy. This aspect brings opportunity, optimism, and the strength to face otherwise tense situations and predicaments. This aspect teaches us a great deal about the hardships of the universe that we face, and we can learn a great deal from other generations. This is a time of breaking through for some, and a time to make decisions not to indulge in the same destructive conduct as previous generations. All around tender care is advised in the effort create some peace. This is a time to face illness as fearlessly as possible and with open eyes and to deal with the physical world as responsibly and actively as possible before the potential for illness to worsen takes its toll.

May 25th Sunday
Moon enters Aries   12:59 a.m. PDT   3:59 a.m. EDT

Spring Gemini Sun and a waning Aries Moon have us up, ready, and rearin'-to-go. This challenging and demanding environment is bound to build up and blow off some heat. Our moods are geared toward working off energy and letting out aggression, although it is sometimes viewed as swift or offensive. Those candid and often satirical quips are usually not intended to hurt feelings; in some cases they are just a childish attempt to raise a few eyebrows. Spring is in the air and the testosterone levels of dominating expression are predictably a bit loud. It may be best just to push past it all and let the energy go to the place we need it most.

May 26th Monday
Memorial Day
Moon in Aries
Venus square Jupiter   12:29 a.m. PDT   3:29 a.m. EDT
Mercury conjunct Venus   5:04 p.m. PDT   8:04 p.m. EDT

There is a desire to take action and press forward through life. Aries Moon calls to us and teaches us an important part of addressing the warrior self on this Memorial Day Monday. This is a time when the force of energy compels us to act ourselves, or to react to the beat of those who are warrior beings. We are all warrior beings on some level. Vitality and energy is a healthy sign of life that we all must maintain, nurture, and find within ourselves on a daily basis. Waning Aries Moon gives us the opportunity to exercise our vitality levels, and encourages us to drop emotional pressures that may be the source of some anger issues in our lives.

Venus square Jupiter (occurring May 20 – 31.) Our experience of beauty and affection is challenged and tested with the difficulty of attracting or acquiring prosperity. Some might say that the act of appreciating beauty is a form of prosperity in itself. Unfortunately, this aspect may create the hardship of our not being able to acknowledge beauty as a form of wealth within itself. This aspect reminds us that something more than love's blindness is required in order for us to fully realize our riches. Love may be blocked from attainment in some of fashion, and traveling lovers may be tested on some level. Those who require beauty through riches are challenged to potentially give up or sell desired objects that fulfill a sense of aesthetic attainment. There may also be a focus on the need to create curbs on spending in pursuit of pleasure. This may be trying, particularly while love is being so ardently expressed with Mercury conjunct Venus. Don't let money matters spoil the beauty of loving affection, but expect the strong possibility that this might well be the case with others.

Mercury conjunct Venus (occurring May 20 – June 28.) Mercury and Venus are conjunct; the energy suggests an emphasis on the need and ability to communicate love. Both communication and love are expressed in a variety of ways. Today's conjunction of Mercury and Venus takes place in the sign of Taurus, and this is deliciously expressed with the ardent and heartfelt joy of sharing luxuries with loved ones. This is the time to articulate our needs, to speak out on what we want and need to have, particularly when it comes to sharing love. These two planets in Taurus lend to this aspect a very strong physical attraction in the communication of love. Any words of love or adoration uttered at this time may come across more easily and with better reception, so long as this expression of love is actually very sincere and genuine in nature. The practical nature of Taurus doesn't mess around; talk of love must be real in its intent. Generally an excellent aspect to discuss love matters, when this conjunction occurs in Taurus, it gives all of this loving communication a delectably down-to-earth bite. As we head on into June, Mercury and Venus remain very connected and proceed into the sign of Gemini. This aspect will repeat on June 20th in the sign of Gemini where the sentiment of love related messages becomes more playful and articulate. Be sure to let those you truly love know it; sometimes it's what isn't said that disquiets the heart. Hold no expectations in the expression of love, and take no offense if your attempts to be loving are in fact poorly interpreted, especially while Mercury and Venus are squaring off to Jupiter and Neptune. Mercury is direct now, what have you got to lose? Taurians often think that what you have is all-important. What you have to lose must be weighed against what is to be gained. Love is worth having. Taurus says: "I have." Taurus in Venus conjunct with Mercury says: "I Have Love! Hallelujah!." Sing your praises of springtime frolic and down to earth love. Know that there is a need to communicate the love that is happening now and the most simple and practical (not overly complex) way to express that love might be best.

May 27th Tuesday

Moon in Aries goes V/C	11:41 a.m. PDT	2:41 p.m. EDT
Moon enters Taurus	1:32 p.m. PDT	4:32 p.m. EDT
Venus square Neptune	12:06 a.m. PDT	3:06 a.m. EDT
Mercury square Neptune	9:18 a.m. PDT	12:18 p.m. EDT

The waning Aries Moon continues to keep our moods both diligent and somewhat restless. For a spell, the void-of-course Moon afternoon brings a tendency towards impatience during those line ups and delays. Later in the afternoon, the Taurus Moon focuses our attention on the need to create more stability, either financially or otherwise. By evening, the overall consensus is that the best position to be in is a comfortable one.

Venus square Neptune (occurring May 22 – 31.) You may find your desires are at odds with your spiritual beliefs, and it may be a hard time for some people to make a personal connection with spiritual teachings. This may also appear to be a hard time to concentrate or meditate on spiritual activities. Faith and belief in love matters may be tested at this time. Feminine expression may be set back by old world beliefs, and love matters may be thwarted by conflicts between belief systems. This is a time to persist with loving expression despite those conflicts. Certainly it is best to avoid arguments concerning spiritual beliefs with loved ones at this time.

Mercury square Neptune (occurring May 5 – June 3.) Now the forward moving Mercury creates a repeat of this aspect for the third time this year. This may be the time when many are coming across unsettled disputes concerning spiritual matters that are still unresolved. Fortunately Mercury is no longer retrograde, or squaring to Mars, so the attempts to address spiritual issues may not be as disquieting as they were earlier in the month. See May 12th for more details on Mercury square Neptune.

May 28th Wednesday
Moon in Taurus
Venus square Mars begins (see 6/5)
Sun trine Neptune begins (see 6/3)

Moon in Taurus wanes down darkly. This is a time of preparation and refinement. Taurus Moon fixates our moods on the important focuses of the physical world. An assessment of our finances is common at month's end. The need to continue spring cleaning practices calls to us. There is also an emphasis on selling, buying, shifting and moving physical possessions. This means having to face a lot of emotional baggage attached to letting go of the physical possessions that have piled up in our lives. Taurus Moon often brings a sentimental attachment to the things we are working on.

May 29th Thursday
Ascension Day
Moon in Taurus goes V/C   8:53 a.m. PDT   11:53 a.m. EDT
Moon V/C in Taurus all day and night
Sun sextile Jupiter begins (see 6/4)

Before us is a perfectly fine spring day with a long line of confusion and mix ups ready to affront us as the day progresses, or in some cases, digresses. All afternoon and all evening the Moon is void-of-course in the sign of Taurus. This is not a good time to be moving. The most common occurrence we can expect to see are forgetting, misplacing and losing things. Stubborn and lazy moods may also be a symptom of today's darkly waning void Taurus Moon. Worry over where the money is going to come from is likely to be common. To make matters more dense, we are on the brink of a solar ecliptic New Moon set to take place tomorrow. Confusion and perhaps even a bit of uncertainty are bound to create stagnation. Getting through this month is testing some folks at this time. Hang in there; as in all particularly dark lunar phases, it will pass.

May 30th Friday
New Moon in Gemini - Solar Eclipse
Moon enters Gemini   2:32 a.m. PDT   5:32 a.m. EDT
Moon conjunct Sun   9:20 p.m. PDT   12:20 a.m. (5/31) EDT

The **New Moon / Solar Eclipse in Gemini** (Moon conjunct Sun) allows for new thoughts and ideas to begin to flow, and new feelings about the way we are thinking will begin to emerge. Solar eclipse energy brings a dark mood for some folks, and it is wise to apply caution during this time to what we say and how we communicate. New Moons are like clean slates. It's time to begin again a process of strengthening and celebrating your energy, to plan new vistas for growth, particularly the emotional well-being of your mental growth. This represents a time for paying attention to those newer thoughts, ideas and caprices in the wind. This would be a good time to initiate a new round of creative writing, or apply a new discipline of thinking in a particular manner that will eventually become more personally beneficial. Making a new attempt at reaching out to an old friend or opening up communications with a new circle of friends will bring great new insights to one's field of knowledge.

May 31st Saturday
Moon in Gemini

The Moon now begins a cycle of waxing in the sign of Gemini. Sun and Moon in Gemini is a busy time for the mind and the engaging and communicative part of our beings. Things happen with the Sun and Moon in this placement, and there is a strong underlining current urging us to take note of all those curious details of life as they go fluttering by faster than we can contain them. A childlike fascination fills the air, and there will be an endless stream of chatter and babble. The dark phase of the Moon and yesterday's solar eclipse have begun to lift past our moods, and all the discussion and talk of this time serves as an outlet for people. Distracting as this outlet might be, it is necessary, to save time and troubled feelings, to be a sport and lend a listening ear.

June 1st Sunday

Moon in Gemini goes V/C   1:55 p.m. PDT   4:55 p.m. EDT
Moon enters Cancer   2:27 p.m. PDT   5:27 p.m. EDT
Jupiter trine Pluto begins (see 7/1)

SO MANY ASPECTS THIS CRAZY MONTH!:

At this time a number of aspects and shifts are busily at work to test some of us on challenging levels, while providing relief for others.

Curious and busy minds are at work on this Gemini Sun and Moon Day. The young Gemini Moon now waxes and the mood setting is youthful, inquisitive, talkative, and of course, easily distracted by a number of details. There are places to go, people to see, things to do. For a short time this afternoon there is a gap in the time space continuum of keeping the details straight. It all becomes a blur while the Moon is briefly void-of-course in Gemini. It is wise to pay attention and stay on track as much as possible. By 2:27 p.m. PDT / 5:27 p.m. EDT, the Moon enters Cancer and our moods shift over into a more sensitive, perhaps even guarded or withdrawn state. Feelings are surfacing and putting us in touch with our instincts. This is the time to nurture the heart, pamper the soul, enjoy the best there is in a comforting home environment. We all have to work out our kinks, especially on the home front. Home is where we work out a number of kinks in our lives and are at liberty to display a wider variety of moods and feelings about what matters. This mind bending Gemini day is tempered by a flow of emotion, some venting of the feelings, and a good strong hunch about what kind of month this will be by the way in which it began.

June 2nd Monday

Moon in Cancer
Jupiter opposite Neptune   7:58 p.m. PDT   10:58 p.m. EDT
Mercury square Mars begins (see 6/10)
Sun opposite Pluto begins (see 6/9)

Moon in Cancer impresses our moods with the need to get in touch with our feelings and the ways in which we show care and concern. A home oriented focus continues to be emphasized. Waxing Moon in the water sign of Cancer is an ideal time to transfer plants and shrubs in the garden and to plant seeds.

Jupiter opposite Neptune (occurring Jan. 11 – July 4.) Jupiter opposite Neptune has been actively occurring since January 11th and continues through July 4th of this year. This aspect is reaching its peak again, just as it did on February 16th this year (see Feb. 15th for more details.) While this aspect took place back in February, Jupiter was retrograde. Now Neptune is retrograde, and Jupiter moves forward. There is no question that these two sizeable planets are having a little dance this year. Jupiter opposing Neptune may, to some degree, cause our sense of economic growth to be thwarted by our spiritual and religious beliefs. Career moves are affronted by spiritual concerns and a sense of well being is questioned. We are made acutely aware of the need to excel in the economics of the big picture, while having to balance the ways our beliefs and spiritual comforts fit into our travels and advancements in the world. While Jupiter moves in a direct fashion, this is the time to open up one's visionary talents, and attempt to understand why certain focuses of life appear out of hand or disruptive. For the most part, this aspect brings a better understanding of the spirit world, an expansion of our beliefs, and the interplay of Spirit within our daily lives. While Neptune is retrograde, spiritual growth is best focused internally. In mythology, Jupiter is the god of joviality and prosperity, and this force of high hopes and dreams come true exists whenever we are openly advancing towards economic growth. Neptune is the god of the sea, the place where our ancient soul remembers. There is an acute awareness in the air with regard to the ways in which we are progressing, and of the beliefs, customs, and memories we are compromising for the sake of our true will. Some may be asking themselves, "Is this direction my career now takes going to dampen my spirit?" Neptune is in Aquarius; the spirit will **know**. Jupiter is in Leo, and brings the prosperity that comes from the power of personal will. Keep your spirits bright!

June 3rd Tuesday

Moon in Cancer goes V/C	9:27 a.m. PDT	12:27 p.m. EDT
Saturn enters Cancer	6:32 p.m. PDT	9:32 p.m. EDT
Sun trine Neptune	7:28 p.m. PDT	10:28 p.m. EDT

Feelings are building up now as the Moon is in Cancer and waxing steadily. This month has a great deal of celestial activity, making it one of the most complex months of activity and change this year. This morning the Moon goes void-of-course for the entire day, and emotional currents seem to run throughout the course of daily events, slowing down progress. For every action there is an equal and just as time consuming reaction to the way things are going. Territorial disputes are likely to crop up. Let the feelings flow; Saturn is now entering Cancer and the Moon is aligned in this place, affirming that there is no sense denying what we can all feel happening.

Saturn enters Cancer (occurring June 3, 2003 – July 16, 2005) Approximately every 2 to 3 years, depending on the retrograde periods, Saturn enters a new zodiac sign. The expression of Saturn in Cancer focuses the realm of discipline into an emotionally charged, home oriented and conscientious mode of work. Ahhh, Saturn. So much to do about Saturn. This is the planet that puts us in touch with reality, and challenges us to apply discipline and a sense of limitation if we are to stay on track enough to survive. Saturn is the great teacher and the grim reaper all in one. Saturn is where the line is drawn in every chapter of the story of our lives. Beginnings and endings occur when Saturnian experiences penetrate our lives. Saturn is our teacher, our guide and our sense of limitation. Our sense of discipline and our sense of being on guard also resides with Saturn related events. There is a hard edge to creating new disciplines as well as giving up old ones. Saturn reflects time constantly and doesn't skip a beat. Time waits for no one.

During Saturn in Gemini, it became important to recognize the two-sidedness of living freely and intelligently, to know that we apply our intelligence as well as take responsibility for our choices. Saturn makes us realize sometimes we are driven to make choices we do not want to make, and sometimes we are forced to participate in a system with which we don't agree. In our quest to perform our true will, to accomplish important goals, we are beset by obstacles, challenged by difficulty, and overwhelmed by the unpredictable factors of a vastly changing world. Saturn is the planet which gives us the edge to proceed with clarity and focus. It is also our protection mechanism, our lock-and-key to the issues in our lives on which we choose to work, determining when and how these matters are to be unlocked and completed. Saturn represents where we truly deem to place our focus in life; it is where we manage and maintain some control in our lives. Saturn in Gemini affects the nature of applied intelligence. Having a grip on the mental world and the psychology of how we are judged, and how we let this affect us is essential for our social and career oriented survival; while Saturn was in the mutable sign of Gemini, we were all constantly reminded of this unavoidable fact. In North America, our leaders forced us to take sides in the war on terrorism, and the broad spectrum of the subtleties that constitute terror became a controversial issue. The discipline to decipher and to become clear on exactly what that means for us personally has been a delicate matter over the past couple of years. Gemini's nature facilitates observation of the dualities before us, and allows us to reason our way through the complexity of our responsibilities. Gemini people will not deny the past few years have been a time of hard work, and there has been no way to avoid responsibility. Take it easy, Gemini, this Saturn influence is now completed! Now the master of discipline and focus, Saturn, wends its way through the sign of Cancer. Saturn is the ruler of the sign of Capricorn, the polarized opposite of Cancer; therefore, Saturn is unfortunately considered to be in "detriment" in the sign of Cancer. The consequent disadvantage is a result of placing the serious and unfeeling properties of defence and discipline on the highly perceptive, adeptly sensitive and intuitive realms of the Cancer character. Saturn in Cancer also imposes responsibility and work on our Cancer friends for the next couple of years. Discipline and setting limits will now be emphasized in the home, as Cancer represents the place from which we draw our nurturing spirit, the place where we take refuge. Now that the computer age is fully upon us, perhaps while Saturn is in Cancer there will be a strong emphasis on people working at home. Saturn in Cancer may play a strong role in society's influence on what takes place in our homes. Cancer is ruled by mother Moon, and the lunar quality of how we care for, nurture and raise our children may undergo some form of structural change, particularly as Saturn merges from Cancer into Leo. Real estate will no doubt undergo some big changes as numerous kinds of homeowner restrictions, property taxes, and economy shifts will affect the home owner's choices. This could also mean the elimination of welfare programs involving halfway houses or low income housing. New regulations may arise in the building and inspection codes. On some levels, we may have to be more aware of our emotionalism and curb our feelings in order to apply the discipline needed to keep the home structure intact. Now the cardinal signs of the zodiac go into a disciplinary mode, for as Saturn goes through Cancer, the Aries and Libra people will experience Saturn's squaring affect to their natal Sun signs over the next couple of years. Aries and Libra's lives will be more focused on cleaning up unfinished business, solving relentless problems, undergoing tedious kinds of work and overcoming personal limitations. Saturn in Cancer will be opposing Capricorn, creating more of an acute awareness on the part of our Capricorn friends. The work levels and disciplines in their lives will be trying and overwhelming at times, and occasional bouts of exhaustion will inconvenience the lives of Capricorns. Saturn in the water sign of Cancer will trine with the other water signs of the zodiac, Pisces and Scorpio, to activate and stimulate these folks' abilities to identify with the need for order and structure in their lives. This will give them a greater sense of ease in applying their work and creating more structure where they need it. Taurus and Virgo people are likely to experience more career opportunities and get a better grasp on their personal discipline as Saturn goes through a sextile to their natal Sun signs. Saturn is there to remind us of the work required to deal with the harsh realities of life. When this is done, our efforts are often rewarded with a sense of real accomplishment, so long as we act responsibly on the things of life that really matter.

Sun trine Neptune (occurring May 28 – June 10.) This aspect particularly affects those Gemini people celebrating birthdays this year from May 28th through June 10th. These Gemini birthday folks are experiencing the favorable trine aspect of Neptune to their natal Sun. This brings gifts of spiritual encounters and awareness as well as a calming effect on one's life. This serves as a good time (particularly for these birthday folks) to seek visions, apply prayer and meditation, and to explore spiritual avenues and beliefs that are being presented at this time.

June 4th Wednesday

Moon enters Leo   12:25 a.m. PDT   3:25 a.m. EDT
Sun sextile Jupiter   12:13 a.m. PDT   3:13 a.m. EDT
Mars trine Saturn begins (see 6/22)

A Moon in Leo spring day enlivens our spirits as our childlike qualities come out and play. Waxing Leo Moon brings on self-awareness, and the desire to feel important and look good stands out today.

Sun sextile Jupiter (occurring May 29 – June 9.) This aspect brings those Gemini people celebrating birthdays this year from May 29th through June 9th into a favorable natal Sun position to Jupiter. This represents a time of opportunity and expansion for these birthday folks, and there are good times in the works for these people so long as they act on their desires and work towards their goals. Skills that are introduced to these folks throughout this year will support the overall schemes of career and fortune building. This serves as a grace period for these birthday folks, and for a short time now, fortune and opportunity will shine. The sure to take the time right now to enjoy life and smell the roses! Keep an eye out this year for opportunities that could become most beneficial!

June 5th Thursday

Moon in Leo goes V/C   11:18 p.m. PDT   2:18 a.m. (6/6) EDT
Venus square Mars   4:54 p.m. PDT   7:54 p.m. EDT

This is a good time to enhance some aspect of one's personal life, and work on improving one's personal outlook. Many people will appear to be calling out for attention, and the need to surround oneself with uplifting people and places is strongly emphasized. Waxing Leo Moon emphasizes family and friends.

Venus square Mars (occurring May 28 – June 13.) Venus is now undergoing what is considered an unfavorable square aspect to Mars. This creates tensions and obstacles between the forces of love and the forces of defense. The archetypal images of Venus and Mars are largely that of feminine and masculine counterparts, and in this sense there could be trouble between women and men in relationships. On the other hand, these energies can create a dynamic and animated expression of love. The square makes it difficult to harmonize these energies, and letting certain obstacles remain to be dealt with later may be necessary at this time in order for tender egos to mend. One cannot go wrong with putting beauty on the pedestal for awhile, but to be expectant of a loving response at this time is futile. Love requires tender care and the space to enjoy pampering, even while conflicts are brewing in unseen and subtle ways. Let off the steam of personal conflict at this time, but don't let the obstacles become an issue. The pain of separation or the martyrdom of unrequited affection may be evident. The rocky boat of romance is due to have some notable ups and downs this month as numerous aspects mount up like a traffic jam. When It comes to relationships, remember this: don't sweat the small stuff!

June 6th Friday

Moon enters Virgo   7:51 a.m. PDT   10:51 a.m. EDT
Uranus goes retrograde   11:59 p.m. PDT   2:59 a.m. (6/7) EDT

The waxing Moon of Virgo encourages us to put important matters into order. Curious and investigative moods abound. Record keeping and reference guides are all around us, waiting for us to find and use them. Analytical tendencies are brought out with Virgo Moon.

Uranus goes retrograde (Uranus retrograde June 6 – Nov. 8.) Uranus, the outer planet that represents revolution, chaos, and big changes, turns back through the degrees of the zodiac at the cusp of Aquarius/Pisces. Outer planets move slowly, and this one will take five months to backtrack only four degrees before it moves forward once again. This long retrograde pattern of Uranus is quite common. We are bound to experience revolution everywhere with regard to the issues of mankind's beliefs as Uranus plays havoc on this zodiacal cusp. Uranus at the Aquarius/Pisces cusp challenges us to realize what we know and what we believe in, to work with great volumes of information, and to use our intuition in order to be prepared for the times ahead as this new century unveils further dimensions of the dawning age. Learning to not only live with chaos, but to also work and function with chaos, is the key to realizing Uranus influence. The skeptic might say that if you can stay calm while chaos is all around you, then you probably haven't completely understood the situation. Chaos demands awareness. In the midst of upheaval, if we need to respond wisely if we do not wish to get burned out in the process. When retrograde, Uranus influence teaches us to handle uncertainty. Many aspects of chaos tend to be sporadically repeated until the boundaries of restriction are loosened up enough for one to move around more freely and not go stir crazy. Uranus liberates, although for some, the retrograde process may seem to be excessively inhibiting, particularly if one's surroundings do not allow for much freedom. Be sure to set a standard for a certain degree of freedom in your life, so that you can stop and smell the flowers this summer and on into autumn while Uranus is retrograde. Don't let this valuable time of the year slide by without allowing the inner rebel to take up his or her heels once in awhile. Freedom is always a worthy thing to claim, even if it is only a temporary state of being. How could we of the precedent setting western world know of freedom's virtues if we do not appreciate the price paid for it?

June 7th Saturday

First Quarter Moon in Virgo
Moon square Sun   1:28 p.m. PDT   4:28 p.m. EDT
Venus square Uranus begins (see 6/12)

Throughout the day, there is a strong investigative curiosity at work with the Sun in Gemini and the Moon in Virgo. This is the First Quarter Moon in Virgo (Moon square Sun.) Both these Mercury ruled signs (Gemini and Virgo) are emphasizing the need to maintain fluidity both on a logical and practical level of application, particularly with regard to circulation of information. This is often a busy time of spring when the quickening of summer is upon us, and the preparation for the long days of the Sun turn energies once more towards the fruition of the warmer days ahead.

June 8th Sunday

Whit Sunday / Pentecost

Moon in Virgo goes V/C   9:27 a.m. PDT   12:27 p.m. EDT
Moon enters Libra   12:30 p.m. PDT   3:30 p.m. EDT

A fair portion of the morning PST /afternoon EST brings us a void-of-course Virgo Moon. Skeptical moods create slow progress for awhile. By the time the Moon enters Libra, shifting concerns focus our attention on partners and loved ones. The process of making decisions will be emphasized. Many adjustments will be made, and the tone of the evening will have the reinforcement of more positive energy. Sun and Moon in air signs keep us busy planning and communicating.

June 9th Monday
Moon in Libra
Sun opposite Pluto   1:41 p.m. PDT   4:41 p.m. EDT
Venus enters Gemini   8:32 p.m. PDT   11:32 p.m. EDT

Throughout today, the Moon in Libra focuses our moods on harmony and the requisite decision making process, which will no doubt tug at us all day. The Sun and the Moon are in air signs, emphasizing the need to apply logic and mental clarity to the things we do. Moon in Libra focuses our moods around social and moral issues. Libra Moon encourages us to harmonize with our partners and friends. Group harmony is emphasized and the need for balance in relationships is accentuated. Sun in Gemini keeps us attentive to the two sides of everything we observe, allowing us to be more open and adaptable in our decision making processes.

Sun opposite Pluto (occurring June 2 – 16.) Sun in Gemini is opposite to Pluto in Sagittarius. This means that those Gemini folks having birthdays this year June from 2nd through the 16th are undergoing the long term affects of Pluto in opposition to their natal Sun sign. What does this mean for these people for the year to come? Pluto is in opposition to your identity, and this is the time to accept transition, however overwhelming the circumstances. This is the time to persist in recognizing the empowering differences that each of the various alliances of thought, and generations of people, represent. Gemini folk have had an acute awareness of the dark and mystical manner in which Pluto energy has altered their outlook. Talkative Gemini must be careful what they say and be aware of the audience they are addressing. For some time to come, Pluto will be opposing the sign of Gemini, teaching Gemini people about the necessity of regeneration. Gemini is acutely aware of irreversible change and the power of new generations of thinkers who are defying all the logic of the previous generation. The battle to keep a sense of control and power is an awakening one. Pluto is in Sagittarius connecting us with the act of transforming vision, the vision of the generations now and to come. It is altering our perception of travel and extreme sports, and expanding our awareness of the diseases and cruelties of the world. Those born of this Pluto in Sagittarius generation (1995 – 2008) will be pioneers, creating new ways of seeing the world with transforming philosophies, new ways of travel, new ways of awakening astral travel, and of course, new developments of extreme sports These challenges appear threatening and are often perceived as a painful process of loss and destruction. Gemini birthday folk, do not get hung up on high expectations of life or you are likely to burn out. The downside is that these folks will undergo, or have already come across, a long series of crisis events. These crises have demanded the most thorough participation of those who hoped to persevere through and endure the testing of their spirits, particularly while Saturn was traveling through Gemini the past couple of years. These lessons are meant to be; so open up to the need for endurance and perseverance during this time, using wisdom as your guide. Survival counts! Use your senses and your sensibilities well, but do not resist the forces of great change. Awareness is strong now; use this awareness to make personal breakthroughs. Surviving all of this means the best of life is yet to come, as you will grow to appreciate life in a delightfully transformed way. This is also true for your opposites, the Sagittarians, who are intensely feeling the conjunction of Pluto to their natal Sun.

Venus enters Gemini (Venus in Gemini June 9 – July 4.) Venus, the influence of love, magnetism, and attraction is in Gemini; the personification of duality. There is an attraction towards the need for variety and more than one avenue of expression with regard to affections. Subtle and playful love comes with words. Love matters are submerged in thoughts and mindful observations. Venus in Gemini will create an attraction to writing, speaking on and recording extraordinary love experiences. For some folks, the love nature may vacillate between the giving and the taking process of fulfilling relationships. Gossip and talk concerning love matters may be especially prevalent at this time. Gemini people will be touched by love and may find themselves flirting a lot, as Venus crosses over their natal sun.

June 10th Tuesday

Moon in Libra goes V/C	10:00 a.m. PDT	1:00 p.m. EDT
Moon enters Scorpio	2:39 p.m. PDT	5:39 p.m. EDT
Mercury square Mars	10:49 p.m. PDT	1:49 a.m. (6/11) EDT
Mars conjunct Uranus begins (see 6/23)		

This morning/afternoon (10 a.m. PDT / 1 p.m. EDT), the waxing Libra Moon goes void-of-course and remains void until later in the afternoon. This puts a damper on the decision making process of midday and slows progress considerably. Usually, contingencies and unforeseen or unexpected factors get in the way of decision making, and the void Libra Moon also tends to slow down the thinking process for some folks. Later in the afternoon/early evening the intense but clearly defined mood set of the Scorpio Moon comes into play. The waxing Scorpio Moon awakens our sexual urges and intensifies our moods with passion. Even the least outgoing among us will participate in exhibiting one moment of unbridled passion or wild abandon, although this may be quite imperceptible on the surface.

Mercury square Mars (occurring June 2 – 16.) This is not a time to lose your temper. It is a good time to be especially careful in watching what you say. Think before you speak, as words can be easily taken the wrong way. See May 13 for more about Mercury square Mars.

June 11th Wednesday
Moon in Scorpio
Mercury square Uranus begins (see 6/14)

Today's strongly waxing Moon in Scorpio brings about very intense and vibrant feelings. It may appear quite subtle to the casual observer, yet the underlying emotional pressures of a waxing Scorpio Moon urge us to release tension, to lighten up somehow, to live it up a little, and to wake up. To others, that wake up call leads to exercising extreme caution. This is a time for deeper encounters, strong feelings, intense moments. As with any expression of the Moon it will pass, but at present it serves as an important and essential part of our mood expressing process. Once again, garden fans, the waxing water sign Moon serves as an ideal time to transplant or plant.

June 12th Thursday
Moon in Scorpio goes V/C	2:51 p.m. PDT	5:51 p.m. EDT
Moon enters Sagittarius	3:12 p.m. PDT	6:12 p.m. EDT
Venus square Uranus	3:54 a.m. PDT	6:54 a.m. PDT
Mercury enters Gemini	6:34 p.m. PDT	9:34 p.m. EDT

Sun trine Mars begins (see 6/24)

Yet another full day of the Moon waxing in Scorpio emphasizes the need to apply life's passions. This would be yet another superb day for garden work. This is a time of intensity, when the fulfillment of desires is emphasized, and when limitations are confronted and released through emotional embrace. Psychic buildups are addressed. Personal enemies tend to surface during the intensity of waxing Scorpio Moon. Some folks are awakened abruptly on the emotional plane. They are reminded of the principles of survival and the need to recognize their own limitations, as well as risk the daring plunge to overcome those limitations. By late afternoon PDT / evening EST, the Moon enters Sagittarius and our moods lean towards sports, poetry, and visions of the future. The electrical energy of the Sagittarius Moon is on the brink of its fullness. This is the time to sew up one's plans concerning the fullness of living, that is, confirm upcoming travel plans, enhance or create a personal fitness program, and get in touch with a sense of prosperity and self advancement. This is a good time to explore and make adventures occur in one's life. A Full Sagittarius Moon leads us to places that go beyond the usual boundaries.

Venus square Uranus (occurring June 7 – 16.) Venus, the planet of love and magnetism, is undergoing the square aspect to Uranus. This aspect tends to put obstacles between love and freedom. This influence may be testing the power of your love to withstand chaos. Be assured in self-love and empower affection with personal integrity. For more about Venus square Uranus, see Jan. 3rd, when this aspect last occurred.

Mercury enters Gemini (Mercury in Gemini: June 12 – 29.) Mercury is the ruling planet of two astrological signs: Gemini and Virgo. When in Gemini, Mercury is known to increase our attention to detail, and to cover a wide range of topics and subjects of interest. Mercury in Gemini directs and orchestrates information, like food for the brain, in an interesting and captivating fashion. The thing to remember is that information is not always well researched or even a correct and accurate representation of the truth. Mercury in Gemini, the mutable air sign, is the best known storyteller, and the storyteller is often looking for ways to make the story more interesting. Take the information with a grain of salt. Talk, discussion, tidbits of interest, gossip, and the news media all generate flash news designed to captivate one's interest even if only for one moment. The deeper and more inquisitive thinker often chooses to see the many sides of one topic and explore issues demanding hours of research and examination. Mercury in Gemini brings out the two sides of every explanation, of every story. What we learn on the information highway is for the most part blown over and becomes a blur, but some topics of interest and story worthy explanations later become lifetime studies. The whirlwind of details sometimes captivates us long enough to alter the course of our path in life. Why? Often the reason is simple: the well developed story has merit as a description of the course of our existence. Take careful heed of the storyteller if the messenger happens to be telling *your* story while Mercury is in Gemini.

June 13th Friday
Moon in Sagittarius

Electrical magnetism and energetic forces build to an amazing crescendo, as this late spring Friday-the-thirteenth Full Sagittarius Moon Eve builds visions, and highlights the poetic paradoxes of our existence. Energy and activities run high, and with all the celestial traffic this month, it is best to take this Full Moon in stride as the energy raised during this time is not likely to dissipate all that quickly. This Full Moon comes in like a comet, and expands our minds and hearts with an opportunistic beam of energy and light. We have officially made it past the lunar and solar eclipses of last month when a shadowing effect slowed the forces. This weekend's Full Moon in Sagittarius will reinforce our desires to expand and progress in a forward moving, battery-charged fashion. Sagittarius Moon moods, when raised to full peaks, can gift us with powerful visions and rich insights. These insights show us the way to the future, and give us an opportunity to look outside of ourselves and see what's coming. Life is not always cut and dry, but it is times like this which facilitate opening the porthole to new adventure. The point of the Sagittarius experience is to experiment with exploration, to go beyond the tangible and defy the odds of logic and probability. This is how great achievements are made possible. Times like this make it possible for those who are open to change and further development to see their potential and ride with it. We don't necessarily have to be strong to realize new potential; sometimes our weakest of moments, brought to us by trial, bring us to this philosophical awakening and give us a new outlook. Have a good look!

June 14th Saturday
Flag Day

Full Moon in Sagittarius
Moon opposite Sun   4:16 a.m. PDT   7:16 a.m. EDT
Moon in Sagittarius goes V/C   2:05 p.m. PDT   5:05 p.m. EDT
Moon enters Capricorn   3:38 p.m. PDT   6:38 p.m. EDT
Moon in Capricorn goes V/C   8:12 p.m. PDT   11:12 p.m. EDT
Mercury square Uranus   3:03 p.m. PDT   6:03 p.m. EDT

Early this morning the **Moon is Full in Sagittarius** (Moon opposite Sun) and many are actively seeking to gain new insights about life. Emotional energy runs very high throughout the day. The Full Sagittarius Moon emphasizes sports, travel, exploration of the senses, and encourages a flurry of flag waving on Flag Day. For many, there is a tendency to go way out beyond their usual boundaries and discover new territory. How we choose to perceive and develop our understanding of this new territory is used by what stage in our life we have come to and what kind of philosophy best suits our own individual needs. By afternoon PST / evening EST, the Moon enters Capricorn and allows us to get a more grounded picture of how we might choose to manifest our insights. There will be much to do this busy month; the evening mood is and highly goal oriented. Don't be fooled however. Starting tonight, get ready for the longest void-of-course Moon interlude we've seen in awhile! Two days of feeling industrious but not making much progress probably describes it fairly aptly. Post Full Moon tiredness will abound, while we must show diligence with the demanding and testing Capricorn Moon.

Mercury square Uranus (occurring June 11 - 17.) Communications will be blocked by obstacles and unusual or explosive viewpoints. It is also possible that important news of a radical nature will be obscured by sensationalism or overlooked as insignificant. Mercury has only recently entered the sign of Gemini, emphasizing the need to communicate about absolutely everything, while Uranus has recently entered the sign of Pisces, emphasizing the need to deal radically with issues of belief, religion, and spiritual matters. The two focuses are creating a tension between people discussing beliefs. Religious debates bring out the two sides of an issue repeatedly during this time. This aspect creates mental states of an explosive nature and causes some people to appear overly radical or even offensive with their unbridled liberty of speech. Stumbling blocks concern the rational understanding of the time honored, age old traditions of religion that represent an important foundation to believers. This aspect brings abrasive talk concerning spiritual revolution. Anger over this talk may escalate, especially while Mars is now working its way towards Uranus for a fiery conjunction on the 23rd of this month. Tact diplomacy are likely to go right out the door when religion is discussed. Spiritual harmony is always best achieved when we exercise it with discretion in this world of limiting factors. Be careful what you say and how you say it; stirring up chaos can sometimes cause disruptive damage that is not really necessary, and in this case may be a contributing factor which costs some folks their jobs or something they believe is important.

June 15th Sunday
Father's Day
Moon V/C in Capricorn

Happy Father's Day! The Moon wanes, and the workload before us may appear demanding. Despite this, Capricorn Moon influences urge us to work hard and with discipline. This intensely earthy Moon is a good time to apply some diligent and concentrated effort. A troubling and somewhat overwhelming sense of pressure to do the impossible strikes our moods. Moon void-of-course in Capricorn is likely to bring sluggish moods just as well as working moods. Even if you don't lift a finger today, you'll at least be acutely aware of your own pending workload on some level. When the high expectations of the day aren't being met, there is a tendency to feel discouraged. It's just a temporary lull. Try a kinder, more accepting and forgiving approach to those serious demands and allow for time-consuming setbacks. Capricorn urges us to focus on our accomplishments. This is a good time to enjoy the fruits of one's labor despite the time warp of slow progress.

June 16th Monday
Moon V/C in Capricorn
Moon enters Aquarius   5:41 p.m. PDT   8:41 p.m. EDT
Mars enters Pisces   7:25 p.m. PDT   10:25 p.m. EDT
Venus trine Neptune begins (see 6/20)
Sun conjunct Saturn begins (see 6/24)

A mundane Monday pace, and a record second full day of void-of-course Moon, suggests the beginning of the day will start off like the feisty temperament of a pesky old goat. A stubborn and tenacious mood setting creates an air of serious or guarded emotions. By 5:41 p.m. PDT / 8:41 p.m. EDT, the Moon enters Aquarius and now invites us to break out of the doldrums of fruitless monotony and to explore the brilliance of overcoming drudgery with a more enlightened and knowledgeable worldview. Stepping out of this Full Moon weekend has been a real labor-intensive doozie for some folks! This evening our moods are feeling a lot brighter.

Mars enters the sign of Pisces (Mars in Pisces: June 16 – Dec 16.) Today Mars enters Pisces where it will remain for an extended period of time: until December 16th. Mars is hot in terms of forces in our life. Wherever there is force, vitality, energy, or action -- there is Mars' influence. While Mars goes through Pisces, much activity takes place with regard to music and the arts, not to mention some heated action concerning the politics of our spiritual and religious beliefs. Piscean people will feel lots of hot and busy energy entering their realms as Mars crosses over their natal Sun for the next six months. The nature of Pisces is fluid, passive, and dreamy, and this is the spiritual realm of the constellations. Mars in Pisces opens the gates of active visions and dreams. Intuitive strength is realized. This is a time to activate our creative senses, and to work out hot feelings such as anger in an artful and healthy manner. Mars is also the famed god of war, reminding us to be especially cautious given the fact that hatred, violence, aggression and strife are often touching on the pulse of our belief structures (Pisces.) Uranus is also in Pisces stirring up the radical side of this controversial upheaval and commotion. There is nothing holy about "holy war!" All the while, there is no denying that the troubled religious leaders of the world will not let matters rest while Mars and Uranus are currently stirring up hot energy due to the concerns of their disturbed spirits.

June 17th Tuesday
Moon in Aquarius
Mercury trine Neptune begins (see 6/20)
Sun trine Uranus begins (see 6/24)

Waning Moon puts our moods in touch with the releasing process, it represents the most conducive time to let go of and work out spent emotional pressure. Waning Moon in Aquarius puts us in touch with those aspects of humanity that challenge and awaken us and demand freedom. With greater knowledge comes freedom, yet with an increase of knowledge comes an increase of responsibility. Where then is the freedom? Each circle around the solar year brings a little more knowledge and a lot more responsibility. This serves as a good time to clean away and banish all those emotional stresses attached to our obligations to others. It is best to know when to proceed and when to the system. With steadfast productivity our obligations can be met, but if emotional stress isn't allowed to dissipate, and concerns and fears are not confronted and flushed, there tends to be explosions. This is the time to reinforce all areas of ourselves that acknowledge and enjoy some kind of freedom.

June 18th Wednesday
Moon in Aquarius goes V/C	6:08 p.m. PDT	9:08 p.m. EDT
Moon enters Pisces	10:57 p.m. PDT	1:57 a.m. (6/19) EDT

Saturn trine Uranus begins (see 6/24)
Mars trine Saturn begins (see 6/22)

The Moon continues throughout the day to wane in Aquarius, and the general course of our moods begin to focus on the basic needs of humanity and of the people around us. Moon in Aquarius impresses thoughtful expression on our moods, and emphasizes the role of science, technology, and integrated systems.

Moods are focused on finding the most knowledgeable source available, thus avoiding a lot of time and trouble in getting important projects off the ground. By evening, the void-of-course Moon brings a sense of mental burnout. Too much information and too many details make it difficult to function on the mental plane. Evening is a good time to relax the mind, take a break from study, and to not get disgruntled over a myriad of incorrect details.

June 19th Thursday
Moon in Pisces

The final days of the spring season and the Sun in Gemini are upon us, and the Moon now wanes in Pisces. Our moods shift towards the drifting and dreamy qualities of life. Intuitive perception and creative desires emerge. Music, art, dance and wild abandon become preferred focuses. More relaxed and less limiting environments of mood attract us. Spiritual continuity inspires us as the release of our emotions brings healing. Pisces Moon helps some people tap into their creative impulses and their natural instinctual qualities, and urges begin to emerge. Sun in Gemini and Moon in Pisces bring on bubbly and frivolous expressions of thought and mood.

June 20th Friday
Moon in Pisces
Venus trine Neptune   9:57 a.m. PDT   12:57 p.m. EDT
Mercury trine Neptune   1:36 p.m. PDT   4:36 p.m. EDT
Mercury conjunct Venus   8:53 p.m. PDT   11:53 p.m. EDT
Venus sextile Jupiter begins (see 6/23)
Mercury sextile Jupiter begins (see 6/22)
Venus opposite Pluto begins (see 6/24)
Mercury opposite Pluto begins (see 6/23)

Throughout the day, waning Pisces Moon puts us in touch with our intuitive feelings. This may also be a time of releasing emotional baggage that has built up to this point, or to be aware of the tendency for escapism.

Venus trine Neptune (June 16 – 25.) Venus trine Neptune brings feminine love in harmony with spiritual expression. This aspect is particularly valuable at this time of relentless celestial activity and traffic. When one comes from a place of love, it is easier to draw down a spiritual enhancement of that love. To love unconditionally is a way to acquire gifts of the spirit world. This has something to do with the old adage; what goes around comes around. Feminine expression is emphasized, and there is a greater potential to create a spiritually enhanced atmosphere. In a time of spiritual turmoil for many, Venus trine Neptune helps to ease our woes with a support network of feminine kindness. Art and beauty are accentuated with a dazzling intuitional charm. The visitation of sacred places and favorite sanctuaries brings visions and inner wisdom.

Mercury trine Neptune (occurring June 16 – 23.) Loads of ups and downs are erupting for many folks as this busy and exciting time unfolds. Here is another favorable aspect, a superb aspect for discussing personal philosophies and metaphysical subjects, and a good time to communicate with the spirit world. Mercury trine Neptune brings gifts of encouraging news from Spirit. Out of the upheaval comes a much needed boon. Those who are open to communication and prayer will have a spiritual channel now open to their hearts and minds, to find peace where it is desired. Communicate about spiritual needs with helpful counsel and make breakthroughs; receive gifts of renewed faith in your own beliefs. Accept that some messages are there to uplift you spiritually, despite the clamor of this busy time.

Mercury conjunct Venus (occurring May 20 – June 28.) Mercury and Venus are now conjunct for a second time since May 26th. Once again we are reminded of the need to communicate our love. Mercury conjunct Venus in Gemini is an excellent time to discuss and communicate love matters, and perhaps there's no stopping it, as there is likely to be an endless flow of details being expressed. Love related messages become more playful and articulate with these two planets in Gemini. The sharing of jokes and the love of great stories, particularly love stories, are all brought to the surface. While Mercury is conjunct with Venus, these two planets are also trine to Neptune today; this brings an intuitive, spiritual, and very colorful flare to the expression of our discussions on the matters of love. Be sure to let those you truly love know it: sometimes it's what isn't said that disquiets the heart. Know that there is a need to communicate the love occurring now, and the most thoughtful, easygoing, and lighthearted ways of expressing love might be best.

CANCER

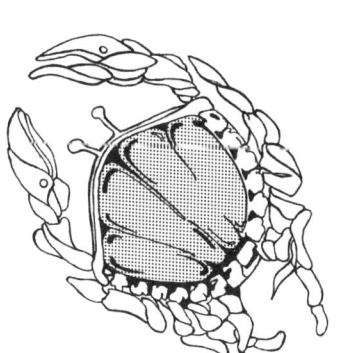

Key phrase "I FEEL"
Cardinal Water Sign
Symbol: The Crab

June 21st through July 22/23

June 21st Saturday
Summer Solstice
Last Quarter Moon in Pisces
Moon square Sun   7:45 a.m. PDT   10:45 a.m. EDT
Moon in Pisces goes V/C   7:45 a.m. PDT   10:45 a.m. EDT
Moon enters Aries   8:06 a.m. PDT   11:06 a.m. EDT

Sun enters Cancer 12:11 p.m. PDT 3:11 p.m. EDT This year's second **Last**

Quarter Moon in Pisces (Moon square Sun) takes place ever so quickly as it goes void-of-course this morning, and shifts swiftly over into the sign of Aries. From a dreamy, mystical, and sublime morning of events comes the new day and our moods are upbeat and ready to tackle the new season before us.

Sun enters Cancer (occurring June 21 – July 22/23.) The Sun now enters Cancer, on solar holiday referred by many a pagan; solar rites practitioner, Druid and Holy Bard as: **Summer Solstice.** This time marks the celebration of the longest day of the year, and today's wealth of solar light is a symbol of life, the life of growing things (crops and livestock) and the sustaining nourishment the growing things will provide. Happy Birthday Cancer people! The sign of Cancer is the elemental expression of the Zodiac known as cardinal water. The element of water can affect a person in deep and unconscious ways. Cancer people are extremely intuitive and often very psychic or perceptive. Cancers are natural born leaders and are often thought of, like the crab, as having hard exteriors. Why so hard? You Cancer folks certainly understand; there is a great deal at stake! Cancers value and prize their deep emotional attachments and treasured memories and feelings -- not just anyone gets to share in their hard earned legacy. Those that do share an experience with Cancer must honor Cancer's special needs to create goals and fulfill them with perfection. When a Cancer is certain about something, there is no disputing their chosen path. Moon rules the sign of Cancer and the need to love and be loved, and nurture and be nurtured in a gentle and motherly fashion is indeed a part of the Cancer makeup. Cancers must be free to protect and defend themselves as they please, and because their depth of feeling tends to run deeper than most, they need a lot of extra armour. When the need arises, they can reach out in very convincing ways and have the attention of everyone concerned. Cancer is a home based sign, and the focus of making the home a well loved place is of great importance at this time. Barbecues, home improvements, and home oriented events are the focuses of many folks during Cancer Sun days. Now that Saturn has moved into Cancer's domain, there is a greater emphasis on home security as well. Moving and setting up new home boundaries and perimeters is potentially a very emotional event during Cancer days. Others may choose to travel and become conscious of home and home life in a whole other fashion. Cancer focuses on security and the importance of being protected and prepared at all times. Happy Summer everyone!

June 22nd Sunday

Moon in Aries goes V/C	8:28 p.m. PDT	11:28 p.m. EDT
Mercury sextile Jupiter	10:55 a.m. PDT	1:55 p.m. EDT
Mars trine Saturn	9:17 p.m. PDT	12:17 a.m. (6/23) EDT

Hot energy builds although the Moon wanes in Aries. It is best to keep the temperature down as much as possible, and consciously release aggression throughout the day, and especially into the evening when the Moon goes void-of-course.

Mercury sextile Jupiter (occurring June 20 – 24.) This is a most favorable, although short lived, aspect that brings the potential to receive good news of expansion and prosperity to those who are open to broadening their awareness. Mercury brings news while Jupiter brings wealth and prosperous advancement. For some folks this serves as an advantageous time to ask for a job or a loan. This is an especially good time to look openly for opportunity when sharing information, and to promote oneself and one's actions. For some folks this may even be a good time to start a new enterprise.

Mars trine Saturn. (Occurring June 4 – Aug. 30.) The events occurring now bring gifts, provided with there is an application of discipline and timing. This may be a time for those who are affected by this aspect to become noticed or actively acknowledged. Mars trine Saturn affects our actions with a sense of good timing. This is a favorable time to apply diligent practice to one's favorite sport, especially those physical activities which demand precision and perfect timing. Offensive and defensive forces tend to work harmoniously with this aspect. For some, though not all, this aspect will be helpful, and this may be just the time to favourably put an end to those factors in life which have held us back from a sense of achievement. A gift of strength of will and the rewards of hard work harmonize to bring positive results. To benefit from this aspect, one must be persistent in taking action regarding important matters. It is the action of doing something with the application of energy (Mars) while applying responsibility and awareness of limitation (Saturn) that allows the perfect timely quality of completion as well as new beginnings to occur with this strong but favorable aspect. This is a time of emergence, when endings and new beginnings are merged. Mars is now in Pisces emphasizing activities of artistry and spiritual quests, while Saturn in Cancer sets up perimeters and puts the focus on having as well as taking possession of our heartfelt needs, especially in matters of real estate and things of value for the homestead. There may be a surge of house, business, and career moves happening at this time. This serves as an especially favorable aspect to take action with respect to control or discipline. This would be the time for ending a bad habit, especially bad eating habits, or applying oneself to actively use discipline in order to accomplish a goal, particularly goals which foster a deep emotional sense of personal achievement. Happy Training! This aspect will repeat again this year on August 12th and November 13th.

June 23rd Monday

Moon V/C in Aries morning and day
Moon enters Taurus	8:15 p.m. PDT	11:15 p.m. EDT
Mercury opposite Pluto	9:44 a.m. PDT	12:44 p.m. EDT
Venus sextile Jupiter	11:07 a.m. PDT	2:07 p.m. EDT
Mars conjunct Uranus	1:03 p.m. PDT	4:03 p.m. EDT

Opinionated, pushy, obstinate, and perhaps even overly curious and mildly irritating gestures of interaction make this a typical day of enduring the moods of a void-of-course waning Aries Moon. Later in the evening, the Moon enters

Taurus and our moods become more preoccupied with grounding and enjoying some soothing luxury.

Mercury opposite Pluto (occurring June 20 – 26.) Mercury, now in Gemini, opposes Pluto in Sagittarius. Communications are likely to focus acute awareness on powerful transformations taking place. The intense and grotesque aspect of the news is being emphasized, and this often causes horror, fascination, realization, and for some people, a kind of triumph takes place as well. News is being highlighted around power issues, and there is a struggle going on that often requires an eye opening breakthrough. This aspect will only be evident for a few more days, but the long term affects for some folks may be unforgettable, especially those Cancer folks celebrating birthdays during this aspect from June 20th through the 26th this year. Mind boggling awareness abounds at this time as the need to comprehend the powerful issues being awakened comes through in our thoughts and discussions.

Venus sextile Jupiter (occurring June 20 - 27.) This aspect leads matters concerning love and attraction to a favorable opportunity to allowing for advancement to more prosperous realms. This serves as an excellent time to shower loved ones with gifts and compliments. A lover's get away may be just the ticket to recapture some romance. Keep those gifts of love flowing. This is the time to allow expansion to occur in love matters, and to take the next step towards enlivening and enhancing a love relationship. A greater opportunity for advancement at work, or towards increasing your skills or enhancing your livelihood is available, especially if you focus on doing what you love.

Mars conjunct Uranus (occurring June 10 – July 12.) Summer is really upon us! As the busiest celestial pileup of the year continues to keep us hoppin', this intensely energetic aspect brings hot and heavy events. Mars, which governs all activities and forces of action, is in an alignment with the explosive and chaotic energies of Uranus. Both of these planets are charged with forceful energy and vitality, and are known for creating violent and unsettled energy at times. Masculine forces are erupting abruptly and loudly right now and the outlook is very fiery, although not necessarily completely destructive, as these masculine forces are slightly tempered by the feminine element of the mutable water sign, Pisces. This may be a time of violence, accidents and upheaval in the world. Revolutionaries tend to stage explosive or violent acts during this aspect, and with both these planets conjunct for the first time this century in the sign of Pisces, the activities are likely to be about issues touching on religion, the arts, drugs, our dreams and those hypersensitive spiritual issues. Those who are affected by this aspect are likely to be stir-crazy and in strong need of a revolution or revolt. Anger and frustration can be stifling at times, causing the need for freedom and for a definite breakthrough. Take caution with your actions, and be aware of the potential for accidents and unexpected outbreaks of emotion when the need to vent some heat arises. This aspect will come very close to occurring again this year from Aug. 20 – Oct. 25.

June 24th Tuesday

Moon in Taurus
Sun conjunct Saturn   6:39 a.m. PDT   9:39 a.m. EDT
Sun trine Uranus   8:06 a.m. PDT   11:06 a.m. EDT
Saturn trine Uranus   4:34 p.m. PDT   7:34 p.m. EDT
Venus opposite Pluto   6:57 p.m. PDT   9:57 p.m. EDT
Sun trine Mars   8:55 p.m. PDT   11:55 p.m. EDT

Waning Taurus Moon says its time to ground out and release the emotional buildups that are occurring as a result of the busiest celestial traffic day of the year!

Sun conjunct Saturn (occurring June 16 – July 2.) Once again the birthday folks of this time have their work cut out for them as the Sun conjunct Saturn in Cancer especially affects those Gemini and Cancer people having birthdays this year from June 16th through July 2nd. Saturn is currently in conjunction with your natal Sun, birthday people, and this creates a perfect time to focus on: out with the old and in with the new. Saturn is also reminding you to take charge of your life more responsibly, and to recognize the importance of your limitations. Maybe its time for an overhaul, at least until certain areas of your life become more comfortable once again, as opposed to agitating, chaotic, and impractical. Saturn is urging you Gemini/Cancer birthday people to connect with a perfectly sound dose of responsibility that fits your lifestyle and energy level. This may be the time to tune into the body and give it what it needs, as health matters are calling to be cared for and dealt with. This year, incorporate a healthy exercise and diet routine that is fun and works, and be sure to drink lots and lots of pure water. Don't be so hard on yourself either; remember to pamper yourself throughout this year with each measure of work's progress -- it's good for the soul. It's time to make up for lost time and apply some self-love and nurturing to your renewed self-discipline. Hang in there and get to work, Gemini/Cancer birthday folks, and don't be so glum; the tedious work in which you are immersed now and throughout this time of your life will bring you genuine reward. You'll see.

Sun trine Uranus (occurring June 17 – July 1.) This aspect favorably affects our Gemini and Cancer friends celebrating birthdays this year from June 17th through July 1st. This aspect puts the radical forces of Uranus in the favorable trine position to the natal Sun of these Gemini/Cancer folks. This is the time for these Gemini/Cancer people to make the breakthrough. Don't hold back: chaos is here to stay for awhile. Left the experience be positive so long as this aspect brings gifts. Expect restless desires for freedom and the need to break out of one's personal prison. Freedom knocks loudly and the course of change for these people is inevitable in the next year. These challenges are a necessary part of these Gemini/Cancer folks' growth patterns, and these impressionable changes are positive in nature, though on the outside they may seem harsh and overbearing. Gemini and Cancer birthday folks of this time are undergoing a positive state of chaos. Just know the madness that has been occurring in your lives is there for a reason. You will find a clearer picture in the long run by keeping up the good fight to preserve your need for inspired intelligence and logic (Gemini), and heartfelt defenses and mood swings (Cancer.) The trine aspect gives gifts of triumph, and this may be a good time to let chaos be the force to bring freedom.

Saturn trine Uranus (occurring May 4 – Aug. 3.) This very important aspect began in early May, and we can expect to be under the influence of this aspect until August 3rd. It doesn't necessarily stop there either, as getting over the events of such an aspect will take a long, long time, and this is not really the kind of thing that someone ever totally gets over. Three years ago (May, 2000), Saturn was in the square position to Uranus, contributing to the heavy changes of the past few years. Examples of this manifestation has accompanied such events as the December, 1999 riots at the WTO conference in Seattle, an exhaustive overkill of Y2K stress at the turn-of-the-century, and (in relation to Saturn in Taurus) the volatile ups and downs of an uncertain economic market. Stock commodities became available to the public to buy, sell and trade through the Internet for the first time in 2000. The dance of Saturn and Uranus continued to bring on radical events at an accelerated rate. Things did change, particularly as a result of Saturn's interplay with the outer planets. Uranus was in Aquarius, opening the eyes of humanity in powerful and eccentric ways, changing the course of our thoughts quite profoundly, and forcing us to deal with issues that make us think at an accelerated rate. As for Saturn, the most obvious change of all happened in late summer 2001 when Saturn in Gemini was opposite to Pluto, and the famous attacks on America forced us to really wake up. The opening of this century has put us in the definite throws of what the Mayans call **"Big Chaos!"** Take heed: it is always vital to keep our thoughts positive in nature, to face these challenges with the greatest self-respect, and preserve our confidence in humankind, no matter how weird it all becomes! But despite the losses and sacrifices, humans have survived such atrocities throughout history before, and despite the hardships, we will just have to face the music and dance. That square of Saturn and Uranus three years ago certainly contributed to the definite overthrow of the established order of things! Here's the good news: Saturn and Uranus are changing their tune now, as they have both recently entered the water signs of the zodiac, and are currently in the favorable trine aspect. This brings a positive note to our changing world. Saturn represents defense lines, disciplines, and responsibility in whatever form they take. Uranus represents an influence creating the need to break free of old guidelines and outmoded lifestyles, as the Uranus effect has explosive impact! The trine aspect creates a harmony between these two powers which are very much like opposites. Here, the concept of change for the better is emphasized, and the need to end one thing and begin another has been causing many of us to make important decisions. Those who don't make these decisions could find that radical and chaotic energies may force them to the brink, and the transition from one way of life to another may not be so methodical or easy to assimilate. Lifestyles are not the only things that change during this aspect;

ideas, attachments, desires, and unfinished projects which do not reflect the needs of this time may never get off the ground. Expect radical challenges as unforeseen limitations in the world are likely become even more serious. Timely matters may be but downright abolished due to Uranus' volatile nature coming up against Saturn's very serious custom of finishing up old business. Saturn is in Cancer now, placing an emphasis on further establishing and perfecting security systems for our homes, particularly in America (America is a Cancer sign.) It's time to make changes which benefit the security of our homeland in a way that allows us to hail and retain our freedom; Uranus is the radical force that always relates to freedom. Uranus is newly in Pisces, demanding that the overall spirit and artistic nature of the people of this world undergo a genuine spiritual change. However difficult it may be to release our attachments to the old Aeon modes of thought, there is no stopping chaos and the revolutionary rate of change in society. Yet people will try to prevent change because they preservation of the old ways continues to be highly regarded on many fronts, sometimes causing unbelievable disasters when the ways of the past and the trends of the future collide and unfold. Keep an open mind, and remember this aspect is positive in nature and can brings gifts and breakthroughs in support of protecting our freedom.

Venus opposite Pluto (occurring June 20 – 29.) Venus in the sign of Gemini now opposes Pluto in Sagittarius. This creates an acute awareness of the generation gap among kinfolk. Love may be challenged by dark forces, particularly by those in places of power. This is a time to support those we love, despite the challenges that appear too harsh to us. This aspect may well bring on an acute awareness of the love that some folks have for power, and the need to have power over loved ones. Such power truly only exists with the act of letting a loved one be free to choose the objects of their affection. Counterfeit or manipulative love loses its power of attraction through the test of time. No one, no matter how powerful, can tell us what we love, who we love, or how we are to love. Deep in our hearts lies the real truth.

Sun trine Mars (occurring June 12 – July 5.) This day and this month mark a milestone, a venerable onslaught of activity in the stars. Finally, on this longwinded day of aspects, we come to Sun trine Mars. Gemini/Cancer people celebrating birthdays this year from June 12th through July 5th are under the favorable trine position of Mars to their natal Sun. As if you don't have enough things to think about this year, Mars trine your natal Sun sign brings a strong need to activate your personal life, and to accomplish goals by taking action and putting out your energy, as opposed to just receiving the energy. There is a major force at work that will no doubt prompt you to action. Creative work abounds. There are special gifts of triumph for those who activate their dreams and desires at this time, and upon doing so, the energy which is naturally there to harness will come easily. Positive energy allows you to handle this chaotic and work-demanding phase of your life. This is a time to exercise the will and the internal sense of primal might which brings your personal agenda into a state of action and movement. Heated matters will come to the surface in a an advantageous manner. Through the act of making things happen, personal achievement will shine forth like a long needed blessing in the year to come for these birthday folks. Keep it active, Gemini and Cancer birthday people; if you don't think you're alive, circumstances of this time and the year to come will certainly awaken you!

June 25th Wednesday
Moon in Taurus goes V/C 6:41 a.m. PDT 9:41 a.m. EDT
Moon V/C in Taurus all day and night

Today, the void-of-course Taurus Moon closes this month and the busiest celestial traffic jam of the year with the cool love of beauty, of sensual pleasures, and of living in the lap of luxury. If none of that is true, then for sure we are still yielding to an immense anxiety about our finances. Relax! Clear conscientious focus will get us through ANY economic setback so long as we are diligent about the attempt. In the fixed earth sign, we must not forget that Moon in Taurus is what astrologers call "exalted," meaning there is pleasure and beauty to be found. It is essential to find peace in all the drama of making ends meet. So when you have gone out and done your best today, do no more; this is the time to relax and take pleasure in the beauties of life despite lazy moods and those seemingly infinite setbacks.

June 26th Thursday
Moon enters Gemini 9:13 a.m. PDT 12:13 p.m. EDT

By morning on the west coast and just past noon on the east coast, the Moon enters Gemini and is now waning down darkly. Gemini Moon puts the focus of our moods on communicating and receiving information. Activities revolve around writing, speeches, conversations, and secretarial duties. On the surface, a lot of the information drifts past our ears. Through seemingly meaningless detail, eventually more significant, more useful and more practical information is attained. Sifting through details seems costly for some, but not to the trained investigator who is reluctant to draw conclusions, and just connects all the pieces of the puzzle wherever they snap into place. As you go along, trust the details of the day to fall into place. Be careful not to overtax the nervous system with too much coffee, caffeine products or sugar.

June 27th Friday
Moon in Gemini

The waning Moon in Gemini keeps our moods focused on activities involving writing, speech, lectures and conversations. This Moon in Gemini permits our moods to let go of a lot of emotional tension through the process of communication. Talking our way through problems relieves stress and is a very common activity with waning Gemini Moon. There is much to talk about, as this has been an extremely busy time of celestial activity. An overwhelmed feeling may be a symptom of all this, coupled with the classical nervous energy that the cerebrally oriented Gemini Moon energy brings. If the mind is busy but scattered, fear not, this is a normal reaction to so much going on.

June 28th Saturday

Moon in Gemini goes V/C   7:31 p.m. PDT   10:31 p.m. EDT
Moon enters Cancer   8:52 p.m. PDT   11:52 p.m. EDT
Mercury trine Uranus begins (see 6/30)
Mercury conjunct Saturn begins (see 6/30)
Mercury trine Mars begins (see 7/1)

Gemini and the general course of moods begin to focus on personal curiosities and puzzling concerns. The thought process is emphasized, and the need to keep details in order becomes mesmerizing. A darkly waning balsamic Moon in Gemini stimulates our concerns about baffling details and deep rooted thoughts and discussions. This is a time of chatter and talk, but is mostly characterized by introspective thinking and plotting. New ideas are being circulated, and it may be easy to become preoccupied with an endless string of irrelevant concepts and notions. Restlessness and exited energy keep us busy, and by the close of the evening, those who have not paced themselves wisely may seem very tired. Later on, the Moon shifts into the sign of Cancer. This is the darkest phase of the Moon in Cancer, encouraging us to release old feelings and make way for the new.

June 29th Sunday

New Moon in Cancer
Moon conjunct Sun   11:39 a.m. PDT   2:39 p.m. EDT
Moon in Cancer goes V/C   11:39 a.m. PDT   2:39 p.m. EDT
Mercury enters Cancer   3:17 a.m PDT   6:17 a.m. EDT
Sun conjunct Mercury begins (see 7/5)

The **New Moon in Cancer** beckons our feelings and our moods to acknowledge new feelings about ourselves. The New Moon inspires a new experience, the desires to nurture the child within, and to build up a new outlook on our home life. Cancer focuses on the nurturing strength of the mother and initiates new feelings of great depth. This is a time when we learn to realize new things about ourselves emotionally. It is a good time to bring new things to the home and brighten up one's outlook with nurturing and uplifting moods and feelings. The past couple of days have emphasized the need to drop and banish old feelings; now is the time to initiate and feed new and welcomed feelings, and enjoy the boundless beauty of summer. All that having been said, bear in mind that the Moon is void-of-course and there is a tendency for extreme moodiness to accompany all these new feelings.

Mercury enters Cancer (Mercury in Cancer: June 29 – July 13.) For a couple of weeks, Mercury will be in the sign of the crab, Cancer. Now the shift in communications turns from attention to detail (Mercury in Gemini) to a focus on feelings (Mercury in Cancer.) This is a time when many will appear to intuit their way through conversations. Thoughts will tend to blend with mood as the emphasis on emotional expression takes the stage. As Mercury now goes through Cancer, take special note of the tendency for people to talk more specifically about their feelings, their defenses, and their need for nurturing. Mercury in Cancer makes some people more intuitive to the thoughts of others, and this may be an easy time to interpret people's thoughts by feeling their emotions.

June 30th Monday
Moon V/C in Cancer
Mercury trine Uranus   8:26 a.m. PDT   11:26 a.m. EDT
Mercury conjunct Saturn   6:14 p.m. PDT   9:14 p.m. EDT

As this month comes to a close, the newly waxing Cancer Moon remains void-of-course for the entire day and night. Much of the emotionalism that abounds at this time is a reaction to so much celestial activity. Let the feelings flow and nurture them with love, care, and pampering kinds of activities.

Mercury trine Uranus (occurring June 28 – July 3.) This good news for rebels and unconventional types. Mercury trine Uranus emphasizes breakthroughs in communications among anarchists and in all matters concerning a revolutionary process. Mercury emphasizes matters with regard to the transmission and exposure of news and information. Mercury is now in the favorable trine position to Uranus, an energy which emphasizes the need for chaos, and not for any particular natural order. This aspect brings news of disorder and calamity that represents a gift, probably a gift of freedom. There are many premature or radical breakthroughs in the course of human discovery, and Mercury trine Uranus often brings us news of these discoveries. Perhaps there is something on our news channels now that will encourage us to persevere through this extremely chaotic time. Mercury trine Uranus also allows for brilliant concepts to shine through and be worded in a way to actually make sense. This is a good time to record thoughts and take delight in brilliant thinking and reassuring news.

Mercury conjunct Saturn (occurring June 28 – July 3.) Mercury conjunct Saturn brings talk about putting an end to the unwanted components of our lives. This aspect also sets a tone of discipline and limitation on our speech and attempts at communication. There is a discerning quality of strategy at work, and there is a strong drive to sustain and act on new forms of thought, making this aspect a very good one for speakers and writers to inspire, initiate and capture vital thoughts. News concerning the end of a term is likely to occur more often at this time. Examples include retirement announcements, job loss, proclamations of relationship break-ups, and possibly even the news of a notable death. This may be the occasion to make that very timely speech, or to commit important matters to memory. Overall, Mercury conjunct Saturn tends to bring out a strong tone of seriousness in communications. Often our thoughts are at work with some system of boundary lines. There is a restriction, a discipline, a carefully considered emphasis of our thoughts placed on communication. There is a serious intent to get the word across in no uncertain terms. Governments may make new and restrictive proclamations for order. There is the strong implication at work that we be seriously responsible for what we say, particularly around authority. Serious emotional issues are strongly at work with Mercury conjunct Saturn in Cancer.

July 1st Tuesday Canada Day

Moon enters Leo	6:13 a.m. PDT	9:13 a.m. EDT
Jupiter trine Pluto	5:40 a.m. PDT	8:40 a.m. EDT
Mercury trine Mars	5:06 p.m. PDT	8:06 p.m. EDT

Happy Canada Day, eh? The month comes in with a restless lion's roar. The waxing Moon in Leo is very young so the roar may sound like a smaller cat. June, 2003, was some month! Last month's planetary activity may have felt like killer bees doing the Do-si-do and the Watusi on our heartstrings. This month settles down to a quieter round of commotion, allowing some of us to assimilate all the planetary activity that just came down the celestial pike. It will take more than a month to get over some of the changes occurring in people's lives at this time. Despite a slower pace, the opening of this month brings the benevolent lash of the June dragon's tail. Have no fear; even though celestial activity remains strong at this time, it will slow down into a easier pace through these days of July.

Jupiter trine Pluto (occurring June 1 – July 28.) Jupiter represents expansion, prosperity, social advancement, and opportunities towards growth, just to name a few of its qualities. Pluto represents transformation, power, fate, and the transfer of lifestyles from one generation to the next. Through this aspect, various different power structures will be taking their fill and will of advancement in the world. This aspect is likely to bring an economic shift which will bestow many gifts of opportunity and promote advancement towards some form of new power for some of those hard working folks among us. Strong power plays and shifts in the economy are at work on the international market at this time. This is an advantageous time to take note of companies making strong advancements, as they are likely to become more prominent over the long term in international markets. This aspect brings some relief and greater ease when facing up to the troubles left by the previous generations. Jupiter trine Pluto aids us in a powerful way when we are advancing beyond an old standard of life towards something more prosperous. There are likely to be powerfully influential gifts bestowed with regard to an inheritance during this aspect of Jupiter trine Pluto.

Mercury trine Mars (occurring June 28 – July 4.) This aspect brings news, thoughts, and communications into a most favorable position when it comes to taking action. Mercury trine Mars activates the world of communications with an energetic punch that often persuades people to take immediate action regarding whatever the subject matter requires. Thoughts, words and intuitive speech inspire activity, and the messages coming across often give us the incentive to get into the action. The trine aspect acts like a gift, and this is a superb time to communicate and receive positive and uplifting information which will inspire others to take affirmative action where needed.

July 2nd Wednesday
Moon in Leo
Venus trine Uranus begins (see 7/6)

Playful moods allow for jovial encounters under the youthfully waxing Leo Moon. If the lion does not sleep or play, his hunger leads him into the most serious effort of stalking prey. Keep your bellies full and your spirits light, and there won't be much trouble keeping peace on the plains. Remember: cats are territorial. Energy at this time is upbeat and full of vigor and animal magnetism. Playful fun among friends and family is a valuable source of amusement. Those who are inspired do not rely on others to provide them with entertainment. This is a good time to indulge in a favorite hobby or personal project. Be your own source of enlightenment.

July 3rd Thursday
Moon in Leo goes V/C	11:06 a.m. PDT	2:06 EDT
Moon enters Virgo	1:16 p.m. PDT	4:16 p.m. EDT
Venus conjunct Saturn begins (see 7/8)		

A lively morning gives way to a couple of hours of confusion as the Leo Moon goes void-of-course and enters Virgo by the afternoon. This is a time of retracing steps, getting all of the scattered elements in order, then pausing throughout the evening to ponder the expenses incurred by the start of a new month. Virgo Moon moods focus our attention on the need to hold back, reassess, and devise a much more grounded strategy for living up to the high expectations we have for ourselves.

July 4th Friday
USA Independence Day
Moon in Virgo goes V/C	9:15 p.m. PDT	12:15 a.m. (7/5) EDT
Venus enters Cancer	10:39 a.m. PDT	1:39 p.m. EDT

A Virgo Moon Independence Day USA holiday is upon us. Once priorities are set strait and strategies are in place, anything is possible; that is, anything that will not defy the laws of physics or the doubt ridden and scrutinizing perfectionism of the Virgo demeanor. The Moon keeps warning us: be cautious, be prudent, be accurate, be precise, and be anatomically correct. It's summer, it's holiday time, and it's hard to heed such warnings. As long as we learn to read the signs, listen to our instincts, and apply the laws of the elements properly, the best experience can be made to manifest.

Venus enters Cancer (Venus in Cancer: July 4 – 28.) The expression of love, magnetism and attraction, shifts towards a focus on feelings and intuitive understanding. Venus in Cancer generally represents pure love and the expression of deep affection. There is an attraction to the home and the security of home's comforts. There is a love of nurturing and the maternal expression of care and affection. The love of Mother and maternal duty are best expressed with Venus in the sign of the mother Moon. This is a superb placement of Venus for the display of American patriotism today, especially since Venus rules love. America itself is a Cancer sign country (July 4th, 1776), which gives Americans more of a focus on the love of home - the motherland - and love of the defence and protection of citizen's rights and freedom. The United States forefathers were astrologers who specifically chose this date in history to sign their carefully engineered Declaration of Independence. By the way, the USA's birth chart does have Venus in the sign of Cancer. Venus in Cancer focuses our affections on the nurturing qualities of love's purest expressions. Venus in Cancer brings love and adoration into the lives of Cancer folks at this time.

July 5th Saturday

Moon enters Libra	6:20 p.m. PDT	9:20 p.m. EDT
Sun conjunct Mercury	3:21 a.m. PDT	6:21 a.m. EDT
Venus trine Mars begins (see 7/11)		

Today's Moon in Virgo keeps us focused and interested in a sense of progress, particularly in cleaning up the immense physical mess so typical of a holiday weekend. On the other hand, the challenging little detail of the Moon being void-of-course all day may well be creating havoc with our refined sense of order. Avoid giving sales pitches or asking for handouts, or merely discussing touchy money subjects, if you don't wish to be snarled at. As with all lunar expressions, this mood will soon pass. By 6:20 p.m. PDT / 9:20 p.m. EDT, the Moon enters Libra and our moods are more geared towards making adjustments and creating more harmony among loved ones.

Sun conjunct Mercury (occurring June 26 – July 7.) This aspect creates a much more thoughtful, communicative, and expressive year ahead for those Cancer people celebrating birthdays this year from June 26th through July 7th. This is your time (Birthday Cancers) to record ideas, relay important messages, and pay close attention to your imaginative thoughts as they are touched by Mercury, creating the urge to speak and be heard. Your thoughts will reveal a great deal about who you are at this time and in the year to come.

July 6th Sunday

First Quarter Moon in Libra
Moon square Sun   7:32 p.m. PDT   10:32 p.m. EDT
Venus trine Uranus   11:19 a.m. PDT   2:19 p.m. EDT

The Sun is in Cancer, emphasizing activities of the home, the world of our feelings, and the need to preserve our emotional attachments. The Moon now waxes to the **First Quarter mark of Libra** (Moon square Sun.) First Quarter Libra Moon encourages us to harmonize with our partners and friends. This is the Moon that brings out a focus on the need to create balance in various kinds of relationships, particularly close relationships. This would be a good time to connect with our loved ones. We may be challenged at this time to tread softly with regard to the dreams of others, and to read between the lines concerning the inconvenient qualities of facing the difficulties of life. Waxing Libra Moon brings a positive team spirit. Its all about making adjustments.

Venus trine Uranus (occurring July 2 –11.) Venus trine Uranus brings a favorable attraction to revolutionary concepts. Often this aspect creates harmony between the lines of love and chaos. This is a time of freedom fighters and rebel love. This is an aspect that creates an attraction to the unusual. Youth is attracted to and more highly susceptible to rebellion during this aspect. Dangerous love and taking chances become common occurrences. Love at first sight is explosive at this time, but not necessarily long lasting.

July 7th Monday

Moon in Libra goes V/C   3:23 a.m. PDT   6:23 a.m. EDT
Moon enters Scorpio   9:43 p.m. PDT   12:43 a.m. (7/8) EDT

A long day and evening of the Moon in Libra being void-of-course makes this a day of going around in circles while making unnecessary adjustments the whole time. It might not really be all that bad, but one set of decisions is likely to set off a whole new round of discussion and further consideration. This will prove to be a difficult day to sit through committee meetings, to attempt to get decisions made with a group or team of workers, or to simply achieve equilibrium with a partner or loved one. Avoid petty arguments and disagreements - its just not worth it. On the other hand, don't be surprised if some form of disharmony begins to crop up throughout the day.

July 8th Tuesday

Moon in Scorpio
Venus conjunct Saturn   1:30 a.m. PDT   4:30 a.m. EDT

The Sun is in Cancer and the Moon is in Scorpio, these are water signs and the general theme of today focuses on the emotional flow of our senses. Waxing Scorpio Moon puts our senses and defenses on the line. Sexual prowess and the passion of Eros and Psyche are ascending on the horizon. Summer excitement and drama is in full swing.

Venus conjunct Saturn (occurring July 3 – 13.) During this aspect is a favorable time to apply discipline with regard to art and love related matters. It represents the diligent application of taking care of the people and things we love. It may also indicate there is a strong timely quality about love matters taking place, or that love matters are undergoing a restriction, or possibly even closure of some kind. This aspect can go either way on the positive-negative scale, since the loving attraction of Venus can be either encouraged or thwarted by the responsible, serious, and limiting discipline of Saturn's energy. Venus conjunct Saturn can bring an intense focus on guarding and protecting loved ones. Love oaths are emphasized, and love commitments at this time will be taken extremely seriously as a whole. This could be the ideal time to apply the discipline to clean up and to produce art and beauty where it has been badly needed, or to create a security system to protect valued objects. Take good care of the ones you love at this time, and be sure to share your affections sincerely as the stability of love matters will no doubt be taken seriously.

July 9th Wednesday
Moon in Scorpio goes V/C   10:58 a.m. PDT   1:58 p.m. EDT
Moon enters Sagittarius   11:48 p.m. PDT   2:48 p.m. EDT

Moon of Scorpio awakens our moods to strong depths of emotion with the Sun in Cancer. Emotional currents tend to run deep and there is a strong need to express and unleash personal tension. This is a very creative time of the soul. This is also a time of emotional healing. Sexual passions run deep. Scorpio Moon keeps us busy and creative, and this is a time when many of us may be touched deeply by personal concerns. Some creative diplomacy may be required to combat the conflicts of personal desires. Delays, setbacks, and minor disturbances that come with the Moon being void-of-course all day don't help the intensified emotional quality of the mood. Scorpio Moon reminds us to keep releasing tension as much as possible and not to be so hard on one's self.

July 10th Thursday
Moon in Sagittarius

The Sagittarius Moon waxes strongly and brings on the warm glow of a tempering spirit. This is a time to set our priorities straight with a philosophical application of life's complexities. The Sagittarius Moon inspires us to reaffirm our sense of vision with the flash of insightful fortitude. This is a time to build on our talents and skills, when we are drawn towards the need to explore and find opportunity wherever possible. Here we can reflect on our understanding of past events and transform them into a better picture of what the future holds. It is best to seek our good fortune today as tomorrow's progress will be slow. This seems to be the summer of reoccurring long void-of-course Moon days. Perhaps Mother Moon is telling us to take it easy on our expectations and go with the flow this month .

July 11th Friday

Moon in Sagittarius goes V/C   8:53 a.m. PDT   11:53 a.m. EDT
Venus trine Mars   12:28 a.m. PDT   3:28 a.m. EDT

Today it will seem like everyone sees everything in a way that's entirely different from the person standing next to them. This is usually true, but on days like today when the Moon is void-of-course all day and night in Sagittarius, our views are likely to differ wildly. Philosophical discussions are an attempt to smooth over the apparent slow progress that's happening, but too much philosophy and not enough good service will no doubt conjure a few sighs.

Venus trine Mars (occurring July 5 – 17.) This is a terrific aspect for promoting harmony in the relations of feminine and masculine counterparts. There will be lots of excitement as well as clever, imaginative, and thoughtful love at play. This is a good time to get to know your mate better, and to work towards obtaining gifts of understanding with regard to how the opposite sex (or alternative lifestyle) can share so much in common, even though this often seems to defy understanding. As a general rule, when Venus and Mars are well harmonized by this ideal aspect, there is a greater opportunity for peace and healing in relationships, and often great gifts are bestowed between people. These are gifts which help people to understand how masculine and feminine expressions are harmonized. It starts with the effort to make things better, concentrating on the positive, not the negative, and continues with the persistence to bring out the best in your partner, no matter how stubborn at first (s)he may seem. Give it a try this weekend while the energy is still ripe!

July 12th Saturday

Moon enters Capricorn   1:21 a.m. PDT   4:21 a.m. EDT
Full Moon Eve

Today begins the cycle of the Moon's preparation for peak fullness now that she has reached the sign of Capricorn. Diligence and serious intent affects the mood pattern which is building at this time. Tonight marks the eve of the Full Moon, and there is no doubt that the wolves are howling somewhere. Today serves as a good day to get some work done. Tonight is a good time to celebrate the beautiful Moon: the first full Moon of summer.

July 13th Sunday

Full Moon in Capricorn
Moon opposite Sun   12:21 p.m. PDT   3:21 p.m. EDT
Moon in Capricorn goes V/C   12:21 p.m. PDT   3:21 p.m. EDT
Mercury enters Leo   5:10 a.m. PDT   8:10 a.m. EDT

Full Moon in Capricorn (Moon opposite Sun) is here, and the general course of our moods remains focused, even rather serious as well as work conscious. The Full Moon always suggests a time of celebration, and the earthy Capricorn character focuses on the accomplishment of goals through the application of persistence and diligence. The gold is in your integrity and work. As the day progresses onward, the wave of energy begins to decrease, and the void-of-course Moon throughout the afternoon and evening suggests that it is indeed time to wind down and kick back.

Mercury enters Leo (occurring July 13 – 30.) Mercury in Leo is an excellent time to effectively write or perform screenplays and comedy. When Leo the lion speaks, it's a penetrating sound! Mercury in Leo puts the focus of information, news and discussions on entertainment and the connection of families. This is the time when many kids are turning to, or away from, family, in an effort to find answers. They seek answers with which they can live, answers with regard to determining self-identity, as well as survival skills. Thoughts, ideas and communications shift toward a greater application of charismatic interplay as Mercury enters Leo. This serves as a time when the mind establishes, reaffirms and maintains a self-created identity. Connections with Leos will be easy to make as the expression of thought becomes more colorful and dramatic. Self-expression and fortitude will be more evident in conversation.

July 14th Monday
Moon enters Aquarius   3:38 a.m. PDT   6:38 a.m. EDT

The Moon now wanes in Aquarius and the general course of moods emphasizes the need to break out of routines. A bit of the eccentric or the risk-taker comes out in our moods, and for some people, there is a need to go *off* track for a little while in order to gather a sense of what is necessary to be *on* track again. Knowledge is empowered and confirmed initially from within. There is a general fascination arising for innovative thinking and technology. Unusual capabilities are evident for those who choose to be aware and apply their talent.

July 15th Tuesday
Moon in Aquarius goes V/C   3:57 p.m. PDT   6:57 p.m. EDT

The Moon now wanes in Aquarius. Innovative thoughts and ideas spark our moods and imaginations as we contemplate all the things occurring in the world with regard to the advancement of technology and the persistent need to get a handle on it. Many folks may be feeling bogged down by the work that is mounting with regard to enduring the glitches of this technical age. The struggle to stay ahead of electronics, to not get flustered by machines, is indeed an ongoing challenge, especially during the waning Aquarius Moon. It is best for people to pace themselves and to apply patience with the world of electronics. Evening is an especially good time to rest one's mind and efforts with the Moon void-of-course.

July 16th Wednesday

Moon enters Pisces   8:14 a.m. PDT   11:14 a.m. EDT
Sun sextile Saturn   5:37 p.m. PDT   8:37 p.m. EDT
Mercury opposite Neptune begins (see 7/19)

Throughout today, the waning Moon in Pisces puts the emphasis of our moods on spiritual matters, in some cases moral and religious focuses, and for those who care not about such lofty matters, the wild abandon of parties and escapism also take the stage. Waning Pisces Moon may alternatively cause some folks to become somewhat introverted and meditative. This is a good time to look within and clean up any issues which create personal turmoil or possibly even depression. For some this is a time to "clean house" with regard to the emotions and to banish away or clean up alienated feelings that create confusion or uncertainty. Performing acts that help to create peace and promote spiritual welfare may be very healing at this time. Be careful not to overindulge in emotional calamity or the abuse of substances. While the Sun and Moon are both in water signs, this could easily end up being a very emotional day for many folks, and it is best just to let these feelings flow and not get caught up in inflicting harsh judgements concerning emotionally instigated behavior.

July 17th Thursday

Moon in Pisces

Pisces Moon sets no boundaries on the scope of feelings. The imagination is strong and feelings are absorbed from all around; our feelings also are busy addressing all the post-full-Moon changes in the air. Throughout the day, the Moon in Pisces brings imaginative, poetic and deeply feminine images to the forefront of our emotional awareness. The waning Pisces Moon can be a time when the need to escape from reality is strong. The waning Moon is more visibly veiling her lunar light. This phenomenon brings a greater need for the closure and dissipation of emotional climaxes which have occurred over the past couple of weeks. Pisces Moon brings out our need to quench thirsts, connect with aquatic life forms, and release feelings through art and music. Addictive or compulsive behavior is strong at this time.

July 18th Friday

Moon in Pisces goes V/C   7:49 a.m. PDT   10:49 a.m. EDT
Moon enters Aries   4:20 p.m. PDT   7:20 p.m. EDT

The Moon wanes in Pisces and goes void-of-course early in the day. Dreamy moods continue, and people tend to be rather spaced out through the day. Later when the Moon enters Aries at 4:20 p.m. PDT / 7:20 p.m. EDT, moods shift over into a more awakened state. Aries Moon brings on self-assertiveness and focuses our moods on pushing forward with force and vigor. A waning Aries Moon reminds us to be cautious of other people's need to assert themselves as well. This is not a time to get into a pushing match, though such behavior might be somewhat common. This is the time to disperse disruptive tension with easiness, and discharge hot-tempered flare-ups.

July 19th Saturday
Moon in Aries
Mercury opposite Neptune   2:02 p.m. PDT   5:02 p.m. EDT
Mercury trine Pluto begins (see 7/22)

Throughout today, the Moon in Aries presses our moods forward as the events of the day shape and form them into a perpetual state of emergence. The hustle and bustle of moods are at work, and this is a good time to stay out of the way of the more determined and pushy patrons of various kinds of mood swings. For some this will be a good time to exercise, and be sure to use up excess energy.

Mercury opposite Neptune (occurring July 16 – 22.) Mercury opposite Neptune brings out an acute awareness in discussions concerning disputes or challenges with regard to personal and religious beliefs. It also brings out strong discussions regarding spiritual matters, and there is often a push for a really good argument to ensue. It is wisest to be clear on one's own beliefs, and not to put oneself in a position of having to defend or expose those beliefs before a pack of merciless critics. Beliefs go beyond the physical to the metaphysical realms, where information is accessed and spiritual fortification takes place with one who is a (believer) practitioner. This is not only the realm of belief; Neptune also focuses our modern human curiosity on such issues as escapism, hypnosis, and the concern regarding the use of substances for relaxing and easing life's constant stresses. Perhaps there is a lot of media talk about how we are poisoning ourselves with substance abuse. This aspect often makes us acutely aware of the need to discuss and defend our beliefs about the importance of spiritual growth and enlightenment. When Mercury opposes Neptune, beliefs are challenged by information which contradicts the structure of one's own personal understanding. Let the tests of your beliefs be tests that yet strengthen the course of your sojourn. There is an old saying: "You must stand for something, or you'll fall for anything." Neptune represents the spirit world and challenges us to stand for nothing, to overcome our attachment to the ever-changing relentless material world, in order to be free of stress and worry. Many associate this energy with the need to escape from, or address, personal problems by using substances that either anaesthetize or enhance personal understanding. This controversial subject is ready to spring forth like an unexpected tiger. All of this becomes particularly true as the planet of controversy, Uranus, is now newly in Pisces, the Neptune-ruled sign of the zodiac. Uranus in Pisces is teaching us about the controversial manners in which our age-old beliefs, as well as our newer unconventional beliefs, have become challenged. Mercury opposite Neptune accentuates all of this concern escalating over issues around belief structures.

July 20th Sunday
Moon in Aries

The Moon wanes down throughout the course of the day and, as this evening comes to a close we reach the Last Quarter Moon mark in the sign of Aries. A Last Quarter Moon represents the square aspect of the Moon to the Sun. Barriers occur between one's emotions and one's sense of personal identity. The Moon is in the sign of Aries and this expression of mood has very little trouble inspiring new energies. Last Quarter Moon requires the letting go of intensified emotional energy – unless of course the energy creates a desired and positive response in which case, congratulations! Dropping problems with the ego becomes the key to this Moon, and this is a decision that can only be determined for one's self. One cannot change the stubbornness and selfishness of others, but one can make a difference by setting the right example individually. Be true to yourself.

July 21st Monday
Last Quarter Moon in Aries

Moon square Sun	12:01 a.m. PDT	3:01 a.m. EDT
Moon in Aries goes V/C	12:01 a.m. PDT	3:01 a.m. EDT
Moon enters Taurus	3:48 a.m. PDT	6:48 a.m. EDT

Overnight, we reached the **Last Quarter Moon in Aries** (Moon square Sun) – see yesterday's commentary regarding this Last Quarter Moon. The Moon now wanes in Taurus, and the general course of our moods becomes more down to earth. Taking in the time to enjoy a beautiful view or to improve upon one's appearance and surroundings will bring favorable moods. Waning Moon in Taurus is a good time to clear away and pay up old bills, as well as clean up the atmosphere in general in order to make life more functional and beautiful again. This final day of the Sun in Cancer shines down on our summer. No matter what kind of weather abounds, this serves as a good time to focus on enjoying the beauty around us and getting on with practical concerns.

LEO
Key phrase "I Will"
Fixed Fire Sign
Symbol: The Majestic Lion

July 22nd through August 23rd

July 22nd Tuesday

Moon in Taurus
Mercury trine Pluto   2:36 p.m. PDT   5:36 p.m. EDT
Sun enters Leo   11:04 p.m. PDT   2:04 a.m. (7/23) EDT
Mercury conjunct Jupiter begins (see 7/25)

♌

A waning Taurus Moon continues to focus our moods on practical needs, aesthetic surroundings, and the focuses of having, attaining, financing and paying for those material desires that persevere to keep us working. Overall, the day progresses into the sheer pleasures of nature loving tendencies and earthy moods, and the outlook on the day holds promise.

Mercury trine Pluto (occurring July 19 – 26.) This aspect brings favorable news and optimistic discussion with regard to issues of control and power. See March 31st for more details on this repeat performance of Mercury trine Pluto.

Much later this evening, the **Sun enters Leo** (Sun in Leo July 22 – Aug. 23), and the sign of the Sun's rulership fills the season with strong instinctive fervor and deep fiery desire. Happy Birthday Leos! This solar time of year is Leo's regal, sun-drenched domain. Leo focuses on will, identity, truth, selfhood, integrity, pride, and strength. Yours is a lustful time of year, Leo, and your totem, the lion, is one of the most self-assured of the zodiac's symbols. Sun in Leo focuses our attention on sun related frolic and play, outdoor activities for children and families, and the entire entertainment industry. This is a time for self-development and fulfillment. For many, it is a time of self-affirmation and launching personal projects and hobbies. Sharing affections is a vital part of Sun in Leo activity. Leo says "I Will" and it is important for a Leo to be expressive in the act of will. Leo is ruled by the Sun which symbolizes the building up of identity. The making up of the self consists (in part) of what the individual identifies with. To identify with the Sun is to identify with the self and the source of one's own fire. Just as the Sun projects light and energy, the Leo personality can personify and project great intention. Leos are notoriously great actors and performers. Leos are projection artists. Leo willfully projects and portrays many facets of the identity. This is the fixed fire sign, capable of maintaining whatever fire necessary to persist in a resolute manner towards the achievement of a willed purpose. The Sun in Leo is the time for all you solar types to let your hair down, enjoy entertainment events, and bask in the Sun whenever possible. You are applauded, Leo! Bravo, bravo! Please, by all means, take a bow!

July 23rd Wednesday

Moon in Taurus goes V/C   2:14 a.m. PDT   5:14 a.m. EDT
Moon enters Gemini   4:42 p.m. PDT   7:42 p.m. EDT

This morning, the Moon enters Taurus and as it continues to wane, our moods of this midweek are hard-pressed to allow us to accomplish a whole lot of work. Lazy Taurus moods have us preoccupied with finding a pleasing and comfortable environment while the Moon remains void-of-course for most of the day. Things might not be going exactly as planned, but this must not get in the way of enjoying life. For some, financial concerns create a tailspin of taking care of practical concerns. For others, the need to clean up and beautify the workplace or home is the primary concern. By late afternoon PDT / evening EST, the Moon enters Gemini, making the mood more conducive to communicating and sharing information.

July 24th Thursday
Moon in Gemini
Sun conjunct Venus begins (see 8/18)

Chatter fills the air today as the Gemini Moon atmosphere creates loads of both internal and external conversation. Busy minds are at work, and the manner in which this manifests through the waning lunar expression often builds up confused or mixed feelings. Today there are mutable thoughts at the point of decision. The debates and concepts at work are very prevalent but not necessarily profound or even noteworthy. Gemini Moon can bring nervous energy, and the resulting restlessness may cause many folks to be preoccupied with getting to the point and cutting through the chatter in order to obtain some sense of peace and well-being. Joking and small talk is all a part of getting through this nervous clamor, so if your heart is restless, chatter on!

July 25th Friday
Moon in Gemini goes V/C   2:38 p.m. PDT   5:38 p.m. EDT
Mercury conjunct Jupiter   8:17 p.m. PDT   11:17 p.m. EDT

Gregarious and talkative moods persist throughout the day with the Moon in Gemini. By 2:38 p.m. PDT / 5:38 p.m. EDT, the Moon goes void-of-course and there is a tendency for scattered and mixed up feelings. It is a common occurrence to get the facts mixed up this evening as well. If it's not a sure thing, don't place the bet.

Mercury conjunct Jupiter (occurring July 22 –30.) This aspect creates expansive talk which spreads quickly with news about the economic state of matters. Thoughts and information regarding some form of visionary breakthrough highlight this aspect. On more mundane levels, this is a prosperous aspect for communicating the need for a job or a financial loan. Leo folks having birthdays at this time are about to be showered with a wealth of information and opportunities which are worthy of their time and effort.

July 26th Saturday
Moon enters Cancer 4:23 a.m. PDT   7:23 a.m. EDT

Cancer Moon emphasizes the interaction of our emotions and feelings. Feelings are strong for many, and the need to express them is just as important. The steadily waning Cancer Moon naturally impresses us to drop negative feelings. Giving the home a nurturing and loving atmosphere is an enriching way to go with the flow. Darkly the Moon wanes in Cancer, bringing up old feelings and internalizing them to create a more nurturing emotional outlook. This is truly the time to finish dumping those outdated and useless emotions that might be contributing to a compulsive or bad habit. The common experience of worry, fear, and anxiety needs to be addressed. These feelings also need to be dumped and replaced with positive affirmations. A good cry or a primal scream has its merits. At best, well-adjusted folks apply patience, understanding, and an encouraging word to ease the sensitivity of this time. Moodiness, or the flow of mood, is the essence of lunar expression and Cancer is the Moon's attributed domain. This is the time to apply the motherly touch.

July 27th Sunday
Moon in Cancer

The Moon in Cancer is waning towards a dark stillness and in the core of this stillness our moods are met with the need to look within and assure ourselves. Reassurance is the key today as we approach the New Moon of Leo (tomorrow), and question the course of our emotional realm with the needs to address truth and certainty. Cancer Moon creates moodiness and this is all part of the natural order of such a moon. Cancer is, after all, the natural placement for mother Moon, and to be in touch with one's own personal moods and emotions is to be clear about the occasionally touchy emotional qualities of all those lost, uncertain and confused folks surrounding us during these interesting times. Be assured in your own truth and do not let the uncertain moodiness of others be the foundation of your own moods. Share your cup wisely.

July 28th Monday
Delta Aquarids Meteors
New Moon in Leo

Moon conjunct Sun	11:53 p.m. PDT	2:53 a.m. (7/29) EDT
Moon in Cancer goes V/C	12:25 p.m. PDT	3:25 p.m. EDT
Moon enters Leo	1:17 p.m. PDT	4:17 p.m. EDT
Venus enters Leo	9:25 p.m. PDT	12:25 a.m. (7/29) EDT

Mercury opposite Uranus begins (see 7/31)
Sun opposite Neptune begins (see 8/4)

Cancer Moon in its darkest phase this morning brings a deep sense of anticipation. A shift of energy occurs by the afternoon as the Moon enters Leo. This is the day of the **New Moon in Leo** (Moon conjunct Sun.) This placement of the Moon encourages our moods to attain a new outlook on our personal image. Some may be strongly touched by the need to get a new lease on life. The desire for new attire and a focus on hair is commonplace for this sort of mood setting. The enhancement of our outward appearance can help reinforce the power of how self-image is personified. If low self-esteem sets you back remember that you aren't inherently a failure – that's just an old pattern of behavior. A new pattern of self-image and dignity can be created, and the old beastly pattern will have to be tempered and corrected. Image comes from within and is generated by the sheer magnitude of one's will. Everyone has room to grow if they take the time to apply some self-worth, self-respect, and discipline.

Venus enters Leo (Venus in Leo: July 28 – August 22.) Venus in Leo now brings out the more playful side of the love nature. Venus represents the expression of love and affection, of magnetism and feminine refinement. It represents what we want to attract to ourselves. In the sign of Leo, Venus brings out desires and needs for personal attention. Magnetism is one of Leo's most endearing traits and the application of magnetism brings what Leos want most: loving attention. Charitable and kind-hearted sympathy are brought out in the expression of affections with Venus in Leo. Fashions continue to become unleashed with wild animal prints and eye catching flare. The entertainment industry becomes highlighted as, music, poetry, art, singing and acting are all enhanced with heartfelt expression. The love of looking good, having the best, and being the best is alluring to the ego. Wild lust abounds! The love of fantasies is enhanced. Love affairs can be torrid and dramatic, while affections, when first initiated, can seem very ardent and sincere. One might be hesitant to believe that a too-good-to-be-true relationship is actually happening. It's okay to enjoy a harmonious relationship. On the other hand, if the opposite of a harmonious relationship is occurring, it may be because the love affair is more focused on the demands and needs of one individual and not the harmony of the two. Leo demands a lot of affection, and when Venus comes into play the need for attention sometimes outweighs the need to reciprocate the attention. It is always wise not to have expectations in love matters and to be sure that the joys of love exchanging are balanced.

July 29th Tuesday
Moon in Leo
Mars goes retrograde   12:37 a.m. PDT   3:37 a.m. EDT

The newly waxing Moon in Leo puts us in touch with our pride and our joy. There is pride in the self, pride in the family, and pride in the way we put our own signature on things. Strength, self assurance and vitality are good things to get in touch with during a newly waxing Leo Moon. Sharing affection and playful interactions can be contagious.

Mars goes retrograde (Mars retrograde July 28 – Sept. 27.) Now the god of war, Mars, goes retrograde, and is urging us to face up to those heated events of the past, particularly regarding the actions of the past couple of months. Those who have overextended themselves may be due for a recreational healing period. Mars retrograde is also likely to stir up heated energy in the lives of February born Pisces people as Mars crosses their natal sun. Mars retrograde in Pisces will undoubtedly cause difficulties and numerous energy shifts in the lives of Sagittarius and Gemini people as Mars squares to their sun signs for an extended period of time. Virgo people are likely to feel overwhelmed with hot emotional energy while Mars is retrograde, in opposition to their natal sun. This energy is moving backwards instead of forwards and it will take another two months before all these folks are likely to get their activity modes and energy levels in smooth running order. Immense amounts of energy will be required by these people, and in one fashion or another, it will be there for them. While Mars is retrograde in Pisces, this is really the time to learn to kick back intermittently and relax. Don't get impatient over projects that are slow to take off or hot emotions that might get out of hand. Also bear in mind, for some people this may be a time of vigilance and alarm with regard to emotional calamity. As the red planet travels retrograde through Pisces, Mars' sometimes violent, forceful, or reactionary quality of energy may be seen in the arts, in music, and in spiritual or religious actions which are being stirred. Beware of the tendency to act on dangerous impulses, as Mars retrograde is not a good time to take risks which may lead to disruptive and sometimes fateful accidents.

July 30th Wednesday

Moon in Leo goes V/C	8:46 a.m. PDT	11:46 a.m. EDT
Moon enters Virgo	7:27 p.m. PDT	10:27 p.m. EDT
Mercury enters Virgo	7:06 a.m. PDT	10:06 a.m. EDT

Laziness, forgetfulness, and easily distracted moods will cause this day to be relatively non-productive. Self-indulgence, entertainment, and a vacation frame of mind do come in handy. This may be the day to work on settling ongoing family disputes. By 7:27 p.m. PDT / 10:27 p.m. EDT, the Moon enters Virgo and a more cautious and discerning quality of mood begins to take over.

Mercury enters Virgo (Mercury in Virgo July 30 – Oct. 6.) This is a most advantageous place for Mercury, a place of its rulership. It will be in Virgo for an extended period of time, as it will go retrograde in Virgo (Aug. 26), and remain there through Oct. 6th. Mercury in Virgo will focus our minds more clearly on the pending events of autumn. Mercury in Virgo puts the focus of talk, communications and news on issues such as computers, budgets, systems analysis, harvesting, planning, preparing for autumn, accounting, filing and organizing. Mercury in Virgo also brings out the skeptical and analytical side of every argument and topic of discussion. Mercury in Virgo keeps us on our toes. Those folks who have this planet in this sign (in their natal birth-chart), are often quick-witted, and they're also very intelligent thinkers and planners.

July 31st Thursday

Moon in Virgo		
Mercury opposite Uranus	11:22 a.m. PDT	2:22 p.m. EDT

Virgo Moon keeps us focused on accounting for our resources and making ends meet. This is an excellent time to practice some extra dental hygiene and to focus on caring for our health.

Mercury opposite Uranus (occurring July 28 – Aug. 4.) This aspect generally brings around a great deal of talk and discussion with regard to radical concepts, explosives and outrageous acts. There is news and talk about unusual activities. News coverage may seem out of line or far-fetched and there is a radical principle being examined by many people. Talk spreads extremely quickly and fads are born with this aspect. Ideas may seem bigger than life, and talk seems to focus on concepts which have not been fully grasped but appear to be presented with assured confidence. Radical and sometimes vulgar language can pop your space. Sensationalism is strongly at work with this aspect. There is an acute awareness of the need to speak out for freedom, and the dialogue may appear sharp and explosive. This is a good time to observe openly, but still to maintain a balanced sense of clarity with a healthy dose of skepticism.

August 1st Friday
Lammas

Moon in Virgo goes V/C	2:01 a.m. PDT	5:01 a.m. EDT
Moon enters Libra	11:48 p.m. PDT	2:48 a.m. (8/2) EDT

A new month is here, and today is apparently congested with skeptical questioning, endless doubt, and perpetual analyzing as to how things could be done in a better manner. This all-day Moon in Virgo fiasco makes it difficult to just get on with matters and get things done. It is a day to stop and question, to stop and reassess the necessity of doing things correctly before much more is potentially done incorrectly. Some days are just like this, yet the sharpest sense of humor is often found in the mind of the skeptic. As well, the worst mistakes can be avoided through the wisdom of caution and discernment.

Today marks the solar holiday of **Lammas**, the middle point of summer. This is the time when the crops are thirsty and the green traces of spring season have gone. The fields are straw-like and golden, not green. The Green Man of spring has transformed and he now appears to us as a straw figure popularly known as The Wicker Man. The word "Lammas" comes from the term "loaf-mass" and it traditionally represents the time when the first corn is harvested. The Druids call this festival holiday "Lughnasadh," a time dedicated to Lugh, the Celtic sun god. Just as the first crop is cut, this time represents a sacrifice, for Lugh was killed and he came back to life. After Summer Solstice (June 21st), the Sun's power begins to die, not literally but symbolically, and the rebirth occurs at Winter Solstice (Dec. 21st.) Although the Sun dies, the life of the sun is sustained in the living harvest. Now we begin to feel the first hint of autumn, a feeling similar to when Candlemas (the solar opposite of this time) begins to reveal the first signs of spring. For many people in North America, a slight chill in the air is strongly desired at this time -- this is the heat of summer after all. This is a good time to let unwanted worries and fears die with the sun king and to reaffirm the picture of oneself with the promise of the life contained in the harvest of seeds. Collect seeds of wisdom and contemplate in the heat of summer what part of ourselves must die and what part must remain to be sustained through the pending winter.

♌

August 2nd Saturday
Moon in Libra
Mercury sextile Saturn begins (see 8/4)

Waxing Libra Moon focuses our moods on the need to create harmony and beauty in our lives, and to acknowledge the necessity to create some order with our sense of progress. Friends and partners often become the highlights of our moods and focuses during the waxing Libra Moon. Since the Moon is still quite new in its waxing phase, this may be a good time to initiate a new friendship or revive a sense of newness with an old friend. Libra Moon stirs up book consciousness, as the book writers, buyers, printers, publishers, and distributors all commence the massive juggling act of the pending fall season.

August 3rd Sunday
Moon in Libra goes V/C   6:33 p.m. PDT   9:99 p.m. EDT
Mercury opposite Mars begins (see 8/6)
Venus opposite Neptune begins (see 8/7)
Sun trine Pluto begins (see 8/10)

Waxing Libra Moon is an excellent time to kick back with a friend or partner and enjoy the lovely Leo sun energy of summertime. Friendship is highlighted, and this is a good time to enjoy artful cuisine as well as cultural and social endeavors. At 6:33 p.m. PDT / 9:33 p.m. EDT, the Moon goes void-of-course and this evening may be a good time to avoid getting into domestic disputes. No big deal; just a few extra adjustments will have to be made in order to keep the atmosphere balanced.

August 4th Monday
Moon enters Scorpio   3:12 a.m. PDT   6:12 a.m. EDT
Sun opposite Neptune   7:01 a.m. PDT   10:01 a.m. EDT
Mercury sextile Saturn   8:12 p.m. PDT   11:12 p.m. EDT

Waxing Scorpio Moon calls to our passionate center. Sun is in Leo, Moon is in Scorpio, drama of some sort is bound to happen. Energy rises to the occasion. Activities of cleansing and purification bring troubled occurrences to the shadow world. Spirit releases a death cry, peace is restored. Sales and thefts soar high in the market place.

Sun opposite Neptune (occurring July 28 – Aug. 11.) This aspect especially affects those Leo people celebrating birthdays this year from July 28th through August 11th. Neptune in opposition to these folk's natal sun brings a strong awareness of Spirit, the spiritual path, and the acknowledgment of one's beliefs. The challenge of these Leo birthday folks is to confront and overcome all disrupting personal doubts that cause them to question the practice of believing. These people will be ever so imminently aware this year of the vast shifts in spiritual beliefs, and may feel quite overwhelmed by the confusion and shifts of their own spiritual awareness. This is no surprise -- it is happening strongly for numerous people at this time. However these birthday Leo people in particular are acutely aware of it. This is the time to go to a personal sanctuary of choice and tune into Spirit.

Mercury sextile Saturn (occurring Aug. 2 – 8.) This is an excellent time to do some serious research, and to learn vital lessons concerning boundaries, limitations and responsibilities. This is an opportunistic time to learn about handling responsibility and discipline. Mercury sextile Saturn emphasizes favorable news and communications with regard to matters of restriction and timely completion. Mercury sextile Saturn brings timely news. This tends to be a time when struggles and difficulties are frequently discussed, and many people collectively draw conclusions on how best to handle their problems or responsibilities. This is also an opportunistic aspect for setting up guidelines and communicating work skills. Don't delay; this useful aspect is only here till Friday.

August 5th Tuesday
First Quarter Moon In Scorpio
Moon square Sun   12:28 a.m. PDT   3:28 a.m. EDT
Moon in Scorpio goes V/C   10:22 p.m. PDT   1:22 a.m. (8/6) EDT

First Quarter Moon in Scorpio (Moon square Sun) arouses our moods in deep and impassioned ways. Intense exchanges between people leave strong impressions. Throughout today, this waxing Quarter Moon of Scorpio continues to bring our moods to a strange and intense level of existence. Don't go looking for trouble or you'll surely find it, and this brand of trouble has teeth! The waxing Scorpio Moon often brings out strong sexual appetites and desires. This is a good time to get in touch with one's creative and imaginative side.

August 6th Wednesday
Moon enters Sagittarius   6:11 a.m. PDT   9:11 a.m. EDT
Mercury opposite Mars   6:13 a.m. PDT   9:13 a.m. EDT

The Sun and Moon are both in fire signs, igniting creative and energetic expression and giving us a very lively perspective on the events of the day.

Mercury opposite Mars (occurring Aug. 3 – 10.) Under the influence of this aspect is not a time to lose one's temper. It may also be a particularly common time to observe a number of people doing just that! This aspect creates an acute awareness of the need to let the mind spout off with regard to heated subjects. This is a time to be especially careful to watch what you say, preferably before you speak. Nevertheless words can be easily taken the wrong way. This requires thinking before acting, because this aspect generally brings arguments and debates concerning the actions or active thoughts of others. Mercury opposite Mars makes it difficult for some to justify their actions, or explain why they take a certain stand in life. Communications may be misunderstood if one is too caught up in the action of what is going on. This is a good time to hold off on making comments that might be taken the wrong way, particularly around associates, customers, and strangers. It is best to apply reason and not to take aggressive language personally, particularly if isn't necessarily pointed at you. In other words watch out for signs of hypersensitivity and do not to fall victim to other people's inability to handle their own anger or aggression towards offensive comments. Many may misinterpret communications as being hostile, or perhaps war related news takes an overwhelming tone at this time. A variety of heated talk and action is possible with Mercury opposite Mars.

August 7th Thursday
Moon in Sagittarius
Venus opposite Neptune   9:23 a.m. PDT   12:23 p.m. EDT
Venus trine Pluto begins (see 8/11)
Jupiter opposite Uranus begins (see 8/29)

The waxing Sagittarius Moon encourages us to focus our moods on a visionary process. The need to see ahead is strong, and this is often empowered when we also take an insightful look at the way our recent (and sometimes distant) past has manifested in our lives. Sagittarius Moon encourages us to reach out to new realms of possibility and advancement. The Sun and Moon are in fire signs, and hot energy, full of upbeat and inspiring business, keeps us on our toes.

Venus opposite Neptune (occurring Aug. 3 – 12.) This aspect brings on an acute awareness of the opposing struggle between classic feminine archetypes in today's changing modern culture, and the universal and natural or spiritual expression of femininity, which is often at odds with a new model of beauty. There is a lot of focus at this time on what is and what isn't ladylike behavior, appearance or poise, while there is a need for the feminine spirit to be free and connect with a more divine image of womanhood. This may also be an awakening aspect for the feminine spirit to see the divine within. This aspect will pass in less than a week; those who are being directly affected by it must acknowledge that their own personal prejudices and their confusion with regard to the divine aspect of the feminine are being forced to transform due to the accelerating pace of change in today's global attitudes. A truer understanding of the struggle of the feminine archetype is particularly revealing in other regions of the world where western culture has less of a dominance.

August 8th Friday
Moon in Sagittarius goes V/C   2:01 a.m. PDT   5:01 a.m. EDT
Moon enters Capricorn   9:02 a.m. PDT   12:02 p.m. EDT
Mercury square Pluto begins (see 8/12)

An industrious mood captivates us as the waxing Moon enters Capricorn at

9:02 a.m. PDT / 12:02 p.m. EDT. Throughout the day, a sense of keen focus and a serious determination to get things done make this an excellent time to complete tasks and make some progress on important projects and work loads. Anything important that is left behind today is not likely to get finished very easily tomorrow. Tomorrow's long void-of-course Moon in Capricorn day suggests that although the work won't go away, it is not likely to progress very quickly. Getting the job done takes concentration; make use of the incentive to concentrate today while this aspect is still taking place.

August 9th Saturday
Moon in Capricorn goes V/C   7:57 a.m. PDT   10:57 a.m. EDT
Moon V/C in Capricorn all day and night

What a difficult thing a void-of-course Capricorn Moon can be when it is extended for an entire day and night. This Moon is creating a strong sense of needing to get things done, while at the same time there is little cooperation in the universe to assist with the outstanding goals and tasks. This is a time to remember it is futile to let such setbacks be taken so seriously. On the other hand, there are folks out there with high demands from life, and just because things aren't going as planned does not mean that we need to tie ourselves in hopeless knots. This would be a good time to address serious needs with a gentle persistence which reminds everyone that we must wade through setbacks and mistakes without demanding expectations! Those who must have the job done will do it, but at a price. Try to endure with a smile no matter what, and remember to laugh!

August 10th Sunday
Moon enters Aquarius   12:23 p.m. PDT   3:23 p.m. EDT
Sun trine Pluto   1:39 a.m. PDT   4:49 a.m. EDT

Moon in Aquarius is waxing up to its fullness and the energy at this time is busy and strong. Aquarius Moon puts the focus on the need to apply knowledge. Being in the know is a big part of how we function, and this is certainly a time to gather our talents to fulfill the tasks deserving of our energies. This is a time of technological breakthrough, and a time of sharing our knowledge and feats of discovery with the world at large. Be confident with what you know; it is part of the backbone of helping others to learn from your experience.

Sun trine Pluto (occurring Aug. 3 – 17.) This aspect is creating positive life-altering changes in the lives of those Leo people celebrating birthdays this year from August 3rd through the 17th. These Leo birthday folks are currently undergoing the favorable trine aspect of Pluto to their natal sun, bringing out experiences that involve transformation and encounters with greater powers and fate. It is always difficult to speculate just how the Pluto experience will manifest. For these folks, the concept of being gifted by fate may seem rocky and not particularly advantageous. Have no fear; this is a time to get in touch with your power, birthday folks! It is wise to remember Pluto moves slowly in our cosmos, and powerful encounters that seem deadly or harsh are actually a necessary process. Though unavoidable, matters involving fate can be positive, and the trine aspect does represent a gift being bestowed however unlikely this may seem. Be gratefulness trine aspect brings power issues into your life in a more positive fashion. Observe current events in the life of these birthday folks; it represents a celebration of the newly transformed person. Finding how to use this power is a big part of discovering this fateful gift of Pluto. For these people, the work of destiny bestows untold gifts. This is a time of positive transformation.

August 11th Monday
Full Moon In Aquarius
Moon opposite Sun   9:48 p.m. PDT   12:48 a.m. (8/12) EDT
Venus trine Pluto   10:17 p.m. PDT   1:17 a.m. (8/12) EDT

Today's **Full Moon in Aquarius** (Moon opposite Sun) enlivens our senses with the need to apply clarity and definition. The moods of the day are likely to be blanketed in bizarre and unusual occurrences, and often focus on modern technological breakthroughs and invention. People may seem idealistic and generous in some respects of this lunar expression, or out of control and downright unrealistic in other respects of this full lunar expression of Aquarius. This is a good time to celebrate our knowledge and intelligence.

Venus trine Pluto (occurring Aug. 7 – 16.) This aspect represents a love or fascination at work with regard to matters the work of fate as well as power. This aspect often allows a breakthrough to occur for those who are under stress from accepting the work of fate. There is hope for us to acquire an attraction for the not-so-glamorous aspects of existence. This is also an aspect that allows for adoration and loving energy to flow more easily between generations despite all the differences that have separated us in these vastly changing times. A lot of what seems uncontrollable these days is really in our minds and not our hearts. What is in our hearts speaks the truth, and the unpredictable facets of the hardship of loss or death are often brought to light with this aspect. Venus trine Pluto can often help us overcome the pain of separation when it applies to love. It is the place where love triumphs over death. Replace what is lost with love; pure and true love will conquer all. This aspect last occurred on May 7th.

August 12th Tuesday
Moon in Aquarius goes V/C   11:35 a.m. PDT   2:35 p.m. EDT
Moon enters Pisces   5:19 p.m. PDT   8:19 p.m. EDT
Mars trine Saturn   7:56 p.m. PDT   10:56 p.m. EDT
Mercury square Pluto   8:00 p.m. PDT   11:00 p.m. EDT

The all-encompassing Full Moon energy from yesterday is still going strong, but now the Moon wanes and our energy levels are beginning to quiet down a little. By 11:35 a.m. PDT / 2:35 p.m. EDT, the Moon goes void-of-course and we may be a bit overwhelmed by amazing feats of human stupidity and assumption. Those who are not up to the challenge may find it is best to avoid intellectual disputes and scientific debates today, if at all possible. Just let out a good cacophonous lion's roar and the deed of spewing forth your built-up energy will be done. By 5:19 p.m. PDT / 8:19 p.m. EDT, the Moon enters Pisces and many of us will be content to turn to tranquil, calming activities and favorite pastimes.

Mars trine Saturn (occurring June 4 – Aug. 30.) Due to the retrograde motion of Mars, this prolonged aspect which last occurred on June 22nd is repeating again today. Mars trine Saturn affects our actions with a better sense of timing. This is an especially favorable aspect to take action with control or discipline, and would be an ideal time to end a bad habit. For more information on Mars trine Saturn, see June 22nd. This aspect will repeat again on Nov. 13th.

Mercury square Pluto (occurring August 8 – 19.) This aspect increases obstacles with regard to communicating to those of another generation. This is a particularly difficult time to deal with harsh issues and discuss them in a manner which makes the hardships any easier. Mercury is about to go retrograde on August 28th and this aspect will be repeating on September 11th this year. Without a doubt, the commemoration of September 11th, 2001, continues to be difficult and challenging work. Mercury square Pluto often brings difficult news. Talk is often focused on the corruption of the superpowers and the setbacks of this corruption causes. The effects of Mercury square Pluto focus our attention on the obstacles and the difficulties of communicating about power issues, and the great dangers that our own concepts of being threatened represent. It is especially important to be aware of what we choose to say or think about powers that appear greater than ourselves. These powers are sometimes closer to us than we think.

August 13th Wednesday
Moon in Pisces
Sun conjunct Jupiter begins (see 8/22)

A dreamy, rather psychic expression of awareness takes place with Moon in Pisces. Throughout the day, moods remain somewhat spacey, very clairvoyant, quite artistic, and full of belief, prayer, and meditation. The Pisces Moon, although now waning, remains in essence very full. This for some may be a very emotional time requiring the release of emotional expression. Be aware of the tendency for escapism, and for people to seek to indulge their fantasy world.

August 14th Thursday
Moon in Pisces goes V/C   3:29 a.m. PDT   5:29 a.m. EDT
Moon V/C in Pisces all morning, day, and night

Long before most folks are fully awake this morning, the Moon goes void-of-course and remains so throughout the rest of the day and night. The dreaminess of this time turns downright spacey. It may be difficult to concentrate or perform at optimum levels. This is a time to take it easy on oneself and to enjoy the beauties of life. This may also be a time when those who are prone to depression are feeling the need to escape into a hole and be dormant. Some may find that people's moods are shifting around too unpredictably, and no one really knows how anyone else is feeling. Its all an illusion, except perhaps our spacey moods -- that's no illusion. It's time for the lazy Leos to lounge around for a while.

August 15th Friday

Moon enters Aries   1:00 a.m. PDT   4:00 a.m. EDT
Venus conjunct Jupiter begins (see 8/21)

Today's waning Moon in Aries sets the tone for many people to push their way through traffic and shopping lines, and focus on themselves and their own interests. While some are assured they know exactly what they want, others seem baffled by the tenacity and the fortitude that underlies the push and drive of selfish desires. Self-interest is okay to sport around; we are a self-oriented culture, groping our way through finding our identities and maintaining our egos with some sort of pride. This is fine as long as we are not completely oblivious to the needs of others. This is indeed a time when selfhood is emphasized, and our general moods are based on our own personal needs as well as the needs of those people pushy or powerful enough to insist on coming first! Avoid butting heads if that's not what you're looking for, since it's very easy to do on a waning Aries Moon.

August 16th Saturday

Moon in Aries

The Moon wanes in Aries, bringing out a sense of urgency to make progress throughout the day. This is a time when new projects are developing. Waning Aries Moon brings out the warrior in all of us. Sometimes we must stand up to the things that tie us in knots and make our will be known. Self-importance is both the key and the burden of our sojourn. On one hand we must fight for our rights and be true to our own being, hence, self-importance is aright! On the other hand, too much self-importance can be very threatening to others, and those who do claim supremacy and leadership must have something that captivates and appeals to their subjects. Fear can captivate, while charm can appeal. It doesn't much matter how the commander storms into town, he/she shall seem very important! This kind of lunar expression brings out a reflection of the self, and urges one to look to their own sense of importance, guidance, and leadership. Self-respect is an acceptable practice for the peaceful warrior.

August 17th Sunday

Moon in Aries goes V/C   7:36 a.m. PDT   10:36 a.m. EDT
Moon enters Taurus   11:52 a.m. PDT   2:52 p.m. EDT
Sun opposite Uranus begins (see 8/24)

Morning may have its course of interruptions and delays. After a few head bumps here and there, the kinks in the universe are straightened out and by 11:52 a.m. PDT / 2:52 p.m. EDT, the Moon enters Taurus. Waning Moon in Taurus sets our moods into an earthy, kicked-back sort of expression. There is often concern regarding finances and money management during waning Taurus Moon, and those who don't have money are particularly aware of their poverty at this time. Those who do have money are likely to get hit up for loans. This is a good time to enjoy the warm reverie of summer's beauties, especially nature, as the Taurus Moon puts us in touch with earthly beauty. This may also be a time when we feel somewhat lazy and in need of a relaxing environment after tackling all those financial concerns. Waning Taurus Moon often brings on lazy moods and the strong desire to just plain relax!

August 18th Monday

Moon in Taurus
Sun conjunct Venus   11:04 a.m. PDT   2:04 p.m. EDT
Venus opposite Uranus begins (see 8/22)

Moon wanes in Taurus, and the spirit of the day begins to focus on the need for grounding out, become more sensible, and get on with taking care of more practical needs.

Sun conjunct Venus (occurring July 24 – Sept. 13.) This prolonged aspect particularly affects the love lives of Cancer, Leo, and Virgo people celebrating birthdays this year from July 24th through September 13th. These birthday folks are being filled with the need to have or express love as best as they can. This will be the year for these birthday folks to address love matters in their lives. There is an attraction or draw to beauty, romance, and love when Venus connects with the natal solar degrees. The issue of love is unavoidable, and these people's love needs become evident whether the affected character wishes to acknowledge this or not. It is through the attraction magnet of Venus that the personality (sun sign) is assured of what they choose to identify with and be affected by or attracted to. Sometimes sheer magnetism is unavoidable and cannot be chosen -- it just happens. This can encompass not only love matters, but also such focuses as artistic, esthetic or beauty oriented needs and desires. These folks seek beauty and love and those things to which they are attracted. They are in a place in their lives where the influence of Venus will guide them to focus on their personal attractions. This will be a year of love, birthday people.

August 19th Tuesday

Last Quarter Moon In Taurus
Moon square Sun   5:48 p.m. PDT   8:48 p.m. EDT
Moon in Taurus goes V/C   9:29 p.m. PDT   12:29 a.m. (8/20) EDT

Today marks the time of the **Last Quarter Moon in Taurus** (Moon square Sun), which focuses the general course of our moods on creating some sense of order in our financial situations. It also encourages the need for creature comforts and esthetically pleasing or luxurious surroundings. There is often a focus on cleaning up and/or selling various useful artifacts that have collected in our lives, and the Last Quarter Taurus Moon is a splendid time to partake in yard sales, auctions and flea markets. This is a good time to clean up personal work areas and transform one's atmosphere into a more useful and practical working order. Letting go of attachment to material things that have bogged one down with too much maintenance or disruptive costs may very well be the best move; if ever there is a time to do this, it is during the Last Quarter Moon of Taurus. Through certain kinds of sacrifice comes some very relieving freedom. Overall, the better a person knows the self, the easier it is to be clear about how the material world affects them. Sometimes we just can't know for sure until we take the plunge and do the deed. Giving up responsibility for a beloved object can be very liberating in the eastern cosmology . Those who are more sentimentally attached will have to resolve to commit themselves further to the hard work, financial control, discipline and the dedication required to afford and care for material possessions. For many folks, this is certainly a time to assess their own position. Not only do many have to evaluate their material possessions, sometimes the physical body and the vitality of one's health is in question. It is vitally important to make healthy choices and apply the labor or rest necessary to keep the body, the beloved temple of our life, in good working order. Choose well!

August 20th Wednesday

Moon enters Gemini   12:41 a.m. PDT   3:41 a.m. EDT
Mars-conjunct-Uranus-Non-Exact begins (see 9/21)

Waning Gemini Moon keeps us busily focused on weeding out all those seemingly endless details building up in our minds at this time. There is much talk about events as they unfold. Talking about various subjects of interest and concern can often be very therapeutic, and attempting to open up and be a good listener can be of great service to those we care to guide and help through the learning process. There may be a tendency for people to have mixed feelings concerning certain subjects; with Gemini Moon, the controversial dualities of life always seem to confuse us with both sides of the story. Use your best judgment when discerning what your feelings are really trying to tell you.

August 21st Thursday
Moon in Gemini
Venus conjunct Jupiter   3:23 a.m. PDT   6:23 a.m. EDT

So many details to cover with Moon in Gemini. Many of the details are better ignored while the Moon wanes. Pushing past all the irrelevant information means having to be patient. Eventually, the piece of information that has validity comes to the surface and fits the puzzle nicely. All the while, Moon in Gemini moods focus on talkative interaction and collecting information. Exchanging ideas provides food for thought.

Venus conjunct Jupiter (occurring Aug. 15 – 26.) Here, the influence of beauty, love and attraction (Venus) blends and melds with the powers of production, expansion, and prosperity (Jupiter.) In the sign of Leo these two highly regarded planets are stirring up an awareness and an experience which are very self gratifying or indulgent, as well as entertaining, outgoing and fun loving, and for some, quite fulfilling. This is a time to enhance love relationships and realize the precious value of love in it's most limitless sense, since the influence of Jupiter reminds us the resources of love in the universe are inexhaustible and love's great bounty is designed to be shared. The more love that is spread around, the more there is to partake of and expound on. This is a time when the love of such Leo-related things such as family gatherings and feasting, travel and getaways with a loved one, sporting and showing off proud achievements, theater, and showmanship are all greatly admired and highlighted.

August 22nd Friday

Moon in Gemini goes V/C	11:15 a.m. PDT	2:15 p.m. EDT
Moon enters Cancer	12:44 p.m. PDT	3:44 p.m. EDT
Sun conjunct Jupiter	3:08 a.m. PDT	6:08 a.m. EDT
Venus enters Virgo	4:36 a.m. PDT	7:36 a.m. EDT
Venus opposite Uranus	9:47 p.m. PD	12:47 a.m. (8/23) EDT

Throughout the morning, a busy mindset keeps many of us in a thoughtful reverie. By late morning PDT / afternoon EDT, the Moon goes void-of-course and for an hour and a half, a scattered series of set-backs slows down the process of making sense of anything. By 12:44 p.m. PDT / 3:44 p.m. EDT, the Moon enters Cancer and we are more likely to feel a bit more concerned with the swift current of feelings which seems to be surfacing. Mother Moon returns to her home turf in Cancer and finishes up the old business of bringing to the forefront what has been brewing on the back of the subconscious burner, so to speak. It is time to address those feelings which are surfacing now. This is the time to nurture through reassurance, to unload emotional baggage, and to banish and clear the home and the heart of unwarranted fears and restraints.

Sun conjunct Jupiter (occurring Aug. 13 – 31.) This aspect brings those Leo and Virgo folks celebrating birthdays between August 13th through the 31st into a favorable position of their natal sun to Jupiter. This represents a time of gifts and expansion for these Leo/Virgo folks, and there are good times in the works for these people. Financial or career advancement as well as skill building, exploration and perhaps just plain happiness becomes a bonus for these folks.

Venus enters Virgo (Venus in Virgo: Aug. 22 – Sept. 15.) The love of the harvest comes out in all those who acknowledge the fruits of summer's first harvest. The expression of love and magnetism now comes out in practical and bountiful ways. Virgo people will become more aware of the loving side of their nature as the planet of attraction and feminine vibrations is personified with the meticulous attention to simple gestures of affection. Gentle, subtle expressions of love come out with Venus in Virgo. For some, this expression is touched upon with shyness or prudence since Virgo symbolizes the virgin, and this may be a time when attraction to virginal purity and newness in love is highlighted. All in all, Venus in Virgo is supposed to be "the fall," a time when disappointment in love matters may be evident for some folks; possibly even dual or secret love is emphasized. Keep the faith in your affections at this time.

Venus opposite Uranus (occurring Aug. 18 – 27.) Venus has just entered Virgo, while retrograde Uranus has just stepped back to the zero mark of Pisces. For some folks, this creates radical obsessions concerning love matters, some healthy and some unhealthy. In some cases this aspect may allow for unusual and exciting, although often short-lived, torrid, love affairs. This is a good time for artists to make breakthroughs with their art, and for eccentric people to show a restless side concerning the expression of affection. Issues of freedom, particularly freedom of the spirit and the creative side of our beings, are likely to be raised with regard to love matters. Strong psychic inclinations are occurring more rapidly between people who are linked on a heart level. No matter how you look at it, issues of love are surely being activated with a broadening sense of awareness at this time.

VIRGO

Key phrase "I ANALYZE"
Mutable Earth Sign
Symbol: The Virgin

August 23rd — September 23rd

August 23rd Saturday

Moon in Cancer
Sun enters Virgo   6:08 a.m. PDT   9:0 8 a.m. EDT
Venus opposite Mars begins (see 8/26)
Sun opposite Mars begins (see 8/28)

There are some definite changes in the air as the celestial shifts of the past couple of days have come to us strongly and swiftly. The Moon is waning in Cancer, putting us in touch with our feelings about all these swift changes. The summer sun now sinks lower, and sunset comes earlier. Although the sun on its daily course still touches our skin and emits its warming heat rays, we can now just begin to feel the solar light retreat as the final lap of the season unfolds.

Sun enters Virgo (Sun in Virgo: Aug. 23 – Sept. 23.) We now enter the final round of summer. A more down-to-earth perspective on life now calls to us. Happy Birthday Virgo! This time of year brings on the sudden caution of careful and fastidious harvesting. It is not only the orchards full of ripe fruit and fields of bountiful corn and wheat that call to us to be harvested. We are also called by the need to pull together all those other resources which will get us through the winter. Preparing for the autumn season is a vast and costly endeavor for many. Virgo concentrates the power of communication on the work of the earth and our physical resources. This is the time when rich encounters with the earth bring out fond childhood memories. Fastidious wonder keeps the Virgo spirit preoccupied with maintaining some kind of cleanliness and order on a fairly constant basis. This does not always manifest on the physical level, as some remain locked up in their minds, striving evermore to build thoughts into scholarly mountains of truth. Other Virgos are content to take refuge in gardening, cleaning, pruning and preening the imperfections of their troubled world. Virgos may be content to remain boldly filthy goblins with their hands stuck in pockets full of gold nuggets, always reminding themselves of their worth and value in a hidden sort of way. Or they may just be found fussing over makeup, health products, flossing and brushing, and making sure the details of their fashion statement are in keeping with the proper social event. Virgo's key phrase is "I analyze," and the pragmatic spirit of Virgo sets the busy tone of examining all avenues of life as we know it. It is just like Virgo to pick everything apart, detail by detail, and yet Virgo strives to get as much of an overview of the whole picture as possible. Virgo questions, Virgo doubts, Virgo says: prove it! The Mercury ruled mutable sign of earth is keen, sharp-witted, and not so quick to believe any sort of random information, unless it's painstakingly researched by some reputable source and published in a weighty book. Virgo will question the source every time. Virgo people have swift and practical minds which are often known for hailing the traditional values and following the scientific edicts of observing the laws of nature and the universe with exacting clarity. Without the wisdom of Virgo to assess and pull together as much of the big picture as possible, the efficiency of the harvest would not produce enough nourishment to sustain our needs throughout winter. Virgo's job is immense, and Virgos are famed for their ability to count, calculate and measure everything that must be accounted for. This is why the archetypal Virgos make such good accountants. Stretching out every last dollar and every last grain of food is the gift behind Virgo's prudence. It is the prudent one who is chosen to watch over the bounty of this season, for any other sign of the zodiac might just waste or overindulge in the use of the precious harvest. Be sure to take this time to enjoy the final month of the summer season with the bounty of the harvest at your feet.

August 24th Sunday
Moon in Cancer goes V/C   1:51 p.m. PDT   4:51 p.m. EDT
Moon enters Leo   9:48 p.m. PDT   12:41 a.m. (8/25) EDT
Sun opposite Uranus 3:01 a.m. PDT 6:01 a.m. EDT

Throughout the morning, fastidious care and concern with emotional issues needing to be purged soon gives way to the purging process. By afternoon, the void-of-course Cancer Moon brings numerous contingencies, bothers, worries and concerns. Emotional reactions seem to spread from one area to the next like stop-and-start traffic. Motherly concerns and mother related issues may surface today. Psychic inclinations and first impressions are very good warning signs. Listen to what you are feeling, face the open wounds of the heart and begin the healing exercise.

Sun opposite Uranus (occurring Aug. 17 – 30.) This aspect particularly affects Leo and Virgo people celebrating birthdays this year from August 17th through the 30th. The opposition of Uranus creates an acute awareness of the revolutionary forces in one's life. There is undoubtedly a great deal of chaos occurring, and the challenge (in part) may become the acceptance of the rebel within and to persevere through the drastic and edgy discord. This is the time to go with the flow of unusual and unpredictable occurrences. This is a also good time to learn the Tao of chaos, and to know this awakening force is enlivening a sense of freedom. This is a time of breakthrough, or breakdown if one resists. Survival counts; use your senses and your sensibilities well, but do not resist the forces of great change. Leos instinctively always follow the path of the heart while Virgo often follows the analytical path, applying their carefully considered sensibilities. In the years to come, the Uranus opposition to the tail end of Leo, which is just now affecting the early degrees of Virgo, will both challenge and strengthen our Leo/Virgo cusp born friends to live a life of freedom and stand up for what they believe.

August 25th Monday
Moon in Leo

It's a Leo Moon day, bringing forth the expression of playfulness and the need to keep life interesting and entertaining. Late August Leo Moon instills the need to get the most out of summer, and to indulge the senses in something delicious, appeasing, and completely satisfying. Do something good for yourself today.

August 26th Tuesday
Women's Equality Day
Moon in Leo goes V/C 5:00 a.m. PDT 8:00 a.m. EDT
Moon V/C in Leo all day and night the
Venus opposite Mars 3:18 p.m. PDT 6:18 p.m. EDT
Mars opposite Jupiter begins (see 9/7)

Tender egos are easy to tread on when the Moon is void-of-course all day and night in Leo. Some folks are mulling over the process of internalizing and perfecting self image. A sense of integrity and pride is enhanced through careful self-development, and it is times like this friend the balance and imbalances of the self become clear to those who bothered to notice. People who are more confident and self-assured do not need to force themselves on others for approval. Lions roar for many reasons, but for now mostly just to be heard. This may serve as a good time to listen to the beast within.

Venus opposite Mars (occurring Aug. 23 – 30.) This aspect tends to create an acute awareness of the sexes, and aspect draws our attention to the forces of love in a way that opens our awareness. This is a time when men and women, or masculine and feminine forces, are being made acutely aware of each other. Men and women who meet under these circumstances, or that have these circumstances in their own natal positions to each other, are often obsessed and crazed by the need to understand or accept the phenomenon of their differences. People who have this aspect inherent in their own chart are themselves left bewildered by the antagonism of the feminine and masculine forces that dwell inside them. Oppositions with these personal planets both attract and repel at the same time, and there is a constant need to give and take through the act of compromise. If you are among those somehow caught up in this battle of the sexes, it is important to realize that losses can occur with attempts at moderation just as easily as with extremities. There is no middle ground and arguments are likely to be strong during this aspect. On the other hand, the expanses of these energies create dynamic and animated expressions of love. It is wisest to observe and learn as much as possible. By all means, go easy on your loved ones during this Venus opposite Mars period.

August 27th Wednesday
New Moon In Virgo
Moon conjunct Sun   10:26 a.m. PDT   1:26 p.m. EDT
Jupiter enters Virgo   2:27 a.m. PDT   5:27 a.m. EDT
Venus sextile Saturn begins (see 8/30)

New Moon invites us to start all over again with the growing process of our feelings. **New Moon in Virgo** (Moon conjunct Sun) is a splendid time to organize one's life in a new manner. New Moon in Virgo calls to our feelings a new form of skepticism, a new way of analyzing, and to apply caution. How about a new way of accounting? Or a new set of health practices? School season will soon come, and children experience this practice of preparing for the future by acquiring and contemplating new school supplies and learning tools. New Virgo Moon prepares us for the changes occurring around us in the physical world.

Jupiter enters Virgo (Jupiter in Virgo Aug. 27, '03 – Sept. 24, '04.) For the next thirteen months, Jupiter, the planet of skill, fortune, luck, wealth, expansion, well being, and joviality, will be putting out its expansive opportunities for carefully considered investments and budgetary plans, as this is the nature of Virgo. It is odd to think the expansive, outgoing, thriving, no-holding-back nature of Jupiter can compel the skeptical, analytical, methodical and prudent character of Virgo. Its almost an oxymoron, and yet we must not forget Virgo is the ideal accountant, reminding us that cost cutting measures, prudent spending and saving our money brings wealth back into perspective. In order for growth measures to take place these days, a measure of trust must be placed in a really cautious plan, a logical sounding board based on a keen analysis of our current economic structure. Accountants, analytical scientists, economists, researchers, investigators, writers, secretaries, and health care workers are likely to get into the spotlight with some thriving business over the next year. Expenditures may seem more tediously monitored. Discovering what we have spent as a whole will be astounding, and the measure of what it takes to keep the wheel of fortune turning at this phase of the new millennium will prove to be high spirited, although extremely prudent, measures. There will be an expanding interest in budget plans, as more color and flare will be added to the act of counting up and accessing our valuables. Dormant materials may start to get mobile again, as the resourceful and communicative nature of Virgo will demand more focus on the necessity to find markets for stockpiled goods. The enterprising spirit will be geared towards obtaining practical goods and downsizing whatever is deemed impractical as an expense. Jupiter engages one with a sense of happiness and achievement; this is done in the sign of Virgo with a keen, practical, and accurate method of doing work. Jupiter completes Its orbit around the Sun in a little under 12 years, and since this planet will go retrograde at times (appear to orbit backwards from our geocentric view), it can go through as many as four signs or as few as one sign per year. Now that Jupiter moves through the sign of Virgo for over an entire year, it is evident that economic matters require careful planning. Virgo people will have more opportunities made available to them throughout the pending year. Jupiter in Virgo will allow us to prosper and expand in Virgo things such as savings plans, banking, and cautious investment portfolios. A stabilization of growth and expansion can occur with jovial Jupiter in the practical earth nature of Virgo, reminding us that our basic needs are always something to inspire gratitude and joy.

August 28th Thursday

Moon in Virgo
Mercury goes retrograde   6:42 a.m. PDT   9:42 a.m. EDT
Sun opposite Mars   10:59 a.m. PDT   1:59 p.m. EDT
Pluto goes direct   8:34 p.m. PDT   11:34 p.m. EDT

New feelings with regard to organization and making important connections persistently emerge with the freshly waxing Virgo Moon. This is the time to enjoy the fruits of summer and take in healthy foods as well as implementing more comprehensive health practices.

Mercury goes retrograde in Virgo (Mercury retrograde Aug. 28 – Sept. 20.) For the next few weeks and for the remainder of the summer, Mercury retrograde in Virgo affects communications with skeptical, doubtful, questioning, and mind-boggling technicality. There is likely to be a myriad of tedious detail and research done for what will genuinely seem like rather simple matters that keep getting questioned and disputed. Nitpicking typos will laboriously appear in texts that editors and proofreaders will swear they cleaned up thoroughly 100 times over. Meticulous and tedious care must be given when relaying information if one truly wants to get the pertinent instruction across. Nevertheless, expect communication breakdowns with regard to the rationality of decisions made. As Mercury goes retrograde through an earth sign, it tends to especially affect communications concerning the material things of our lives. Communications are likely to be disrupted during the labeling and delivery of packages, the transfer and handling of funds, the sorting and moving of goods, the charging of accounts -- and the list goes on. A poor sense of timing in communications is always evident with Mercury retrograde. Keep plans and tasks as simple as possible during the next few weeks, and be sure that all messages are carefully relayed. Confirm all vital appointments and schedules repeatedly before endeavoring to make connections; this will insure fewer mistakes and inconveniences which are likely to occur over this time. Pay attention to and read the signs. When people say "yes" and they are actually shaking their head "no" at the same time, this is a powerful clue as to what they're really telling you. Make communication attempts more than once or twice and be persistent as well as patient. At first it may be difficult to sit through everyone's excuses but there is eventually a logical explanation with Mercury related setbacks.

Sun opposite Mars (occurring Aug. 23 – Sept. 3.) This aspect creates an acute awareness of accidents, attacks, illness and anger issues, especially for the Virgo people celebrating birthdays this year from August 23rd through September 3rd. Something strong and full of heat opposes the Virgo character in a way that may cause defensiveness and sensitivity to brazen activities. Mars strikes to warn our Virgo friends they must be on guard and act on life's offensive blows. Being defensive is natural, and acting on this awareness may require a careful approach or the heat may backfire, especially now that Virgo's ruling planet, Mercury, is newly retrograde. Birthday Virgo people will continually be aware of the necessity to take action while controlling anger. There will be an acute awareness of the need to have strength, stamina and courage to face the heated and extremely active matters of their lives. Its not all bad -- this time brings energy too. Use this energy (birthday folks) to make positive change occur in your apparently busy year ahead.

Pluto goes direct (Pluto direct: Aug. 28, 2003 – March 24, 2004) After the long but common five month retrograde period of Pluto (March-August 2003), the planet of transformation now moves into a smooth, direct pattern throughout the year. Since March 23 of this year, Pluto has been going back through the degrees of Sagittarius. Now we can better acknowledge the evolution of humankind's condition in order to survive the changes that are happening on planet Earth. This transformation is about consciousness, without which we would not be. This is not the lifetime to take life for granted; this is a time to participate in making life better by consciously transforming fear into determination and despair into belief in oneself.

August 29th Friday

Moon in Virgo goes V/C	12:26 a.m. PDT	3:26 a.m. EDT
Moon enters Libra	6:41 a.m. PDT	9:41 a.m. EDT
Jupiter opposite Uranus	9:38 p.m. PDT	12:38 a.m. (8/30) EDT
Sun sextile Saturn begins (see 9/3)		

Skeptical morning moods turn to a focus on creating a balance as the Moon in Virgo shifts into the sign of Libra. It is time to take charge, make some adjustments and work it out with others.

Jupiter opposite Uranus (occurring Aug. 7 – Sept. 22.) The big news today occurs this evening (PST) as we come to the exact aspect of Jupiter opposite Uranus, a not-so-common aspect which has been actively occurring from August 7th through September 22nd this year. Jupiter affects our sense of prosperity and our expansion into new realms of fulfillment and discovery. Uranus is known for precipitating every explosive or radical area of our lives. When Jupiter is in the opposite position to Uranus, it makes us acutely aware of our revolutionary capabilities. In some cases, a revolt occurs as a result of economic upheaval. There may be very volatile but bountiful breakthroughs towards freedom and the banishment of fear caused by the need to excel in ways not before ventured. Some folks may feel they are overwhelmed by or forced to take radical measures in order to save a business or company. Jupiter is just newly in the sign of Virgo (see August 27), and our need to prosper in a prudent manner requires quite a bit of downsizing as a measure of lowering and tracking expenditures. Uranus is newly in the sign of Pisces, emphasizing the need to radically change the dominion of the arts and religious institutions. There may be some prudent cutbacks in these areas of life, but for some folks, this process comes as a relief from overwhelming financial and management burdens. Some folks may be playing this aspect the other way; for them, the way to make a financial breakthrough is to take greater risks. This is radical alright, and will undoubtedly challenge these risk takers in a very overwhelming and demanding sort of way. The stock market should really be very interesting through this time. As long as one is working with a process of liberation or is focusing on a freedom quest of some nature, this aspect is giving constant lessons in how to take losses in stride, how to radically expand to great heights, and to empower the pocketbook despite the twists in economy. All of this is a reflection of our ability to live with chaos during those volatile and strange economic shifts throughout the world. This is a time to keep our cool and persist in opening up the field of knowledge which affirms how we can make financial breakthroughs in a positive and productive manner.

August 30th Saturday

Moon in Libra goes V/C   11:37 a.m. PDT   2:37 p.m. EDT
Venus sextile Saturn   4:23 p.m. PDT   7:23 p.m. EDT

Waxing Libra Moon gears up our moods to wrap up the affairs of the month and prepare for the autumn season ahead in these busy final weeks of summer. Its all about making adjustments and finding that quintessential balance between friends, loved ones and partners. Labor Day weekend is classically a busy one. After 11:37 a.m. PDT / 2:37 p.m. EDT, and the Moon is void-of-course and the attempt to create the balance may well backfire. It's quite simply a tough day to please people.

Venus sextile Saturn (occurring May 10 – 17.) Venus emphasizes the vibrations of love, magnetism, beauty and also sensuality. Often there is an opportunity to obtain objects of beauty. Perfect timing brings pleasure. Now that Saturn is newly in the sign of Cancer (see June 3rd) , this is the time to take the opportunity to protect what we love with guidance and nurturing. Venus sextile Saturn last occur on May 14th -- see this date for more details.

August 31st Sunday

Moon enters Scorpio   9:00 a.m. PDT   12:00 p.m. EDT
Venus square Pluto begins (see 9/5)

The final day of the month goes out with a somewhat intense rush as the waxing Moon in Scorpio puts us in touch with the deep-rooted subjects of unavoidable concern. Throughout today, the waxing Scorpio Moon emphasizes a mystical sort of drama as the interplay of moods is intensified with vigilant and undaunted passion. Anything can happen on a Scorpio Moon, and even on the surface there is often a very refined intensity taking place. This is a good time to follow your bliss and act out as well as seek out personal passions. Sexual energy runs high. Matters of fate are often examined, and we are drawn to the need to seek a higher perspective on the wheel of revelation as our life's course progresses. Psychic inclinations run strong today and the need to find our resilient edge comes into play.

September 1st Monday
Labor Day
Moon in Scorpio

All of a sudden, it's September, it's Labor Day Monday, and the waxing Scorpio Moon sets the tone of mood with a sense of urgency and drama. Making the psychological adjustment as each event unfolds may require a bit of reaction time. Scorpio Moon opens up rich emotional issues such as birth, sex, and death. Facing permanent change is not easy for everyone. This is a time to transform the pain, reaffirm the heart, release destructive tendencies or the bothersome worries of other people's troubles, and take joy in the worthwhile pleasures of life. The heavy ups and downs of life are all a part of the journey.

September 2nd Tuesday

Moon in Scorpio goes V/C	3:18 a.m. PDT	6:18 a.m. EDT
Moon enters Sagittarius	11:32 a.m. PDT	2:32 p.m. EDT

Watch your back this morning: void-of-course Scorpio Moon brings us into a lot of direct contact with desperation and despair, possibly even theft or violence. Some may seem to be preying on other people's heartstrings. By 11:32 a.m. PDT / 2:32 p.m. EDT, Moon enters Sagittarius. While the last weeks of summer wind down to an end, the general moods of this day and night are winding up with a fiery fervor. Our moods now shift towards a restless inquisitiveness and visionary awareness as the Sagittarius Moon waxes up. Sports and outdoor activities are emphasized, and there is a need to push beyond the usual bounds and explore.

September 3rd Wednesday
First Quarter Moon in Sagittarius

Moon square Sun	5:34 a.m. PDT	8:34 a.m. EDT
Sun sextile Saturn	11:48 a.m. PDT	2:48 p.m. EDT

Sun square Pluto begins (see 9/10)

Early this morning the **Moon in Sagittarius reaches the First Quarter mark** (Moon square Sun.) Moon in Sagittarius puts the emphasis on such endeavors such as travel and vision quests. With this visionary process comes the desire to expand. While the Virgo sun reminds us to budget our resources for the coming of the changing season, Sagittarius Moon reminds us to extend ourselves while the brilliant beauty of summer is still happening.

Sun sextile Saturn (occurring Aug. 29 – Sept. 9.) This aspect particularly affects those Virgo people celebrating birthdays this year August 29th through September 9th. This aspect helps these birthday folks focus their energy and discipline throughout this year with greater clarity. The timeliness of events hold the promise of opportunity for these people. As Saturn goes sextile over these birthday people's natal sun, there is a greater sense of making progress through their application of discipline. These people may actually begin to see the rewards of their diligent labor in the coming year. This is only true as long as they apply themselves to their work and keep an eye open for beneficial work opportunities as they arise.

September 4th Thursday

Moon in Sagittarius goes V/C   4:23 a.m. PDT   7:23 a.m. EDT
Moon enters Capricorn   2:51 p.m. PDT   5:51 p.m. EDT

The day may seem to get started off rather slowly with the void-of-course Sagittarius Moon. It may be very easy to get lost and end up far off the usual beaten track. Don't push yourself today by expecting to get a lot done: progress and service will assuredly seem slow since so many folks are out there somewhere in the atmosphere getting themselves lost. By 2:51 p.m. PDT / 5:51 p.m. EDT, the Moon enters Capricorn and a more productive, much more serious, confident and determined perspective on our moods comes into play.

September 5th Friday

Moon in Capricorn
Venus square Pluto   2:29 a.m. PDT   5:29 a.m. EDT
Mercury conjunct Venus begins (see 9/7)
Mercury square Pluto begins (see 9/11)

Sun in Virgo and Moon waxing in Capricorn indicate a big focus on business, getting organized, prioritizing, goal setting, management and the development of finances and resources. There is so much to do on the physical plane! Be sure to keep up the pace while you can; tomorrow's long void-of-course Moon day will surely slow down the progress.

Venus square Pluto (occurring Aug. 31 – Sept. 9.) Hold on to your heartstrings: Venus now squares to Pluto in Sagittarius. This aspect last happened on April 12th, 2003. At that time, Venus was in the sign of Pisces; now Venus is in the opposite position, Virgo, where the cautious, shy, or skeptical expression of love and concern is much more evident. See April 12th for more information on Venus square Pluto.

September 6th Saturday

Moon in Capricorn goes V/C   5:43 a.m. PDT   8:43 a.m. EDT
Moon enters Aquarius   7:15 p.m. PDT   10:15 p.m. EDT

Void-of-course Moon in Capricorn fills the day with confusion over goals and priorities, as well as bringing the usual burdens of minor delays, mix-ups and contingencies. Obstacles may seem rather large and obstructive. The workload may seem monotonous and relentless. Serious moods will demand to be taken seriously. Authority figures aren't feeling very flexible and do *not* like to be questioned or contested. No matter -- it all blows over later on when the Moon enters Aquarius and our moods settle down to a much more objective picture of the day.

September 7th Sunday
Moon in Aquarius
Mars opposite Jupiter   1:01 p.m. PDT   4:01 p.m. EDT
Mercury conjunct Venus   10:35 p.m. PDT   1:35 a.m. (9/8) EDT
Sun conjunct Mercury begins (see 9/10)

Moon in Aquarius waxes up strongly as it brings a focus on applying knowledge and learning new skills. This is a time of fairs, social endeavors, conventions, as well as philanthropic and fund raising events. The general mood is outgoing and eccentric. Thoughts and ideas are often unusual and inspired. This is a good time to enjoy social outings and appreciate the late summer with our most inspired friends and comrades as the Moon waxes up towards its fullness.

Mars opposite Jupiter (Occurring Aug. 26 – Sept. 25.) This is a very busy and often overwhelming time to excel in business endeavors. For more information on Mars opposite Jupiter, which is now occurring for the second time this year, see May 5th.

Mercury conjunct Venus (occurring Sept. 5 – 10.) When these two planets are conjunct, the energy suggests an emphasis on the need to communicate love. Both communication and love are expressed in a variety of ways. Today's conjunction of Mercury and Venus takes place in the Mercury-ruled sign of Virgo, and this is often a time when intimate thoughts and secrets are shared, or these thoughts are possibly even doubted and questioned by a loved one. Any words of love or adoration uttered at this time may come across more easily and with better reception, as long as this expression of love is actually very sincere and genuine in nature, despite the tendency to have doubts. Mercury conjunct Venus is generally considered an excellent aspect to discuss and communicate love matters. For some, this means a total bashing around of emotional issues. Be sure to let those you truly love know it; sometimes it's what isn't said that disquiets the heart. Hold no expectations in the expression of love, and take no offense if your attempts to be loving are in fact poorly interpreted. There is a need to communicate the love happening now, and the most simple way to express love might be best.

September 8th Monday
Moon in Aquarius goes V/C   2:01 a.m. PDT   5:01 a.m. EDT

Technical problems? Social foibles and entanglements? Humanitarian decency gone out the door? Are those who are pretending to know just making the problem worse? The Moon is void-of-course in Aquarius all day and night. Much of today's chaos will involve accepting that this is a time of engaging in a learning process. Some must learn to listen, others must learn to keep politics out of the personal realm, most must learn to simply be more patient when the system isn't working for them. Setbacks of the void Aquarius Moon are often centered around issues of knowledge and know-how. The mistakes we make are a factor in our learning process, so take this time to learn from them.

September 9th Tuesday

Moon enters Pisces   1:07 a.m. PDT   4:07 a.m. EDT
Full Moon eve

Sing to the pending Harvest Moon! Rich delights abound. Pisces Moon draws many people to the heart of their beliefs and needs. Addictive tendencies at this time cause some folks to bear the risk of overindulgence. The creative process of performing and enjoying music and fine art are superb ways to celebrate this harvest Moon. Full Moon eve in Pisces is a mystical time which brings strong psychic inclinations and a wide range of emotional expressions and insights.

September 10th Wednesday

Full Harvest Moon in Pisces
Moon opposite Sun   9:36 a.m. PDT   12:36 p.m. EDT
Moon goes V/C   10:41 p.m. PDT   1:41 a.m. (9/11) EDT
Sun square Pluto   2:34 a.m. PDT   5:34 a.m. EDT
Sun conjunct Mercury   6:57 p.m. PDT   9:57 p.m. EDT

The final full Moon of summer lapses into a late summer reverie. Welcome to the time of the Harvest Moon. **Full Pisces Moon** (Moon opposite Sun) brings out the psychic in everyone. People can be very sensitive and as a result some people express themselves in a very artistic or perhaps even nonsensical manner. Dance, music, art, and enchantment set the stage for full Pisces Moon activity. Beware: as extensive drug and alcohol use and the need for escapism are often strong with this Moon. Many people become especially spacey, and parts of them may seem to drift off into alternative states of consciousness. Don't overdo anything as far as trying to accomplish the perfect atmosphere, a very little bit can go a very long way with the full Moon in Pisces. This is a harvest Moon, reminding us to take the best of this harvest season and enjoy it with sweet rapture!

Sun square Pluto (occurring Sept. 3 – 17.) Pluto, the god of the underworld, casts a shadow on us all to some extent when it squares to the sun. This aspect is particularly affecting those Virgo people celebrating birthdays this year from September 3rd through the 17th. These people are now the soldiers of the tests of the Pluto square, and for them this brings disruptive change, and many challenges to overcome the pain of loss, as well as accentuating the severity of transformation. Pisces people born at the exact opposite of this Virgo time of the year must also progress through this necessary process of transformation. Attempting to hold onto past realities is to cause greater destruction on your path of life. This is the time to persevere through the obstacles of hardship. The hardships that are taking place now will resurface in time, so do take note of your current struggles. Realize this trend will be repeated, and will require methods of release and attitude changes in your life in order to survive the anxiety and the stress. Take it one day at a time (Pisces and Virgo birthday people), and do not let fear and worry rule this condition! Know that you are not alone in facing these challenges. Move *through* transformation; stagnation and fear only bring extended suffering.

Sun conjunct Mercury in Virgo (occurring Sept. 7 – 14.) This is a most common aspect which creates a much more thoughtful, communicative, and expressive year ahead for those Virgo people celebrating birthdays this year from September 7th through the 14th. This is your time (birthday Virgos) to record ideas, relay important messages, and pay close attention to your imaginative thoughts as they are touched by Mercury, creating the urge to speak and be heard. Your thoughts will reveal a great deal about who you are at this time and in the year to come.

September 11th Thursday

Moon enters Aries	9:09 a.m. PDT	12:09 p.m. EDT
Mercury square Pluto	10:46 a.m. PDT	1:46 p.m. EDT

Throughout the morning on the east coast, and until 9:09 a.m. on the west coast, the post full Moon in Pisces is void-of-course. Feelings run deep and, in some cases, are very somber. This infamous day for the United States stands before us in all its starkness. The profundity of how the past affects us still remains. As the Moon enters Aries, a vibrant new spirit rises up to greet the day. The Moon now wanes out of a very full state, and tendencies towards tiredness and perhaps a little shortness of temper or patience are to be expected.

Mercury square Pluto (occurring Sept. 5 – Oct. 2.) Due to Mercury being retrograde, this aspect is occurring for an extended time period and will repeat again for another peak performance on September 28th. With Mercury currently retrograde, there is a tendency for trouble to arise over the wrong thing being said, at the wrong time, in the wrong manner, at the wrong place. How many wrongs add up in order to get a right set of circumstances to get busted? This is an excellent time to apply the utmost discretion in all matters of relaying information. Remember that information is easily misconstrued during Mercury retrograde. For more details on Mercury square Pluto, see March 15th, when this aspect last occurred.

September 12th Friday

Moon in Aries goes V/C	6:39 p.m. PDT	9:39 p.m. EDT

Throughout the day the waning Moon in Aries engages our moods to act with courage as well as caution. Aries Moon of September is a restless and impatient time for some: the crops must be harvested and autumn is pending. In other words, it's time for an extra income, or a new roof over one's head, and a budget for winter clothes or snow tires. We harvest what we need. Moods are reflected by the desire to satisfy personal needs and get on with handling the mounting tasks. All of that is hard to believe with such good weather this past season. While the spirit of a strong Aries Moon may seem relentlessly aggressive to some, the necessity to forge the will with precision brings peace and a better sense of well being to others. Taking action towards achieving personal goals is the most natural way to channel this hard driving energy of Aries. By evening it is best to just kick back and avoid creating conflict with the Moon void-of-course.

September 13th Saturday

Moon enters Taurus   7:50 p.m. PDT   10:50 p.m. EDT

It's just not worth it getting oneself in a knot over the slowing down of progress. Senseless aggression is everywhere. Pent-up energy must have an outlet, and sometimes the long void-of-course Aries Moon day reveals a tendency towards high energy outbursts. Getting things started may take several efforts. The build up of masculine energy and aggression must have an outlet. Be on the lookout for accident prone behavior. By 7:50 p.m. PDT / 10:50 p.m. EDT, the Moon enters Taurus and our moods begin to ground out and relax considerably.

September 14th Sunday
Grandparent's Day
Moon in Taurus
Uranus enters Aquarius   8:48 p.m. PDT   11:48 p.m. EDT

Waning Taurus Moon energy brings on the relaxed chore of rummaging through piles of material goods. What we put off doing all summer now needs to be addressed. This is the time to focus on buying important necessities and to clean up the homestead. Earthy focuses are the key today, as the physical realities of this time of year urge us to collect up what we need, and to get to work on making our surroundings comfortable and sound. While the sun is in Virgo urging us to be prudent, the Moon is in Taurus reminding us constantly of our imminently pressing needs.

Uranus enters Aquarius (Uranus in Aquarius April – June 1995 and Jan. 1996 – March 10th, 2003. Last round – Sept. 14 – Dec. 30, 2003.) Today, retrograde Uranus goes back into the late degrees of Aquarius for its final round of being in the fixed air sign of Aquarius. Uranus rules Aquarius, and the dimension that it has taken on during the turn of the millennium has been nothing short of radically bold and has indeed left its impression. Uranus is famous for shaking up old systems of thought and bringing on change at a rapid and often chaotic rate. Since 1995, Uranus has traveled through Aquarius, shaking up big changes in science, technology, and human rights issues, as well as most political and humanitarian issues in our lives. Uranus entered the sign of Pisces on March 10th this year, and the shift of energy has begun to show us how the "Big Chaos" predicted by the Mayans is being stirred in the arts, music, spirituality, religion and substance abuse. Uranus is the freedom fighter and is ill content to accept areas of life that aren't working. These focuses of our lives require a revolutionary process of aggression and strong awareness. Uranus is taking its last explosive punch at being in its home, Aquarius, today through December 30th. Technology will undergo a final shift in our lives as the finishing touches on our inventions reach a new pinnacle in the market. More software companies are likely to fold as the industry giants play out their hands. Scientific breakthroughs are imminent with Uranus boldly completing its journey through Aquarius. Human rights issues may escalate once again over the daunting question of what western freedom represents, and how we can exist freely while upholding the value of our intrinsic differences. Meanwhile, the shaken dogma of the turbulent middle eastern world may well begin to touch on how to integrate into a global economy in order to rebuild the crumbling remains of war-shattered lives. This is particularly essential as the potential for more violent outbreak is the final straw in some bitterly shaken minds. Uranus in Aquarius has explosively opened the doors of global intervention. The precedent of how to rebuild those forever-changed lives is currently being re-examined and addressed as we now send out strong literal and symbolic statements on where the revolutionary process of our humanity must lead us. For the final commentary on the travels of Uranus, see December 30th.

September 15th Monday

Moon in Taurus
Venus enters Libra   8:58 a.m. PDT   11:58 a.m. EDT

Grounded and practical moods fill the air on this Taurus Moon day. As a general rule, our sensibilities are in fairly good working order. The desire to surround oneself with practical beauty and an uplifting atmosphere is strong, and there is much satisfaction to be found in the beauty and delights of nature. Simple and affordable pleasures abound.

Venus enters Libra (Venus in Libra: Sept. 15 – Oct. 9.) Venus enters Libra and now the course of magnetism, affection and feminine perception begins to focus on harmonizing and balancing relationships, marriages, and friendships. Venus will be in Libra today through October 9th, stimulating our Libra friends with a strong sense of affection, and focusing our family and love relationships towards the goal of creating a more harmonized and balanced state of being. Venus is at home in Libra, and brings out a love of libraries, of scholarly works, and there is a greater attraction to large bodies of information. Venus in Libra emphasizes the love of books, education, law and order, friends and loved ones, and particularly, a love and desire for balance wherever possible. Through dealing, compromising, and attempting more sensitivity to others, living with and showing affection to those with whom we have chosen to be, becomes the focus of this time. As autumn approaches, our nesting instincts grow deeper, and relationships that aren't stable enough to undergo the responsibilities and tests of winter are likely to break off: as Venus in Libra strives to apply diplomacy as tactfully as possible. As for the delicacy of love matters; in order to settle on the best choices and decisions possible, Libra strives hard to apply a great wealth of knowledge concerning common law, history, and helpful information regarding relationships.

September 16th Tuesday

Moon in Taurus goes V/C	8:25 a.m. PDT	11:25 a.m. EDT
Moon enters Gemini	8:32 a.m. PDT	11:32 a.m. EDT

This morning the Moon shifts from Taurus into Gemini fairly swiftly. Gemini Moon causes moods and emotions to be easily stirred by our thought patterns. It may be difficult to make up your mind about just how you're feeling today. Restlessness and scattered feelings are common at this time. There are endless details to consider today. Speeches, writings, ideas and discussions run strong. This is a good time to check over lists and plans and to organize.

September 17th Wednesday

Moon in Gemini

Details, details; is there no end to covering the details? The general feeling seems to be that there is no end to the busy mindset that a Gemini Moon puts us through. This is a busy time of year, and the tedious details that take hours of our time to consider must not be overlooked on days like today. Gemini Moon puts many of us in the position of having to explain all the details and communicate the plan of action. Be sure to take the time every now and then to take your mind off matters, stretch, stick your head outside and take a big deep breath!

September 18th Thursday

Last Quarter Moon in Gemini

Moon square Sun	12:03 p.m. PDT	3:03 p.m. EDT
Moon in Gemini goes V/C	8:50 p.m. PDT	11:50 p.m. EDT
Moon enters Cancer	9:07 p.m. PDT	12:07 a.m. (9/19) EDT

The **Last Quarter Moon in Gemini** (Moon square Sun), brings out talkative moods and informative interaction. People will have a lot on their minds today and intellectual pursuits are emphasized. This is the time to enjoy games, puzzles, and social conversations. Waning Gemini Moon is always the time to release those unwanted and frustrating mixed emotions. This is the time to ease the mind by not using it so much to stir those emotions! Later in the evening, the Moon enters Cancer and our moods lean more towards retreating to a quiet environment.

September 19th Friday
Moon in Cancer

♍

The Moon is in Cancer and the entire day stimulates our senses with deep emotional expressions, and focuses our attention on nurturing and instinctual urges. This serves as a good time to brighten up the home and make it feel more comfortable. Deep feelings run through our moods with a waning Moon in Cancer, and there may be a tendency with some people to be distracted and moody. For the most part, this is simply a time when many of us need a little more reassurance and love.

September 20th Saturday
Moon in Cancer
Mercury goes direct   1:53 a.m. PDT   4:53 a.m. EDT
Mercury-sextile-Saturn-Non-Exact Time N/A PDT – N/A EDT
Venus trine Neptune begins (see 9/23)

What is this that is affecting our moods? Waning Cancer Moon puts us in touch with the need to retreat to a more nurturing and calming environment. For a variety of reasons, our emotional patterns are shifting. Cancer Moon reminds us to go with the flow of our feelings.

Mercury goes direct (Mercury retrograde Aug. 28 – Sept. 20 / Mercury direct Sept. 20 – Dec. 17.) Since August 28th, Mercury in Virgo has been retrograde, causing a number of uneasy communication mixups with regard to things such as accounting, keeping track of goods and services, and research. There have been untamed disputes that have raised criticism, skepticism and doubt. Now that Mercury goes direct, expect communications to be a lot more smooth and perhaps less ridiculing. Unsettled contracts can be corrected and negotiated more clearly and swiftly now, and there is likely to be much less difficulty interpreting and translating. From now on, there will be more clarification taking place with regard to those misunderstandings, postponements and disputes which have cropped up in the past few weeks. Now at least, the majority of us who are so strongly affected by Mercury retrograde can move forward in our thinking and our ways of presenting our thoughts. We can interpret others more clearly and get on with business. For now, it's down to the business of celebrating that Mercury has gone direct! Give it a few days for Mercury to move forward and you'll notice the change in the efficiency and accuracy of communications.

Mercury-sextile-Saturn-Non-Exact (occurring Sept. 13 – 27.) Due to the retrograde pattern of Mercury, this beneficial but short lived aspect is taking place for longer than usual. Even though this aspect does not reach an exactness and does not show up on the celestial chart, it comes extremely close to the exact sextile mark today (as close as 00.06 degrees), and is still very influential, although the degree numbers now begin to turn around as Mercury goes direct. Mercury sextile Saturn is the unseen aspect that is very fully at work! For more details on this aspect, see Mercury sextile Saturn on August 4th.

September 21st Sunday

Moon in Cancer goes V/C   3:21 a.m. PDT   5:21 a.m. EDT
Moon enters Leo   7:03 a.m. PDT   10:03 a.m. EDT
Mars-conjunct-Uranus-non-exact time: N/A
Venus square Saturn begins (see 9/25)

Moon in Cancer goes void-of-course very early in the morning, and by 7:03 a.m. PDT / 10:03 a.m. EDT, the Moon enters the sign of Leo. Here we go, out of the waves of minor emotional morning turmoil, staged by the void-of-course Cancer crab Moon, and into the willful determination of the Leo lion. The moods of Leo Moon are heartfelt. The final days of summer wind down to a close this week as our moods focus on family endeavors and activities, as well as friends and entertainment. Personal desires and aspirations are also reviewed and examined.

Mars-conjunct-Uranus-Non-Exact (Sept. 21 – 25 this aspect is at a standstill, with an orb of 0.34 degrees / occurring Aug. 20 – Oct. 25.) Due to the retrograde patterns of both Mars and Uranus, this is a hidden aspect at work that never actually reaches an exact conjunction, but it certainly comes close enough to call this one mighty active. For the next four days, this is as close as it comes with a standstill (almost) conjunction of Mars and Uranus. Retrograde patterns of planets often bring repeat performances of the aspects that take place between them. This aspect last happened in June, and the distinguishable difference is the fact that in June these two were both conjunct in Pisces. At this time, Uranus is taking care of some unfinished business in Aquarius; although the experience now is very similar to the conjunction in June, the dynamics have changed. Heated matters are likely to involve a great deal more radical activity with regard to human rights issues, science and technology. This aspect has extremely hot energy written all over it. For a reminder of what Mars conjunct Uranus entails, see June 23rd.

September 22nd Monday

Moon in Leo

Its here, the final day of summer. Leo Moon now wanes and puts us in touch with the beastly side of our nature. We stand at the precipice of the autumn season, but we still might need to let out the last whooping cries of wild abandon and summertime blues fury. The summer spirit dies hard. Nonetheless, we must begin to rehearse our next moves. The actor in each of us begins to act out new roles in an effort to address the new stage before us. This is the stage of the Autumnal Equinox. It is a time of change, and today we do what we can to strengthen our self image, as we begin to find ways to honor our choices as the days ahead grow shorter. The curtain draws to a close for summer, and there is a commotion backstage. The busy new season is about to begin.

LIBRA
I Balance
Cardinal Air Sign
Symbol: The Scales

September 23rd — October 23rd

September 23rd Tuesday
Autumnal Equinox

Moon in Leo goes V/C	12:33 p.m. PDT	3:33 p.m. EDT
Moon enters Virgo	1:04 p.m. PDT	4:04 p.m. EDT
Sun enters Libra	3:47 a.m. PDT	6:47 a.m. EDT
Venus trine Neptune	10:08 p.m. PDT	1:08 a.m. (9/24) EDT

Throughout the morning Leo Moon captivates our moods with childlike play and family related fun. By afternoon, the Moon enters Virgo and our playful demeanour settles down to the important work at hand. Keeping track of matters and accounting for what's going on becomes an important part of bringing in the new season.

Sun enters Libra (Sun in Libra: Sept. 23 – Oct. 23.) It's Autumn! A mild chill cools the air, the Sun's brilliant light now descends from the northern hemisphere. Today, daytime and night time are equally long: its the magical time of **Autumnal Equinox**. This time of year calls us to reach out to each other and create a support system and a network of helpful friends to prepare for the busy season ahead, and the darker and colder days yet to come. Happy Birthday Libra people! The Sun now enters Libra, and this is a Venus ruled sign that focuses our attention on the power of team work and partnership. Love is the reason behind Libra's hard drive for perfection and harmony. The key phrase for Libra is " I balance," and the key to Libra's happiness comes with a sense of balance. Another factor to take into account for our Libran friends is the perpetual state of adjustment required to meet that balance. Libra could therefore easily say: "I adjust." This action of achieving balance is always facilitated by Libra's unyielding ability to continually make adjustments through life's relentless problems. The cornucopia of life is full of expressions of harmony and beauty. When else is a season so full of a variety and wealth of fruits and delights? Well, perhaps there are fruitful summer harvests, but this autumn harvest time is the plentiful grand finale! It is time to prepare for the cooler days ahead, and this often means securing a mate, as well as balancing and reconciling relationships. Libra focuses on libraries and accesses data and knowledge, particularly concerning law. All kinds of law are considered here: civil and social laws, and morals and dogmas of various proponents are carefully considered or weighed. This sophisticated kind of assessment is done in order to strike a harmony and balance in relationships. Libra strives towards the perfection of the equilibrium of forces to create a stylized harmonious environment. Libra also focuses on matters of law and the court system to justify the actions of those around us. Libra is constantly attempting to perfect the decision making process, always taking into account as many possibilities as conceivable before making a commitment. This is not to say that making decisions comes easily to Librans -- it is only to say that it is a very important process to them. Quite often the decisions people make during the Libra time of year keep them busy throughout the entire autumn season. Libra focuses on education, hence school schedules abound and newly begun classes begin to take a more studious form. Be careful not to take on too much this season if you've already got your hands full. Balancing your schedule is as important as sticking to it. Libra people work hard to keep their relationships stable. Be sure to support them by acknowledging their efforts. This year, the autumnal holiday of equal halves of day and night falls on the 23rd here in North America. May this new autumn season be pleasurable and fruitful for you and all your loved ones!

Venus trine Neptune (occurring Sept. 20 – 28.) Venus trine Neptune brings feminine love in harmony with spiritual expression. This aspect now takes place for the second time this year. For more information on Venus trine Neptune see June 20th.

September 24th Wednesday
Moon in Virgo goes V/C   6:52 p.m. PDT   9:52 p.m.

Throughout the day, the darkly waning Virgo Moon keeps our moods somewhat skeptical, curious, questioning and communicative. By 6:52 p.m. PDT / 9:52 p.m. EDT, the Virgo Moon going void-of-course may bring a wave of overly cautious feelings related to health setbacks, internalized anxiety, and a paranoid attitude. Critical or overly analytical defenses are at work for some folks later this evening, and it may be good just to take it easy. To wallow in doubt is to challenge and test one's own security. Moods are often the darkest right before the New Moon.

September 25th Thursday
New Moon in Libra
Moon conjunct Sun   8:09 p.m. PDT   11:09 p.m. EDT
Moon enters Libra   3:49 p.m. PDT   6:49 p.m. EDT
Venus square Saturn   8:20 a.m. PDT   11:20 a.m. EDT

Though the days grow shorter, this day may seem a little longer as the Virgo Moon remains void-of-course all morning and day, creating a greater potential for critical, scrutinizing, nit picky, and doubtful moods. By late afternoon PDT / evening EDT, the Moon finally enters Libra and the shadow on our moods begins to become more clear, as we start to become a little more objective. **New Moon in Libra** (Moon conjunct Sun), reaches its conjunction with the

Sun tonight at 8:09 p.m. PDT / 11:09 p.m. EDT. This is a time of reaffirming and harmonizing our relationships with friends and partners. It is also a time of new friendship as the shift to autumn activities creates a new working environment for many people. New rules, when diplomatically agreed upon, set the standard for how to create a more harmonious environment in the autumn days to come. This is the first time in this new season the Sun and Moon are both in autumn signs of the zodiac. The commitment to carry out the autumn trends that are beginning to take precedence, now starts to sink into our moods.

Venus square Saturn (occurring Sept. 21 - 30.) Venus square Saturn creates obstacles and restrictions concerning the timely expression of love. This aspect now takes place for the second time this year. For more information on Venus square Saturn, see April 16th.

September 26th Friday
American Indian Day
Moon in Libra
Venus sextile Pluto begins (see 9/29)

Newly waxing Libra Moon gives us the power to focus on our decisions and make adjustments accordingly. This is an important time of establishing new ground rules for creating balance in relationships and partnerships. Libra Moon activities focus on research, teaching, law, courts, the justice system, libraries and information centers. This is a good time to work on harmonizing and balancing unsettled matters which need to be addressed among loved ones.

September 27th Saturday
Rosh Hashana begins

Moon in Libra goes V/C	4:10 p.m. PDT	7:10 p.m. EDT
Moon enters Scorpio 4	4:52 p.m. PDT	7:52 p.m. EDT
Mars goes direct	12:52 a.m. PDT	3:52 a.m. EDT

Sun trine Neptune begins (see 10/3)

Throughout the day, Libra Moon activity focuses our moods on those areas of life requiring the most immediate attention for the sake of striking a balance. By 4:52 p.m. PDT / 7:52 p.m. EDT, the Moon enters Scorpio and our moods begin to shift to a much more definitive set of emotional responses. Scorpio Moon classically brings a strong and sometimes intense underlying emotional current to our moods.

Mars goes direct (Mars direct Sept. 28, '03 – Oct. 1, '05.) Since July 28th of this year, the planet representing the god of war has been retrograde. Mars has been traveling back through the sign of Pisces, focusing activities on deep emotional and spiritual matters. Mars retrograde through Pisces is likely to have been quite challenging, especially for Pisces, Sagittarius, Gemini and Virgo people. Here's the good news: Mars now moves *forward* through Pisces, and all Pisces people may now apply their energy levels and actions towards matters with much smoother results. Mars gives us what we need to sustain life; however, it can also destroy life. The masculine force of vitality holds the promise of action, and represents the principle that energy can be directed anywhere we choose, and while Mars moves forward it is less likely to spread out of control. Mars energy summons our need for survival, animates us to act in defense, and awakens the urge to live and express one's rage at all the apparent offenses of the world. Wisdom decrees it is best to maintain one's own masculine force with the greatest dignity and integrity. To live is to serve the life force that lives inside each of us. Mars will now assume a forward moving position around the sun from our geocentric perspective for a nice long time: until October 1st, 2005.

September 28th Sunday
Moon in Scorpio
Mercury square Pluto   9:28 a.m. PDT   12:28 p.m. EDT

Scorpio moon is newly waxing and shifts our moods towards the emergence of deeper feelings coming to the surface. Scorpio Moon always tends to steer us towards our emergencies and crucial concerns in life. On a lighter note, Waxing Scorpio Moon is an especially good time to transplant or plant shrubs and trees, your potted plants that need to be in the ground before winter, as well as spring flower bulbs. Don't forget autumn seed planting!

Mercury square Pluto (occurring Sept. 5 – Oct. 2.) For a second time this month, Mercury square Pluto takes the stage. It last happened on September 11th when Mercury was retrograde; now many of the things said and done from that time are undergoing a correction process at this time. Beware: in the attempt to clear up what may have been construed as the latest "verbal abuse," there may be a tendency at this time to blurt out even more obscenities due to a perplexing feeling of unfinished business over some really harsh issues. This is a particularly difficult time to discuss issues in a manner that makes the hardship any easier. The prolonged factor of this usually short-lived aspect doesn't make the drama any easier, and boldly demonstrates the need for many folks to speak out against corruption, prejudice, greed and oppression. It won't be long now (4 more days or so), and this aspect will pass, though its affects may linger among the unforgiving.

September 29th Monday
Moon in Scorpio goes V/C   5:08 p.m. PDT   8:08 p.m. EDT
Moon enters Sagittarius   5:57 p.m. PDT   8:57 p.m. EDT
Venus sextile Pluto   10:50 a.m. PDT   1:50 p.m. EDT
Sun square Saturn begins (see 10/6)

The Moon waxes in Scorpio and our moods become intent on deeper emotional feelings and concerns. A sense of secrecy and cautious suspicion fills the air, and many restless souls are on the prowl to satiate personal desires. By 5:57 p.m. PDT / 8:57 p.m. EDT, the Moon enters Sagittarius and to look forward into the month and season ahead. Visions and hopes for the future begin to captivate our imagination.

Venus sextile Pluto (occurring Sept. 26 – Oct. 2.) Venus sextile Pluto points to the opportunity to grow and transform as a result of love related struggles. This aspect now takes place for a second time this year. For more information on Venus sextile Pluto, see March 19th.

September 30th Tuesday
Moon in Sagittarius

A waxing Moon in Sagittarius brings out the adventurous side of our moods as the final day of the month unfolds. Curious and exploratory thoughts captivate our moods and our insights, and high hopes are currently running strong. This serves as a good time to break the usual pattern, take a new route and learn something new. Discoveries made at this time open one up to a richer perspective on life. A different perspective may just be what is needed in order to carry our energies over into the swiftly changing energy of the new month ahead.

October 1st Wednesday

Moon in Sagittarius goes V/C	7:25 p.m. PDT	10:25 p.m. EDT
Moon enters Capricorn	8:21 p.m. PDT	11:21 p.m. EDT

Enthusiastic moods brighten our outlook on this new month as the waxing Sagittarius Moon invites us to explore all avenues of possibility. Miraculous feats always seem to take place on the first of the month and while the Moon waxes in Sagittarius, these achievements might require going beyond the usual bounds and stretching the limits in order to make ends meet. The sweet young autumn air hints of change. If we are astute and willing to watch for the signs, a vision of the month ahead illuminates our senses. A picture or a vision can be magnified with a positive affirmation. Perfect and empower the vision. A sincere effort to achieve logically follows a clear vision. Later tonight, the Moon enters Capricorn and a serious, more pensive tone of mood brings the evening to a close. We must be practical; October's storms will come and we must be ready.

October 2nd Thursday

First Quarter Moon in Capricorn		
Moon square Sun	12:09 p.m. PDT	3:09 p.m. EDT

First Quarter Moon in Capricorn (Moon square Sun) brings a strong emphasis on the need for serious labor. Some staunch determination is required. There is a steadily mounting concern to achieve a notable level of accomplishment or completion of projects. The late harvest ripens, and the physical force of the world is hard at work. October festivals and banquets require a tremendous amount of preparation. People's moods are greatly moved by the acknowledgement of merits. The need to hunt for a steady job, a marketing edge, or a secure investment keeps us vigilant and focused. Punctuality in business matters is stressed. Some may feel isolated by constant work and no play. No one likes feeling rushed, particularly when high standards must be met.

October 3rd Friday

Moon in Capricorn goes V/C	3:40 p.m. PDT	6:40 p.m. EDT
Sun trine Neptune	8:23 p.m. PDT	11:23 p.m. EDT

The Capricorn Moon waxes onward, instilling in our moods the need to maintain a certain level of concentration and skill. Dedication pays off. A sense of loyalty and responsibility to the work will bring the cherished result. By 3:40 p.m. PDT / 6:40 p.m. EDT, the Moon goes void-of-course. Although there is still a strong drive to keep up the pace, daunting pressures, obstacles and unforeseeable circumstances may greatly limit our abilities to concentrate and focus. The best strategy for tonight is to kick back, or at least lighten the pace.

Sun trine Neptune (occurring Sept. 27 – Oct. 10.) This aspect particularly affects Libra people celebrating birthdays this year from September 27th through October 10th. These Libra birthday folks are experiencing the favorable trine aspect of Neptune to their natal sun. This brings gifts of spiritual encounters and awareness, as well as a calming affect on one's life. This serves as a good time (particularly for these birthday folks) to seek visions, to apply prayer and meditation, and to explore spiritual avenues and beliefs presented at this time. An altruistic sort of harmony can be achieved with Sun trine Neptune, and this will be the year for these Libra birthday people to strike a balance in their spiritual outlook on life as they develop a better understanding of the direction their beliefs are taking.

October 4th Saturday

Moon enters Aquarius	12:45 a.m. PDT	3:45 a.m. EDT
Venus trine Uranus begins (see 10/8)		

The Sun is in Libra, the Moon is in Aquarius and this young October Saturday stands before us. This is a time of clarifying and declaring the terms of our life in regards to education, law, documentation, and research. A busy shuffle rustles through the halls of large institutions. Waxing Aquarius Moon puts the spotlight on such focuses as science, charities and humanitarian issues. Unusual and eccentric people are spurred to expose their creative genius. The general mood is outgoing and eccentric. Moon in Aquarius brings on a full day of inspired moods, openness towards learning, and exploring new viewpoints on the people around us. Aquarius Moon focuses our moods on seeking knowledge as well as innovative and unusual avenues of thought and problem solving.

October 5th Sunday
Moon in Aquarius
Venus trine Mars begins (see 10/10)

♎

Festive and philanthropic endeavors continue through this Aquarius Moon weekend of early October. Open minded, inventive, and refreshing viewpoints are sought and circulated. We are living in the age of Aquarius, and every month having an Aquarius Moon reminds us more and more of our social development and personal obligations to the world, as well as the challenges we must confront in the world of science and technology, whose presence grows more ominous with time. Today, our moods are encouraged to face the issues of humanity, raising questions about ourselves and our conduct in the world. Knowledge and how we use it are the keys to discovering how to perfect our personal approaches to the new millennium. Applying what we know makes us stronger, and as far as the mind is concerned, those who don't use it lose it. Today is a good day to get in touch with something that broadens the awareness.

October 6th Monday
Yom Kippur

Moon in Aquarius goes V/C	6:06 a.m. PDT	9:09 a.m. EDT
Moon enters Pisces	7:20 a.m. PDT	10:20 a.m. EDT
Sun square Saturn	6:40 a.m. PDT	9:40 a.m. EDT
Mercury enters Libra	6:28 p.m. PDT	9:28 p.m. EDT

Sun sextile Pluto begins (see 10/11)

Early morning PDT / late morning EDT, the waxing Moon enters Pisces and sets the tone for a day of intuitive and expressive moods.

Sun square Saturn (occurring Sept. 29 – Oct. 13.) This aspect particularly affects those Libra people celebrating birthdays this year from September 29th through October 13th. These birthday folks are undergoing personal challenges with regard to patience, feeling out of control, losing a sense of time, having poor timing, etc. This challenge represents overcoming obstacles that intrude on one's sense of discipline and accuracy. Often, false starts occur during the phases of one's life when Saturn squares the natal sun. This challenge will pass, but it also teaches those who are affected to take a good look at what does matter in their life, and to appreciate life for what it is and not what they're conditioned to think life is supposed to be about. This may be a time of sacrifice, loss or compromise, and of complexity and insecurity for these Libra birthday folks experiencing the Saturn square natal sun challenge. Saturn represents those things in life we are willing to work for and maintain. Just because there is a challenge in the way does not mean it is time to give up. Saturn represents our sense of discipline and the application of effort and focus. Here, we learn about our limitations as our strengths are also realized. This is a time for these birthday folks to conserve energies and to take losses and difficulties in stride. Through the tests of Saturn, a stronger human being emerges to take on future tests with greater ability. Running away from hardship now will only make life more difficult later. This is a time to learn from your mistakes and make adjustments accordingly. The Libra in you knows this.

Mercury enters Libra (Mercury in Libra: Oct. 6 – 24.) Mercury in Libra brings the general course of communications, talk, conversation and discussion into focus on the importance of mindful balance, diplomacy, tact and the need to connect with friends and loved ones. Libra is the autumn sign that emphasizes balance and adjustment. Now through the 24th of this month, Mercury in Libra brings us a mental focus on the acts of harmonizing and adjusting to the changing season. This is a good time for people to converse by gathering and collecting important information, as our decision making process kicks into high gear.

October 7th Tuesday

Moon in Pisces goes V/C   4:30 p.m. PDT   7:30 p.m. EDT

Today, our moods drift into and out of a series of flowing and changing imaginings and impressions. As the Moon travels through Pisces, a mystical and timeless element of perception captivates our moods. Bubbly, artistic, enchanting, and dreamy moments allow us to access some hidden sanctuary where the soulful or prayerful part of ourselves is unleashed. Today, many folks will be drawn towards the need to seek out a favorite space or refuge from the mundane, to find a place that recharges the batteries and allows faith to be renewed. By evening, the Moon will be void-of-course for the rest of the night. People tend to be hypersensitive under these circumstances. Beware of the tendency for some to overindulge in any variety of substances. Night time is a good time to relax and let the tranquil, unburdened comforts of a safe environment ease the heart and soul.

October 8th Wednesday

Moon enters Aries   4:07 p.m. PDT   7:07 p.m. EDT
Venus trine Uranus   9:47 p.m. PDT   12:47 a.m. (10/9) EDT

The overall consensus is that this is not likely to be a particularly high performance day. This will be a day to work out emotional issues, addictive tendencies, and the need to escape or alter reality. A wide variety of subconscious concerns that have finally begun to surface are appearing before us as strong symbols and signs. Go with the flow and look for the signs. By 4:07 p.m. PDT / 7:07 p.m. EDT, the Moon enters Aries. It is a heavily waxing Moon emerging towards its absolute fullness in the sign of the ram. Energetic and enthusiastic sparks fill the air.

Venus trine Uranus (occurring Oct. 4 – 13.) This aspect creates harmony between the lines of love and chaos. Outlandish fashion and fads are often highlighted or created under this aspect. For the second time this year, Venus is trine to Uranus. See July 6th for more details.

October 9th Thursday

Moon in Aries
Venus enters Scorpio 11:56 a.m. PDT 2:56 p.m. EDT
Full Moon Eve
Jupiter sextile Saturn begins (see 11/1)
Mercury trine Neptune begins (see 10/12)

♎

It's Full Moon Eve. The spirit of cardinal fire burns through to the next stage of life, leaving in its path unfinished business and a creative or impulsive course of action which often brings new light to a situation. This almost Full Moon in Aries is a restless and impatient time for some. There is a competitive air building for many folks. Strength and vitality our blessings which Aries Moon encourages us to access and which allow us to complete the mounting tasks of the autumn in preparation for the pending storms of the season. This is a good time to seize the initiative and tackle projects. While the spirit of Aries Moon may seem relentless to some, the necessity to temper the will with precision and expertise brings a better sense of well being. Taking action to complete personal goals is the most natural way to channel this hard driving energy of Aries.

Venus enters Scorpio (Venus in Scorpio: Oct. 9 – Nov. 20.) The planet Venus, which influences matters of love, beauty, art, and attraction now takes us through the astrological expression of Scorpio, which brings out deep and passionate levels of care and concern. Venus in Scorpio brings out a love for and attraction to the more passionate experiences of life: birth, sex, death and rebirth, and transformation. Magnetism runs strong with Venus in Scorpio, and love affairs are often torrid and well hidden. Sometimes the dark side of our love and our hidden fears surface with regard to loved ones while Venus is in Scorpio, forcing us to come clear on what's haunting us and to take strong measures to ensure a functional harmony with those whom we love. Venus is considered to be in "detriment" in Scorpio. This may be a time to work out anxiety, fear and emotional stress concerning love. Sexual love is a strong outlet for many folks at this time. Love with passion is an empowering thing, but it is always wise to be sure that the experience does not hinder the well being of those who are close to us. The nature of Scorpio love can sometimes drag a loved one down with its intensity. Love shines best when it is mutually expressed. In this there is great passion.

October 10th Friday

Full Moon in Aries
Moon opposite Sun 12:27 a.m. PDT 3:27 a.m. EDT
Venus trine Mars 1:32 p.m. PDT 4:32 p.m. EDT

Today we can finally begin to rest, satisfied as we complete the full moon journey. All the accumulated high pomp and hype of the second half of this week comes to a crescendo marked with the burning and wilful force of Aries Moon activity. In the wee small hours of the morning, the **Moon reached its**

Full mark in Aries (Moon opposite Sun.) As we awaken to this day, the full Aries Moon is now waning and our impulse to provoke speedy reactions begins to settle down. Much of the impetuous edge and straightforward tenacity of our moods begin to dissipate and slow to a more steady pace. All the while, the cardinal fire heat of strong intent, the drive that urges us onward, is ever present throughout the day. What a great time to celebrate life-affirming energy with gusto!

Venus trine Mars (occurring Oct. 5 – 16.) This is an excellent aspect for promoting harmony in the relations of feminine and masculine counterparts. Venus is in Scorpio and Mars is in Pisces; there will be lots of excitement as well as deep, imaginative, and inspired love at play. This aspect last took place on July 11th and it's the second occurrence this year. See July 11th for more details on Venus trine Mars.

October 11th Saturday
Sukkoth

Moon in Aries goes V/C	1:31 a.m. PDT	4:31 a.m. EDT
Moon enters Taurus	3:05 a.m. PDT	6:05 a.m. EDT
Sun sextile Pluto	4:31 a.m. PDT	7:31 a.m. EDT
Mercury square Saturn begins (see 10/14)		

The Moon wanes in Taurus. Many folks are now taking the time to assess their values and needs. We are currently in the post-full-moon stage of the month. Tiredness and laziness are natural for many folks, and whenever possible, the luxury of relaxation is especially prized. Don't push yourself if you are tired or the potential for illness may arise, particularly sore throats -- Taurus rules the throat area of the body. Cold and flu season approaches. Some people have a tendency to burn themselves out on the Full Aries Moon, and the waning Taurus moon calls for the practical measure of tending to our physical maintenance and care. Nurture your body with vitamin enriched food. Enjoy the sensual pleasures of comfortable fabrics and textiles. Use warm, rich colors to melt away cold emotions. Keep warm and dry.

Sun sextile Pluto (occurring Oct. 6 – 16.) This aspect particularly affects those Libra people celebrating birthdays this year from October 6th through the 16th. This brings opportunity that may appear demanding and vast, perhaps even endless. These Libra birthday people are undergoing the sextile aspect of their natal sun to Pluto, giving them the opportunity to take charge and step up into positions of power, as well as to address great audiences of disparate generations in diverse levels of dominion. These birthday Librans are undergoing a powerful transformation in an opportunistic fashion. This will be the time for these Libran folks to empower what they identify as their own, especially because their long trials of the past our now concluding. Though life may have had its difficult trials, this is the time for birthday Librans to rise above! Go thee forth and conquer, Libra masters! Your time to triumph is always available when your will and persistence to achieve is balanced and in tact. This, of course, holds true for all signs of the zodiac!

October 12th Sunday
Moon in Taurus
Mercury trine Neptune   6:57 p.m. PDT   9:57 p.m. EDT

It's now back to basics, and the Moon in Taurus urges us to address our finances, shop wisely, and to seek out practical methods to meet personal demands. The need for stable and practical security calls out to many of us. In order to feel balance in our lives and to make adjustments in this Libra time of year, we must address those unavoidable obstacles concerning money related matters. Taurus Moon puts us in touch with our sensibilities and lets us know what we will need to outfit ourselves for the season.

Mercury trine Neptune (occurring Oct. 9 – 16.) This is a superb aspect for discussing personal philosophies and metaphysical subjects, and a good time to communicate with the spirit world. This aspect brings gifts from Spirit. Those who are open to communication and prayer, will have a spiritual channel with which to open their hearts and minds, to find peace where it is desired. Communicate about spiritual needs and breakthroughs. Receive gifts of renewed faith in your beliefs.

October 13th Monday
Columbus Day / Thanksgiving (Canada)
Moon in Taurus goes V/C   2:02 p.m. PDT   5:05 p.m. EDT
Moon enters Gemini   3:45 p.m. PDT   6:45 p.m. EDT
Venus square Neptune begins (see 10/17)

Taurus Moon is an excellent time to indulge the senses in epicurean delights, and to enjoy natural accents such as simple and creative table settings highlighting the beauty of the season. By late afternoon PDT / evening EDT, the Moon enters Gemini and our focus on beautiful surroundings turns to the activity of lively conversations and storytelling. In fact, there might be a moment when it is quite evident that a chorus of innumerable voices are all speaking and harmonizing concurrently, and oddly enough, all making sense simultaneously. We couldn't do this all the time! It's a good thing that Gemini people have only one mouth and two ears like everyone else!

October 14th Tuesday
Moon in Gemini
Mercury square Saturn   7:49 a.m. PDT   10:49 a.m. EDT
Venus sextile Jupiter begins (see 10/18)

The spirit of the Gemini Moon shifts our moods towards a curious and communicative outlook on the day. Many will be confronted with mixed feelings concerning issues that are being raised at this time. Gemini Moon gets us looking at both sides of matters and raises important questions that often concern us directly. The Sun is in Libra and the Moon is in Gemini: this is a time of research, teaching, and speechmaking. The world focuses on the law of the land, and at times like this we commonly seek to have a say in every jurisdiction that directly affects our lives.

Mercury square Saturn (occurring Oct. 11 – 17.) This aspect makes it difficult to put a message out there and be taken seriously. Some may be struck with the feeling that they are limited or restricted in what they can say. This aspect is now occurring for a second time this year. For more details on Mercury square Saturn, see March 17th.

October 15th Wednesday
Moon in Gemini
Mercury sextile Pluto begins (see 10/17)
Venus trine Saturn begins (see 10/20)
Sun conjunct Mercury begins (see 10/25)

Sun in Libra and Moon in Gemini focuses our attention on law matters, justice, and the application of information, bringing out a number of issues that require a second look. It is best not to let mixed feelings lead to confusion. Search for the balance and meaning in all the sides being presented, and try not let emotional issues cloud your mind. Feelings teach us about ourselves: it is beneficial to listen to them as well as to influence them with our thoughts, which often have significant power to influence them. Use your thoughts gently and carefully to stir your emotions with wisdom, and peace of mind will follow.

October 16th Thursday
Moon in Gemini goes V/C	2:54 a.m. PDT	5:54 p.m. EDT
Moon enters Cancer	4:41 a.m. PDT	7:41 a.m. EDT

Sun trine Uranus begins (see 10/22)

Waning Cancer Moon tends to make some folks especially moody or defensive. The common course of worry, fear and anxiety needs to be addressed, dumped and replaced with positive affirmations. At best, well adjusted folks apply patience, understanding, an encouraging word, and perhaps several methods of banishing. This is a good time to apply cleansing practices, particularly emotional cleansing, and make the home sparkle with beautiful charms and inviting specialty foods. Cancer Moon is an appropriate moon for home and food related pleasures. Be careful not to indulge unduly; overeating is a common way to combat feelings of not being loved, and to drown out personal troubles or family conflicts. Feed the hunger, nurture the soul. Moodiness is the essence of lunar expression and Cancer is the Moon's attributed domain. This is the time to apply the motherly touch. Nurture all ills and wounds, and focus on emotional health and well being.

October 17th Friday

Moon in Cancer
Mercury sextile Pluto 1:25 a.m. PDT   4:25 a.m. EDT
Venus square Neptune 8:47 p.m. PDT   11:47 p.m. EDT

♎

The Moon now wanes in the sign of the crab, and is all set to reach the Last Quarter mark tomorrow morning. This is the time to focus on our private lives and our emotional support networks. Many of us may be amazed at our own subconscious response mechanism which is revealing intuitive and instinctual warnings and clues of what is to come. This does not mean we should blow our grocery money on a gambling hunch and blame it on the Moon. It simply means with a little extra observation, and a keenly considered educated guess, our intuition and our psychic awareness may well lead us to success.

Mercury sextile Pluto (occurring Oct. 15 – 19.) Communications and discussions are enhanced, with an opportunity to make a breakthrough in negotiations with a strong power. Mass media may well be entranced by a notable event, or by news concerning world superpowers, or challenging power issues during this aspect. Information and news at this time will be noteworthy. This is an opportunistic time to reach out to those of another generation and make an attempt to communicate something vital.

Venus square Neptune (occurring Oct. 13 – 22.) You may find your desires are at odds with your spiritual beliefs, and it may be a hard time for some people to make a personal connection with spiritual teachings. This may also appear to be a hard time to concentrate or meditate on spiritual activities. Faith and belief in love matters may be tested at this time. Feminine expression may be set back by old world beliefs, and love matters may be thwarted by conflicts between belief systems. This is a time to persist with loving expression despite those conflicts. Certainly it is best to avoid arguments concerning spiritual beliefs with loved ones at this time.

October 18th Saturday

Last Quarter Moon in Cancer
Moon square Sun   5:31 a.m. PDT   8:31 a.m. EDT
Moon in Cancer goes V/C 5:31 a.m. PDT   8:31 a.m. EDT
Moon enters Leo   3:41 p.m. PDT   6:31 p.m. EDT
Venus sextile Jupiter 2:32 a.m. PDT   5:32 a.m. EDT

The moon wanes down to the position of **Last Quarter Moon in Cancer** (Moon square Sun.) Some types of emotional healing take time. The emotional concerns that are surfacing at this time require that extra bit of nurturing and understanding. Feelings must surface sometime during the month, and the void-of-course Cancer Moon today most certainly spells out the need to address emotional currents. Later in the afternoon PDT / evening EDT, the Moon enters Leo. Tonight will be a good time to break out a little and enjoy personal hobbies and favorite kinds of entertainment.

Venus sextile Jupiter (occurring Oct. 14 – 21.) This serves as an excellent time to shower loved ones with gifts and compliments. This aspect is now occurring for a second time this year. For more details on Venus sextile Jupiter see June 23rd.

October 19th Sunday
Moon in Leo

Waning Leo Moon creates a hunger for attention, and quite often there is a need for acknowledgment of individual efforts. This is a good time to encourage people around us by acknowledging them with compliments and praise for their recent efforts. A small compliment can go a long way and to reassure someone that their efforts are not in vain. If you look, you can find a way to give people credit and support for their hard work!

October 20th Monday

Moon in Leo goes V/C	9:18 p.m. PDT	12:18 a.m. (10/21) EDT
Moon enters Virgo	11:01 p.m. PDT	1:01 a.m. (10/21) EDT
Venus trine Saturn	2:48 a.m. PDT	5:48 a.m. EDT
Mercury trine Uranus begins (see 10/23)		
Sun trine Mars begins (see 10/30)		

Throughout this day, Leo Moon brings the focus on the self and the need to satisfy personal needs, as well as effecting a sense of family comradeship. Complimenting, validating and commending others for their personal efforts in life brings about good feelings and a warmth of spirit. As it sometimes goes with waning Leo Moon, some folks may seem a bit overbearing with their need for attention, or their desires to have you listen to the long saga of their complaints. Be clear with people and let them know how you feel about their approach towards you. Keep affections as warm as possible, and generate a playful and loving mood-set among family and friends. Your efforts will bring a shining rewards!

Venus trine Saturn (occurring Oct. 15 – 24.) This aspect brings the timely gift of love. Venus trine Saturn allows for some peace in the closure of a love relationship. This aspect is now occurring for a second time this year. For more details on Venus trine Saturn, see March 21st.

October 21st Tuesday
Orionids meteor showers
Moon in Virgo

Virgo Moon turns our moods towards the need to communicate and to tend to practical concerns, personal hygiene, and the focus of collecting and distributing vital resources. Virgo Moon keeps our moods busy working on matters requiring keen, focused attention. Our desire for health inspires us during a waning Virgo Moon to flush toxins, to drop or curtail bad health habits, and to clean up our surroundings. Prudent resourcefulness allows us to squeeze pennies from unknown sources and eventually account for the hidden gold. Don't spend it now: account for it. See what you've got, and apply your rational sensibility as you picture all the ways in which your money could be spent while it remains in your bank account unscathed. This doesn't mean business can't be conducted; it just means it may be wiser at this time to put off spending until you've got all the facts in order. It is why is to get the better part of your work done today. Tomorrow's long void-of-course Moon day is bound to slow down progress.

October 22nd Wednesday

Moon in Virgo goes V/C	6:19 a.m. PDT	9:19 a.m. EDT
Sun trine Uranus	1:17 p.m. PDT	4:17 p.m. EDT
Neptune goes direct	6:55 p.m. PDT	9:55 p.m. EDT

Throughout the day, the void-of-course Moon in Virgo brings the challenge of fussy moods that range from fault-finding, skeptical and doubtful qualities of expression, to sometimes even ridiculing or melancholic tendencies. High expectations of ourselves and others do not bring good results if we are too critical. This is a time to accept what comes along, despite the raw imperfections of attitude and outlook.

Sun trine Uranus (occurring Oct. 16 – 29.) This aspect favorably affects our Libra and Scorpio friends celebrating birthdays this year from October 16th through the 29th. It puts the radical forces of Uranus in the favorable trine position to the natal sun of these Libra and Scorpio folks. This is the time for these birthday people to make the breakthrough. Don't hold back; chaos is here to stay for a while. Let the experience be positive as long as this aspect brings gifts. Expect restless desires for freedom and the need to break out of one's personal prison. Freedom knocks loudly, and to change of course for these people is inevitable in the next year. The above-mentioned challenges are necessary components part of these Libra and Scorpio folk's growth patterns. These influential changes are positive in nature, though on the surface they may seem harsh and overbearing. This represents a positive state of chaos. Just know the madness that has been occurring in your life (birthday folks) is there for a reason. You will find a clearer picture in the long run by keeping up the good fight to preserve your inspiration, intelligence, and logic. The trine aspect gives gifts of triumph, and this may be a good time to let chaos be the force to bring freedom.

Neptune goes direct (Neptune direct: Oct. 22, '03 – May 16, '04.) Finally, Neptune resumes a direct-moving course after five months of being retrograde. This will regenerate the process of our spiritual and intuitive work and facilitate our progress. Neptune is in Aquarius, influencing and assisting the nebulous flow of Aquarian age tactics, and is also affecting the evolutionary process of humankind's belief systems. Neptune is the master of illusion, while Aquarius demands scientific proof. Somewhere in the realms of the spirit world, human beings are learning to achieve a higher and freer sense of spiritual awareness as Neptune proceeds further into Aquarius, giving us a sense that something divine is occurring, even though it cannot be explained on mortal territory. What many of us are finally coming to realize, or acknowledge more often, is the notion that we are spiritual beings having a human experience and not human beings having a spiritual experience. A good meditation, when sincerely applied, does help to discharge one's dirty emotional baggage. Neptune's calming and forgiving nature helps us let go of all malicious and non-productive crystallized thought and melts away cold-heartedness. Invoke often the spiritually uplifting meditations that work for you, and you will soon find that you are on a positive and regenerative track with regard to your spiritual evolution.

SCORPIO

Key phrase "I CREATE" or "I DESIRE"
Fixed Water Sign
Symbol(s): The Scorpion,
The Eagle, and The Phoenix

October 23rd — November 22nd

October 23rd Thursday
Moon enters Libra 2:27 a.m.
Sun enters Scorpio   1:09 p.m. PDT   4:09 p.m. EDT
Mercury trine Uranus   1:56 p.m. PDT   4:56 p.m. EDT
Mercury trine Mars begins (see 10/27)

Overnight the Moon enters Libra. Waning Libra Moon focuses our moods on the need for peace and forgiveness. Relationships that need mending at this time require structure and some ground rules in order to generate trust. This is the time to flush away and banish those moods and emotions that prevent us from harmonizing and generating good feelings with others.

Sun enters Scorpio (Sun in Scorpio: Oct. 23 – Nov. 22.) Happy Birthday Scorpio! This time of year, like the Scorpio personality, creates an air of mystery and mysticism. This is a time when people are more attentive to their hidden agendas and their needs to get in touch with their own passion and compassion. Scorpio focuses our attention on the most important events of life: birth, sex, death and regeneration, or transformation as this sign is ruled by the underworld god, Pluto. Everyone has his or her own perspective on the need to make breakthroughs with difficult transitions in life. For our Scorpio friends, it is that difficulty and challenge of transformation that inspires and allures the senses. Scorpio is not known for being docile and passive. Scorpio is not hindered by laws or rules of society. When it comes to fulfilling and reaching out to one's own deeper passions and desires, there is no stopping the Scorpio expression of life, or death. This all goes further still: the realm of Scorpio deals with the powers of hidden meaning, the need for secrecy, and the deeper, psychologically ensnaring struggles with the self-destructive nature of humans and beasts. The totem of the sign of Scorpio is classically the desert dweller known as the scorpion. The scorpion sting can kill; indeed, if it is not careful, this lethal critter can sting and kill itself. This is the violent or criminal side of the Scorpio personality. If the matter at hand is one about which there is deep passion, the Scorpio will do anything to protect, or offend, often violently. In more sophisticated spheres and social situations, the sting is just as deadly, though in the early stages of delivery it will tend to appear more subtle and refined. There are other totems: the eagle and the phoenix. These higher aspects of the Scorpio personality relate to the eagle's ability to observe from very far away, and to see a larger and more objective picture of life while noting all the details essential to life itself (like that small field mouse dinner targeted from several yards above.) The Phoenix totem represents the ability to rise above the burning rays of the sun as a transformed and enlightened being. Pushing through and surviving the perilous difficulties and dangers of life is practically a requisite personality trait of the sign of Scorpio. The Scorpio archetype demands some respect or else -- Ouch! Scorpios are frequently stereotyped for having a desire to live richly and often dangerously. There is always the more esoteric version too: the way of spirit, the mystical and spiritual path, or the acknowledgment of one's own truth.

Mercury trine Uranus (occurring Oct. 20 – 27.) Mercury in Libra is trine to Uranus in Aquarius, stirring up an intelligent thought process that is well defined and interpreted with clarity. This is a good time to record thoughts and take delight in brilliant thinking and information. This aspect happened back in the busy month of June, and is now taking place for a second time this year. See June 30th for more details on Mercury trine Uranus.

October 24th Friday
United Nations Day
Moon in Libra
Mercury enters Scorpio   4:20 a.m. PDT   7:20 a.m. EDT

Libra Moon now wanes down to the darkest phase. All imbalances that exist between friends seem to surface at this time, and it requires an effort to create some harmony.

Mercury enters Scorpio (Mercury in Scorpio Oct. 24 – Nov. 11/12.) Today

Mercury enters Scorpio, and the general course of our communications and discussions now focus on more intense fixations. Mercury in Scorpio is often a time when communications are veiled in secrecy, and talk revolves around matters of intensity and sensitivity. Passionate issues are communicated in a wide range of depth, creativity and intuition. This is a time to take caution with regard to matters of secrecy. It is also a time to be aware that a sharp tongue may easily cause a violent or challenging reaction. It is through this medium of Mercury in the sign of Scorpio that the expression of communications is seemingly fearless, obstinate, reckless, and passionate deep down. From the wide range of indecent babble, to the subtle perfection of clear articulation, discussion frequently delivers a powerful punch while Mercury occupies Scorpio. As we approach Halloween, often the time when Mercury is in Scorpio, talk becomes more creatively grotesque and gory in nature. Communications are relayed on all levels, not only by how we choose our words but also in the appearance we choose for ourselves, which sends out the message of who we are. The mask we choose for the grand masquerade of autumn's darkening days teaches us much about ourselves.

October 25th Saturday

New Moon in Scorpio

Moon conjunct Sun	5:50 a.m. PDT	8:50 a.m. EDT
Moon in Libra goes V/C	1:30 a.m. PDT	4:30 a.m. EDT
Moon enters Scorpio	3:08 a.m. PDT	6:08 a.m. EDT
Sun conjunct Mercury	2:58 a.m. PDT	5:58 a.m. EDT
Saturn goes retrograde	4:43 p.m. PDT	7:43 p.m. EDT

Some may say that the "Hecate Moon" is the **New Moon in Scorpio** (Moon conjunct Sun); others may say it's the New Moon closest to All Hallows (Halloween, October 31st.) Still others may say it's the New Moon of October that represents Hecate Moon. As for this New Moon of Hecate, all of that is true. The moon known as Hecate's Moon occurs around the dark moon or New Moon of the Wiccan New Year holiday, Halloween. Hecate is the Wiccan goddess of the underworld who leads us through death towards a cycle of rebirth. She guides lost souls to their final destiny and can be called on at this time to guide those who have passed on, especially those who have met their ends under challenging circumstances such as violent death or suicide. Hecate cures the ills that accompany death. To honor her, take eggs, black bread, and beer to a Y shaped path or crossroad where an old tree stands. Give this offering to her and ask her to oversee the souls of the dead whom we want to see safely through to the other side. Honor her with your respect; she is a serious and powerful spirit to summon and no immature or insincere request will be granted by this goddess of the dark moon. If the wind kicks up or you receive a chill on the back of your neck, fear not: that's the spirit of Hecate confirming her presence. She will not hurt you as long as you respect her. New Moon in Scorpio puts us in touch with a new understanding of the passionate depths of life we experience through birth, sex, death and transformation.

Sun conjunct Mercury (occurring Oct. 15 – Nov. 5.) This is a most common aspect which creates a much more thoughtful, communicative, and expressive year ahead for those Libra and Scorpio people celebrating birthdays this year from October 15th through November 5th. This is your time (birthday people) to record ideas, relay important messages, and pay close attention to your imaginative thoughts as they are touched by Mercury, creating the urge to speak and be heard. Your thoughts will reveal a great deal about who you are at this time and in the year to come.

Note: turn clocks and timepieces BACK one hour this evening before going to sleep; Standard Time begins in North America tomorrow.

Saturn goes retrograde (Saturn retrograde Oct. 26, '03 – March 6, '04.) Saturn now goes retrograde, which means that the influence of time and restriction goes through a backtracking process in our lives. Saturn, representing our acts of discipline with regard to responsibility and the tenacity required to get the job done, is retrograding until March 6th, 2004. We'll need to backtrack on all the obligations as yet unfulfilled until after we've weeded out the mess of so much to do or achieve in so little time. There will be some sacrifices made to fulfill a sense of completion and accomplishment. Discipline is the key to saturnian perseverance; while Saturn is retrograding in Cancer, it is focusing our disciplines on stabilizing our responsibilities to nurture ourselves and on keeping the home front safe and secure. For some, this will be a time of completion, of ending the treadmill of old cycles, and of reinforcing the stronger points of our characters in order to overcome the losses that our weaker points suffer during saturnian tests. When Saturn is retrograde, it is a difficult time to begin new endeavors requiring structure, investment of time, and commitment. This is a time when we may be haunted by incomplete projects, and unsolved problems of the past dominate the stage, requiring added work to finish up unfinished business. For some folks, being careful of what they commit themselves to may prevent having to drop the commitment at midstream. If you haven't already dropped a few of your responsibilities, you may have to do so soon, but don't use this as an excuse to obscure your will and your objectives. Learn how to delegate your jobs fairly; don't give a job away if you're hoping to take credit or get paid for it. Keep a steady check on quality control. Rejoice in your lessons as the tests of today create a stronger you for the call of tomorrow.

October 26th Sunday
Daylight Savings Time ends
Moon in Scorpio
Jupiter-square-Pluto-Non-Exact begins (see 12/22)

Today time shifts, and the same old rule still applies. It's a good rule to remember: "Spring forward, fall back!". This refers to the close of Daylight Savings Time and the return of Standard Time here in North America. Remember to turn clocks BACK 1 hour at 2:00 a.m. to STANDARD time.

The Moon is still dark, still new, although now waxing in Scorpio. This is a time for renewal, and for many, an opportunity to come to new terms with regard to transformation in one's life. There is an initiation process of the soul taking place for those who are open to rebirth. Mystery and intrigue resonate throughout the day. New Moon in Scorpio is a splendid time to drop late autumn seeds expected to rise next spring. There are also seeds of dreams and seeds of the heart. This could be the day to accomplish something new, something that feels right.

October 27th Monday

Moon in Scorpio goes V/C   12:15 a.m. PST   3:15 a.m. EST
Moon enters Sagittarius   1:55 a.m. PST   4:55 a.m. EST
Mercury trine Mars   4:29 p.m. PST   7:29 p.m. EST
Mercury square Neptune begins (see 10/30)
Sun square Neptune begins (see 11/2)

Sagittarius Moon keeps our sights open to all the visionary possibilities unfolding at this stage of autumn. Philosophical outlooks abound out of the need to get a handle on the rapid changes emerging. Moon in Sagittarius allows for exploratory moods and adventurous feelings. Studious efforts will go far today. As the wind kicks up, anticipation of the Halloween fun begins, and a long line of mysterious images beguiles our imagination.

Mercury trine Mars (occurring Oct. 23 – Nov. 1.) This aspect activates the world of communications with an energetic punch, and is occurring now for a second time this year. For more details on Mercury trine Mars, see July 1st.

October 28th Tuesday

Moon in Sagittarius
Venus square Uranus begins (see 11/1)

The newly waxing Sagittarius Moon directs our moods towards a congenial, cooperative and flexible expression of service. Keep an eye out for opportunity. Exploration and a little bit of risk-taking are highlighted. This is a time when our moods are more prone to consider a greater number of possibilities and alternatives. Good food, travel, plays, and research are all strong Sagittarius Moon focuses.

October 29th Wednesday

Moon in Sagittarius goes V/C   12:51 a.m. PST   3:51 a.m. EST
Moon enters Capricorn   2:37 a.m. PST   5:37 a.m. EST
Mercury sextile Jupiter begins (see 11/1)
Mercury trine Saturn begins (see 1/11)

The dedicated and serious people are likely to stand out today, and to be diligently on-the-ball, and very devoted to the progress of their particular focus. Capricorn Moon tends to bring serious moods. Those who know not what they serve may very well feel used. Be confident that you are free to serve in the type of work you choose, and do not let others try to make you feel inferior. Self-confidence in one's work over time brings a personal sense of reward. Even mundane work is the precious commodity known as the Salt of the Earth, and this work is worthy of our respect. The lunar aspects of the day are dominated with sextile positions to the other planets. This brings opportunity and is, indeed, a good time to expect progress!

October 30th Thursday
Moon in Capricorn
Sun trine Mars   7:55 a.m. PST   10:55 a.m. EST
Mercury square Neptune   11:46 a.m. PST   2:46 p.m. EST
Sun trine Saturn begins (see 11/5)

The Witches' New Year is almost here on this "Mischief Night" before All Hallows Eve. Our moods continue to be down-to-earth and purposeful with the Moon waxing in Capricorn.

Sun trine Mars (occurring Oct. 20 – Nov. 11.) This aspect particularly affects those Libra and Scorpio people celebrating birthdays this year from October 20 through November 11th. Mars is in the trine position with these Libra/Scorpio folks' natal sun this birthday year. This brings a strong sense of the need to activate one's personal life, and to accomplish goals by putting out one's energy as opposed to just receiving energy. There is a major force occurring that will no doubt prompt an action or a reaction to numerous situations arising in the coming year. Creative work abounds. There are special gifts of triumph for those who activate their dreams and desires at this time, and upon doing so, the energy which is naturally there to harness will come easily. This is a time to exercise the will and the internal sense of primal might, inspiring our personal agendas into a state of action and movement. Heated matters will come to the surface in an advantageous manner. Through the act of making things happen, personal achievement will shine forth like a long needed blessing in the year to come for these birthday folks. Keep it active.

Mercury square Neptune (occurring Oct. 27 – Nov. 3.) This aspect is occurring for the fourth time this year due to the retrograde patterns of Mercury. Looks like we have had a lot of harsh communication with regard to spiritual issues this year! See April 13th for more details on Mercury square Neptune.

October 31st Friday
All Hallows (Halloween) / Samhain / Witches' New Year
First Quarter Moon in Aquarius
Moon square Sun   8:25 p.m. PST   11:25 p.m. EST
Moon in Capricorn goes V/C   12:07 a.m. PST   3:07 a.m. EST
Moon enters Aquarius   5:41 a.m. PST   8:41 a.m. EST
Mars opposite Jupiter begins (see 11/20)

We have now reached the time of the **First Quarter Moon in Aquarius** (Moon square Sun.) Waxing Aquarius Moon and **Samhain** put the spotlight on humankind's eccentric and unusual breakthroughs. The eccentric quality of this Moon is perfect for creating novelty Halloween costumes laced with brilliant concepts. Controversial subjects are strongly influential as we cross this Scorpio Sun bridge from October to November, and this time is intensely affected by a very busy pileup of celestial traffic. November is going to be a busy month, and even now we are all aware of great shifts of energy. HAPPY HALLOWEEN! HAPPY NEW YEAR! This holiday is here to stay! This is the New Year of the witches' calendar, and for most witches of the old tradition, this is the time to celebrate. The slumber of the plant and animal world deepens, and the crops and seeds of the fields go to their rest with the promise of returning one day. This time represents the honoring of the dead, and is a classic time to invite the beloved spirits of our ancestors to join us in a feast of celebration and reunion. Some believe that from sunset until dawn the spirits of deceased loved ones are able to roam the earth and converse with the living. This is a particularly important time for the names of those who have passed away (especially within this past year) to be spoken aloud, and for them to be honored with the food, drink and song we know our loved one enjoyed during their life. This is a time to awaken the memories of and to explore a metaphysical relationship with those whom we adore and who have passed on. Don't forget to set an extra plate of food and drink aside for your deceased loved ones at dinner this evening and leave the window or door open a crack (if only for a short time), as this is the tradition of old; how else will they get inside? Autumn is truly here! Again, Happy Halloween to everyone, and have fun!

BOO !

November 1st Saturday
Day of the Dead / All Saints' Day
Moon in Aquarius
Mercury sextile Jupiter   4:48 a.m. PST   7:48 a.m. EST
Mercury trine Saturn   5:17 a.m. PST   8:17 a.m. EST
Jupiter sextile Saturn   9:11 a.m. PST   12:11 p.m. EST
Venus square Uranus   4:42 p.m. PST   7:42 p.m. EST
Sun sextile Jupiter begins (see 11/5)
Mars trine Saturn begins (see 11/13)

There is an ancient saying of magicians and the like: "As above, so below." Complexity now builds up in the heavens; here on planet Earth we ride the wave. Earth's Moon sets the tone of the overall group conscious mood of the day. Today, Moon in Aquarius steadily waxes, increasing our awareness and putting us in touch with the quickening pace of events now increasing to meet the challenges imposed by the high celestial traffic. This will be an amazing day.

The festival of the "Day of the Dead" is celebrated on November 1st all around Mexico and in Mayan and Aztec cultures. Colorful altars with decorative skulls, photos of the dead and symbols of death adorn the streets, and the love of the dead is celebrated. The Sun is in Scorpio bringing forth all the holidays reminiscent of the Scorpio mysteries.

Mercury sextile Jupiter (occurring Oct. 29 – Nov. 3.) This favorable aspect may bring good news of expansion or prosperity. For some folks, this serves as an advantageous time to ask for a job or a loan, or even to start a new enterprise. See June 22nd for more details on Mercury sextile Jupiter.

Mercury trine Saturn (occurring Oct. 29 – Nov. 4.) Mercury trine Saturn brings favorable discussion with regard to where to draw the lines. This is a good time to make an impression, to teach and to communicate to others those important matters requiring clarification. News with regard to the end of a long and arduous task brings relief.

Jupiter sextile Saturn (occurring Oct. 9 – Nov. 24.) Jupiter and Saturn are the two social planets of our solar system. There is an old Greek myth that the god Saturn ate up all the gods in the solar system except for jovial Jupiter. Why? Well, it's simple really: Saturn represents time and from our perspective, time eats up everything. Time consumes and eventually alters our feelings (Moon) and our memory (Mercury.) Time has been known to eat up our love affairs and our potency or fertility (Venus.) Time eats up our battles and struggles with life as well as our strength and vitality (Mars.) Time, through the process of aging, eats up our identity and our personality (Sun.) But, according to this myth, there is one thing time (Saturn) is unable to consume, unable to devour, and that is the joy of expansion and prosperity for all humankind (Jupiter.) How could Saturn destroy and consume something that is always growing, and always superseding time and space? Jupiter constantly supports expansion and is the facilitator that allows us to see beyond the boundaries of the universe, giving us insights on the depth of our joy. Jupiter sextile Saturn brings out a favorable and opportunistic place and time to plant the seeds of immortality, and to invest in a project that will go far beyond space and defy the limitations and restrictions of time. When we do something that will benefit others in the future, we have performed a Jupiterian deed. We have extended a part of ourselves that will grow, and leave its mark for others to expound on. This is a good time to invest in sound markets of reputable merit and to take action with regard to retirement plans, financial investments, and investments concerning future welfare. It is also a good time to make some kind of statement that will go far beyond your life span, and may make a difference a hundred or more years from now. These deeds need not be complex and expensive; simple acts of helping to improve and broaden the skills and philosophies of others can go a long, long way. As for time; it is Jupiter that reminds us time is merely an illusion, a human concept measuring our collective worth through the course of our earthly sojourn. With every ending, there is always a new beginning. Take joy in your work! Live by example, and the bounty of your disciplines will bring reward. In the science of the Tarot symbolism, Saturn is represented as The World card, or Universe card. It is the place (our world) we must be masters in order to hold a triumphant position on the Wheel of Fortune (Jupiter), the measure of our joy and grandeur.

Venus square Uranus (occurring Oct. 28 – Nov. 6.) Venus, the planet that governs love and magnetism, is undergoing the square aspect to Uranus, creating chaos and disruption in matters of love. Expect to have relationships tested by minor explosions, and be careful not to become too personally affronted by radical love matters. Be assured in self-love and empower affection with personal integrity. It is essential to let love take its course with regard to issues of personal freedom.

November 2nd Sunday

Moon in Aquarius goes V/C	11:40 a.m. PST	2:40 p.m. EST
Moon enters Pisces	11:52 a.m. PST	2:52 p.m. EST
Venus enters Sagittarius	1:42 p.m. PST	4:42 p.m. EST
Sun square Neptune	10:56 p.m. PST	1:56 a.m. (11/3) EST

Out of the chaos of the human alarm system which has been crazily responding to this busy month's start, Moon enters Pisces this morning PST / afternoon EST. A dreamy, tranquil, and interchangeably moody reverie fills the atmosphere. Moon in Pisces allows us to get more easily in touch with our intuition, our dreams, and our beliefs. and Moon in Pisces often brings deeply penetrating wet weather; a watery, rainy, cloudy, snowy, and all around damp cast to the North American landscape brings misty moods. Perhaps all those things are going on all at once internally? Hot delicious drinks bring comfort to the soul.

Venus enters Sagittarius (Venus in Sagittarius Nov. 2 – 26.) Now the planet of love and the expression of affection are emphasized with the inspired character of Sagittarius. Venus in Sagittarius brings out a love of the arts, philosophy, travel, cultural exploration, outer space, and sports achievements. With this comes an outgoing spirit of camaraderie among people in general, and the effort to take affections beyond the usual bounds is certainly present at this time. Philosophical theories now serve to keep love matters afloat, while the dynamic adjustments of this Scorpio time of year challenge us to endure and proceed ever forward through the depths of autumn's brisk storms. A wide range of exasperating personal and social clamor continues to test us as celestial activities pile up once again.

Sun square Neptune (occurring Oct. 27 – Nov. 10.) This aspect especially affects those Scorpio born people that are celebrating birthdays this year from Oct. 27th – Nov. 10th. Neptune in the square position to these folk's natal sun brings a sense that there are obstacles getting in the way of spirit, the spiritual path, or the acknowledgment of one's beliefs. The challenge for these birthday folks is to overcome the doubts and confrontations that interfere with the practice of believing. Over the next year, there will undoubtedly be some spiritual adjustments, and perhaps even an upgrade of spiritual values is required for those folks encountering birthdays at this time.

November 3rd Monday
Moon in Pisces goes V/C   10:36 p.m. PST   1:36 a.m. (11/4) EST

Before us is the typical soulful drama of a November Scorpio Monday coupled with the instinctual and powerfully reflective insights of the Pisces Moon, and lastly, throw in the factor of the above-average number of planetary aspects all complicating the situation. Today we are under no illusion that the intensity of this time is prolifically producing a long string of emotional reactions. All hands on deck! For some folks, this kind of excitement is a breath of fresh air, while for others it is like a rocky ordeal at sea. Tomorrow's long void-of-course Moon in Pisces day will probably bring contingencies, delays, and confusion due to the tendency for spaced-out-moods. Good luck America! Tomorrow is Election Day!

November 4th Tuesday
Election Day USA
Moon V/C in Pisces
Moon enters Aries   9:02 p.m. PST   12:02 a.m. (11/5) EST

This entire day with void-of-course Moon in Pisces gives us illusive, uncertain and spacey moods which classically bring a great deal of confusion; people will be easily distracted or influenced. Does this sound like a typical setting for a U.S. Election Day? Many of us are still reacting to the overabundance of celestial activity erupting this month. Heavy issues in our lives keep us preoccupied, overwhelmed and full of concern, hope, and prayer. The long and short of it is that many people are busily trying to escape from harsh realities. There is a tendency on the part of many folks to indulge in addictive substances, pain killers, or fantasy. Good food, soothing art and music are among the most creative ways to ease the overburdened senses.

November 5th Wednesday
Moon in Aries
Sun trine Saturn   3:24 p.m. PST   6:24 p.m. EST
Venus square Mars begins (see 11/12)

A brisk new mood is in the air as the waxing Moon in Aries invites us to take charge and get in tune with leadership and self-reliance. Many of the more impatient people among us are no longer putting up with inadequacy, and are now taking matters into our own hands. A competitive, confident, and enterprising level of productivity picks up our moods.

Sun trine Saturn (occurring Oct. 30 – Nov. 12.) This aspect particularly affects those Scorpio people celebrating birthdays this year from October 30th through November 12th. This is a positive time for these Scorpio folks to get a handle on their lives. This auspicious aspect brings a timely gift to our Scorpio friends. This favorable placement may help to make it much easier to take on the responsibilities of life with a lot less complication and difficulty than expected. Now is your time (Scorpio birthday people) to work successfully at putting more structure into your life; the kind of structure you've truly been needing and wanting awaits you in the coming year. It is possible: time (Saturn) is on your side in a favorable manner, and now is a good time to make your move!

November 6th Thursday
Moon in Aries
Sun sextile Jupiter   12:33 p.m. PST   3:33 p.m. EST

The Moon is in Aries, the Sun is in Scorpio; there was a time (before the discovery of Pluto) when the planet Mars was attributed to both Aries and Scorpio. Mars has to do with raising energy, and many folks will be doing this very thing today. Depending on the kind of atmosphere in which we have chosen to be, Aries Moon can create a very defensive or an offensive quality of mood. Dominant moves and plays on others is a direct result of the competitive aggression that is typical of a heavily waxing Aries Moon. As a general rule, it's the same old story of wants and needs; likely concerns at this time include wanting to get ahead, to act on those higher impulses, to stir up some incentive among workers, to be self expressive and reliant, to become motivated by success, to curb the temper when tested by challenge, and at the very least, to harness energy as it is required.

Sun sextile Jupiter (occurring Nov. 1 – 12.) This aspect particularly affects those Scorpio folks celebrating birthdays this year from November 1st through the 12th. This represents a time of opportunity and expansion for these birthday folks, and there are good times in the works for these people as long as they act on their desires and work towards their goals. Skills that are introduced to these folks throughout this year will set the overall schemes of career and fortune building. This serves as a grace period for these birthday folks, and for a short time fortune and opportunity will shine. Be sure to take the time right now to enjoy life and take in each breath with joy! Keep an eye out this year for opportunities which could become most beneficial (Scorpio birthday folks) as a new discovery awaits you.

November 7th Friday
Moon in Aries goes V/C   6:16 a.m. PST   9:16 a.m. EST
Moon enters Taurus   8:29 a.m. PST   11:29 a.m. EST
Mercury square Uranus begins (see 11/11)

Early this morning PST / later morning EST, the Moon enters Taurus. Material needs are today's theme. Last week's wave of celestial traffic has not even begun to dissipate yet, and we are just now entering a Lunar Eclipse Full Moon weekend. Back-to-back events and situations this week have overwhelmed our senses, tested our stamina, and shaped or influenced our outlook somewhat dramatically. Though we have tried relentlessly to exert some kind of control over the busy events occurring up to now, the condition in which we find ourselves today leads many folks back to the basics of our human needs for creature comforts. Taurus Moon, so full, reminds us of our most important and practical needs: money, a secure roof over our heads, warm clothes, a financial plan to get us through the year and the pending holidays, and a full refrigerator to reflect the fullness of the weekend Moon. The challenge of meeting basic personal and family needs is very strong. The Moon will be eclipsed tomorrow, and although the refrigerator may not house everything our hungry hearts had hoped, a steady effort and a bullish attitude to succeed will give us what it takes to win.

November 8th Saturday

Lunar Eclipse
Full Moon in Taurus
Moon opposite Sun   5:13 p.m. PST   8:13 p.m. EST
Uranus goes direct   4:45 a.m. PST   7:45 a.m. EST
Venus sextile Neptune begins (see 11/11)

Full Taurus Moon (Moon opposite Sun) invites us to celebrate beauty and the perfection of the valuable elements of the earth, and brings us an appreciation for the beauty in nature. The Taurus totem is the bull and in all its splendor, the bull is a marvellous and classically stubborn creature of habit. This Full Moon reminds us to take the time to enjoy and create beauty around us, and indulge ourselves a little in some luxurious pleasures or leisure time. Of course, you can expect emotional currents to be full of some unexpected energy with the Full Moon being eclipsed at this time. This highlighted emotional energy focuses on polarizing desires and needs. If you don't have the things you need to live a practical existence, you will be acutely aware of those needs at this time. For most, this usually translates into a lack of money, or a lack of stable surroundings to fulfill personal needs. For those who realize the importance of celebrating planet Earth, now is the time to reflect on what you do have, and how it is that these physical gifts of Earth can be enjoyed. If you don't know how to enjoy the fruits and gems of the physical world, it may be time to redefine your sense of value. If you don't believe you can afford something, it is likely that deep down you think you aren't ready to take responsibility for what it is you desire to possess. The standards we set for ourselves determine the ups and downs of our economy. Start by believing the thing you need is something you deserve to have. Ask Mother Moon to bring you what you need and she will teach you how to sow for the harvest of your desire.

Uranus goes direct (Uranus direct: Nov. 8, '03 – June 10, '04.) Since June 6th, Uranus, known for stirring up calamity, has been retrograde. The crux of explosive and radical tendencies in our culture and around the globe now shift towards showing us the way in which the revolutionary process of humankind moves forward. Uranus going direct may bring a less internal or personal sense of anarchy. The force of chaos now moves outward, onward, forward, allowing for a greater sense of freedom and a brighter, clearer sense of awakening. Over the past five months, retrograde Uranus recapped the story of what its radical force has taught us, having entered Pisces this year (see March 10, '03 Uranus enters Pisces.) Uranus then returned to the heartland of Aquarius on September 15th. Today Uranus progresses forward in the late degrees of Aquarius, and persists in awakening humanity's urgency to make breakthroughs with regard to human rights. The work of radical and revolutionary forces resumes course as Uranus moves direct until June 10th, 2004. We all have the need to break out of oppressed conditions of life. As Uranus moves forward, the ominous quality of its work demands the utmost intelligence if we are to survive its unbridled force. For the final round, the ship of Uranus now sails out of the harbor of its native sign, Aquarius, until the close of this year. It will then return to Pisces and begin to focus on the need for breakthroughs and radical change in music, the arts, and particularly our in beliefs and religious practice. Freedom is sought for the good of all humankind, yet the chaotic force of boundless freedom is often conceived as corrupt and destructive. Aquarius must always apply intelligence and knowledge as each level of urgency is unveiled. Remember to kindle the light of love for humankind's wisdom next time the urge for unabashed rebellion makes you kick up your heels. This is, after all, the age of Aquarius.

November 9th Sunday

Moon in Taurus goes V/C   6:59 p.m. PST   9:59 p.m. EST
Moon enters Gemini   9:14 p.m. PST   12:14 a.m. (11/10) EST
Venus square Jupiter begins (see 11/14)

The Full Moon is waning and Taurus Moon energy is becoming lazy. Post Full Taurus Moon is still quite strong, and while the earthy quality of existence is ever-present, energy is indeed dissipating. Now as emotional attachments wind down, the energy in the air suggests a tired and somewhat sluggish level of output. This is a good time to relax and let the body recover from the taxing activities and emotional stress that runs high during an ecliptic Full Moon. As for today's activities, simple, easy, convenient, and comforting choices are best.

November 10th Monday

Moon in Gemini

The Full Moon weekend is behind us now. A shift of mood occurs with the Moon in Gemini. The nature of the Gemini Moon keeps us curious and inquisitive as well as oriented towards collecting details and sharing ideas. Writing down feelings in a journal will help one become clear about personal emotions, especially if these feelings are mixed about a given subject. Gemini Moon is a good time to participate in a stimulating conversation with a wise friend, particularly with someone who is a master listener. Sometimes talking things over brings a better perspective on life.

November 11th Tuesday
Veterans' Day
Moon in Gemini
Venus sextile Neptune	12:36 a.m. PST	3:36 a.m. EST
Mercury square Uranus	6:04 a.m. PST	9:04 a.m. EST
Mercury enters Sagittarius	11:20 p.m. PST	2:20 a.m. (11/12) EST

As if we haven't seen enough activity this month, today also brings a busy day of celestial events. Gemini Moon keeps us questioning, sorting out and fussing over the details of life. Thinking matters through and exploring a wide range of options gives adaptability and flexibility to our outlook. Communicating, investigating, and examining choices helps us to understand.

Venus sextile Neptune (occurring Nov. 8 – 14.) A great opportunity for love, beauty, and perception of spiritual values to help smooth over some of the challenging heat of other busy celestial activity at this time. This can have a strong healing affect on the soul. This aspect also holds the potential for one to realize profound beauty and the depths of which true love is capable. See January 17th and May 2nd, dates this aspect has previously occurred this year.

Mercury square Uranus (occurring Nov. 7 – 15.) Mercury is at the cusp of Scorpio/Sagittarius, emphasizing the need to communicate about profound realizations, while Uranus is at the Aquarius/Pisces cusp, emphasizing the need to deal with human rights issues and spiritual turmoil. The two focuses are creating conflicts with regard to giving and contributing where they are most needed in the community and the world, versus the need to maintain personal employment and stay on track with a focus on finance for the sake of personal advancement. So many events at this time seem to be bigger than life and rather difficult to put into words. For more details on Mercury square Uranus, see June 14th, when this aspect last happened.

Mercury enters Sagittarius (Mercury in Sagittarius Nov. 11 – Dec. 2.) The planet of communication, information, and news is now beginning its travels through Sagittarius, and is best expressed through this sign with an emphasis on expansion, exploration, and vision. News always comes across with a more philosophical tone when Mercury is in this sign. Emphasis of discussion is now more focused on travel and sports, and more global perspectives are introduced to our complex integrated cultures. People are most curious in their communicative efforts to ascertain what is happening in the world. Mercury in Sagittarius is a good time to share visions with others.

November 12th Wednesday

Moon in Gemini goes V/C	7:57 a.m. PST	10:57 a.m. EST
Moon enters Cancer	10:10 a.m. PST	1:10 p.m. EST
Venus square Mars	9:27 a.m. PST	12:27 p.m. EST

For a little while, there's a semi-confused morning shuffle which takes place as the Moon in Gemini goes void-of-course for a couple of hours, and by late morning PST / early afternoon EST, the Moon enters Cancer. Enliven the home with flowers and therapeutic scents. Moon in Cancer emphasizes the need for a homey atmosphere and a safe and cozy realm to explore one's feelings. When in doubt take a bath, or pamper yourself with whatever works to create a calming and soothing affect. For those working people that don't have time for such luxuries, hang in there and acknowledge that moodiness and emotional traffic are standard by-products of Cancer Moon influence.

Venus square Mars (occurring Nov. 5 – 20.) The rocky boat of romance is due to have some notable ups and downs, especially as holiday pressure now mounts and some people dread pending family gatherings during disquieted marital circumstances. It might be best not to probe the tenderness of such subjects whenever that kind of trouble is obviously brewing. It is also a time to be patient with loved ones, no matter how hard the boat rocks. See June 5th for more details about Venus square Mars.

November 13th Thursday

Moon in Cancer
Mars trine Saturn   9:26 p.m. PST   12:26 a.m. (11/14) EST

Its a watery day of fluctuating moods with both the Sun and Moon in water signs. Another day of the waning Moon in Cancer reminds us that it's times like these that allow us to share our emotions openly and sort through the ebb and flow of our emotional current. The Moon reflects on our emotional cycles. The important thing to remember always in the emotional realm is to keep the energy flowing.

Mars trine Saturn (occurring Nov. 1 – 25.) Our actions bring gifts, provided there is an application of discipline and timing. This may be a good time to apply diligent practice to one's favorite sport, especially those physical activities which demand precision and perfect timing. A timely gift of strength of will, coupled with the rewards of hard work harmonize to bring positive results. To fully benefit from this aspect, one must be persistent and taking action with regard to important matters. This is the third time this aspect is occurring this year. See June 22nd for more details.

November 14th Friday

Moon in Cancer goes V/C   5:39 a.m. PST   8:39 a.m. EST
Moon enters Leo   9:48 p.m. PST   12:48 a.m. (11/15) EST
Venus square Jupiter   7:34 p.m. PST   10:34 p.m. EST
Venus conjunct Pluto begins (see 11/17)
Mars square Pluto begins (see 11/26)
Sun square Uranus begins (see 11/21)

A moody day greets us, especially with the waning Cancer Moon going void-of-course this morning and remaining void all day and night. If you must work among a decidedly crabby crowd of moody folks, pace yourself and don't let the negative qualities of such moodiness get to you. There are likely to be traffic jams and delays. Those feeling particularly run down at this time are probably highly susceptible to getting colds or the flu. Rest, drink lots of liquids, and take vitamins if the signs of illness are evident. Every once in a while a good Cancer Moon comes along and impresses us with the need to tend to the emotional side of our being. Nurture yourself and be sure to release those useless and pent-up emotions in a safe direction. This is the time to let moods flow, and it is important not to take other people's moodiness personally.

Venus square Jupiter (occurring Nov. 9 – 20.) This aspect may create the hardship of our not being able to acknowledge beauty as a form of wealth within itself. Instead, it may remind us that something more than love's blindness is required in order for us to fully realize our riches. There may be emphasis placed on the need to create spending limits on pleasures, travel, and entertainment. See May 26th for more details on Venus square Jupiter.

November 15th Saturday
Moon in Leo

A fun-filled Leo Moon weekend now unfolds as the emotional ups and downs of the past few days begin to dissipate. Family-oriented focuses and pleasures will be the themes of this mid November weekend. Life has its plateaus, its vistas, and even its precipices in which we find ourselves. Leo Moon puts us in touch with our domain -- that place where we rule and carry the big stick. Self-image is reviewed from this plateau. Is there a sense of satisfaction with all that has been brought to this supposedly chosen lifestyle? Are there self-worth and respect present? Do we pass the test of selfhood, or is some substandard image staring us back in the face when we look into the mirror? Everything with which we have identified up until now surrounds us in a cloud of reflection. Sometimes the beastly image doesn't suit our self worth. This is the time to stroke the ego firmly, take pride in and be forgiving of the exceptional uniqueness of the identity, and to do this despite the atrocities that have tested and maimed the character. Take the time to enhance self-image with a positive affirmation. Take pride in self-worth; show dignity and poise. Take measures to clean up and dress up your image in the manner that best suits your individual needs.

November 16th Sunday

Last Quarter Moon in Leo
Moon square Sun 　　　　　　　　 8:15 p.m. PST 　　 11:15 p.m. EST

We now come to the **Last Quarter Moon in Leo** (Moon square Sun.) Today, people will need to be entertained and to get their minds on enjoying life. When the Moon is waning in Leo, it urges us to take special care of ourselves as well as the children in our lives. Projects of interest are sometimes considered to be children as well. If you have a hobby of special interest, take the time to brighten and enliven this work which represents your own talent and bears the mark of your own approval. The Moon simply calls for more playfulness, and the warmth of loving hearts in the chill of autumn. Throughout the working (or playing) day, jokes will fly, toys of special interest will be admired, and moods will reflect childlike frolic and revel. If you're serious about not being distracted by such playfulness, perhaps a quiet workspace is the key. If you must work with others, allow the frivolity to flow. The work will get done, but the child in everyone has to play now and then.

November 17th Monday

Moon in Leo goes V/C 　　　　　 4:38 a.m. PST 　　 7:38 a.m. EST
Moon enters Virgo 　　　　　　　 6:36 a.m. PST 　　 9:36 a.m. EST
Venus conjunct Pluto 　　　　　　 5:48 p.m. PST 　　 8:48 p.m. EST
Mercury sextile Neptune begins (see 11/18)

This will be a time to focus on health and a sense of well-being. Early morning PST / mid-morning EST, the waning Moon enters Virgo. However mundane the task may seem, the need to maintain, clean, perfect, and upgrade our surroundings is ever present. Waning Virgo Moon is driving home the reality that we must tend to and exercise those basic but important health practices.

Venus conjunct Pluto (occurring Nov. 14 – 22.) This aspect last occurred on January 25th and now comes full circle once again, uniting the power of love with the unrelenting, transformational sting of fate. Many of the December born Sagittarius people are experiencing a strong connection to love and power issues with the combination of these energies. Gemini people (born at the opposite of this Venus/Pluto conjunction in Sagittarius) are experiencing quite the opposite effects with regard to this aspect. Many Gemini people are finding it difficult to overcome power struggles and to feel connected with love matters since Venus and Pluto are opposing their natal sun. Those born around the midpoint of Pisces and Virgo are all riding out the hardships of love and power related struggles at this time, with this conjunction squaring to their natal sun. It is important for these folks to pace themselves and to be patient with loved ones during difficult tests.

November 18th Tuesday

Moon in Virgo
Mercury sextile Neptune   11:48 p.m. PST   2:48 a.m. (11/19) EST
Mercury square Mars begins (see 11/23)
Mercury square Jupiter begins (see 11/22)

Once again our health calls to us during a waning Virgo Moon to flush toxins, drop or curtail bad health habits, and clean up our surroundings. Prudent resourcefulness comes in handy during waning Virgo Moon. It's all a question of how to narrow down complex matters. Virgo asks many questions. As ever, caution and skepticism fill our moods. With the proper banishing of illness that has transpired and still lingers, the critical nature of our moods can subside. Cleansing our surroundings helps to combat sluggish feelings.

Mercury sextile Neptune (occurring Nov. 17 – 22.) This short lived but beneficial aspect is a good time to communicate with those who are of assistance in spiritual matters. Mercury sextile Neptune serves as an opportunistic time to apply the work of dreams, hopes, prayers and spells. This would be a good time to internalize thoughts and beliefs and meld them into a workable understanding.

November 19th Wednesday

Moon in Virgo goes V/C   6:15 a.m. PST   9:15 a.m. EST
Moon enters Libra   11:42 a.m. PST   2:42 p.m. EST

Throughout the morning, waning Virgo Moon goes void-of-course and at 11:42 a.m. PST / 2:42 p.m. EST, the Moon enters Libra. Out of the common reluctance to face up to the morning's dirty work, our moods focus on relationships. It may seem to some that keeping their balance in a relationship requires a tremendous amount of patience and encouragement. In those extreme cases where caring and loving efforts do not solve the problem of an inharmonious relationship, waning Libra Moon may be a time for some folks to face up to the prospect of ending the relationship. Sometimes a court judge, arbitrator, or mediator must intervene in a boldly decisive manner. It is difficult to lay the law down sometimes, yet the fact remains that relationship break-ups, however hard to face, do happen much more frequently than ever before. Bringing a sense of closure to a relationship can be a necessary step. With or without a lover or friend the up-and-down cycles of life are still prominent. As we weigh the pros and cons of our complex relationships, we must remember the more we learn through experience from our interactions, the better chance we have at keeping them balanced and harmonious.

November 20th Thursday

Moon in Libra
Mars opposite Jupiter   5:59 a.m. PST   8:59 a.m. EST

It is up to each of us individually to set a precedent, or plainly laid guidelines, on what does and doesn't work in our relationships. A good working relationship usually undergoes a fairly regular readjustment process. This is a good time to educate and teach tolerance. Positive affirmations towards teamwork, compromise, and cooperation bring us closer to a sense of peace. Mars and Jupiter in their opposition to one another are both squaring off to Venus in Sagittarius. Attempting love and affection does have its challenges right now, particularly when traveling. Consider yourself an excellent diplomat if you are managing well with your close relationships at this time.

Mars opposite Jupiter (occurring Oct. 31 – Dec. 4.) For the third time this year Mars is opposing Jupiter, and heated attitudes are often coupled with acute awareness of economic shortfalls. Actions taken now may have a more difficult time prospering. For more about Mars opposite Jupiter, see May 5th.

November 21st Friday

Moon in Libra goes V/C	11:44 a.m. PST	2:44 p.m. EST
Moon enters Scorpio	1:24 p.m. PST	4:24 p.m. EST
Sun square Uranus	9:13 a.m. PST	12:13 p.m. EST
Mercury conjunct Pluto begins (see 11/24)		

We have made adjustments and transformed ourselves right along with the seasonal changes. The final day of the Sun in Scorpio is here. This morning, Moon in Libra continues to focus our moods on the importance of team work and the interaction of our friends and loved ones. By early afternoon PST / late afternoon EST, the Moon enters Scorpio. We are now gearing up for the final lash of the scorpion's tail. The waning Moon in Sagittarius includes a solar eclipse this Sunday when it reaches the New phase. Today's darkly waning Scorpio Moon atmosphere requires delicate perception and astute vigilance. A lunar occurrence such as this may bring out a very dark-night-of-the-soul kind of desperation. Beware of swindlers, crooks, thieves, and distraught associates who may turn out to be dangerous people. These people tend to cross the lines in unexpected ways under these lunar circumstances. Secrecy, mistrust, suicidal feelings, emotional breakdowns, and foul play are all possible symptoms of a darkly waning Scorpio Moon. Take extra precautions and keep the atmosphere as light and as safe as possible for children.

Sun square Uranus (occurring Nov. 14 – 28.) This aspect particularly affects those Scorpio and Sagittarius people celebrating birthdays this year from November 14th through the 28th. The square of Uranus to these birthday folk's natal sun brings about a strong dose of unrestrained chaos and a multitude of challenging events. This may be the year for you birthday folks to surrender to those aspects of life that are truly out of your control, and concentrate more rationally on those facets of life over which you do have control. Sometimes Uranus influence produces a better aftermath, but with the square aspect at work, it is likely these birthday people will feel personally challenged. It is important to understand that some kinds of personal challenges are best left undisturbed, while other challenges must be confronted directly without causing destructive damage, particularly to the self. On the other hand, birthday folks, if your life has no foundation, there is no point in holding on to the illusion of stability at this conjuncture in your sojourn. This aspect will pass, and it is vital not to give this rapid change too much resistance, lest you be subjected to the setbacks of trying to fight chaos with logic at a time when it is futile. Matters will settle down in due time; try not to be so attached to the chaotic events as they occur and the outcome will seem less costly to your sensitive personal outlook. If you need it, project the picture of peace and it will be there for you at the other end.

SAGITTARIUS

Key phrase "I SEE" or "I PERCEIVE"
Mutable Fire Sign
Symbol: The Centaur

November 22nd through December 21st

November 22nd Saturday
Moon in Scorpio
Sun enters Sagittarius　　　　9:44 a.m. PST　　12:44 p.m. EST
Mercury square Jupiter　　　　7:10 p.m. PST　　10:10 p.m. EST

This is a very dark time of the emotional realm. This balsamic phase of the Moon touches the darker sides of our feelings and represents a good time to purge and cleanse the areas of our lives where there is decay or destructive tendencies. A protected and safe environment may be essential in addressing and releasing the dark emotions. This is a good time to face up to the truth and be aware of the tendency towards lying and deception. From the place of true desire, Scorpio's expression allows us to create a new incentive to live every moment of life with the precious awareness that life is rich and death is certain.

Sun enters Sagittarius (Sun in Sagittarius Nov. 22 – Dec. 21.) Sun in Sagittarius represents the final stage of autumn and ushers in the shortest days of the solar year. Happy Birthday Sagittarians! The Sagittarius expression "I See" opens our eyes to some new discoveries during this time. This mutable fire sign achieves visionary awareness by reaching out into the world of possibilities, the stars, and beyond. The Sagittarius time of year, often thought of as early winter, is actually within the fall season and sees to the closing of autumn by putting to sleep the last of the restless foliage in preparation for the pending winter's great slumber. Sun in Sagittarius days focus on prospering through the shorter daylight hours of the season. Jupiter is the ruling planet of Sagittarius and inspires the sign of Sagittarius to excel, expand, and prosper. As the holidays begin and the Christmas season unfolds, the pressure to consume elaborate foods and purchase gifts while keeping the great economic wheel turning can be a monumental task for absolutely everyone. We are often required to pull together an enormous and outstanding number of social events and to increase personal expenditures. The concept of prospering has no doubt been tested to the extremes each time this season unfolds, and it is therefore very important to get back to the basics of what one identifies as prosperity. Often, the stresses of this pending season inspire within us a great sense of relief when the holidays are finally over. The true challenge for many of us will be met when we finally reach out towards the higher vision of what prosperity really means. Sun in Sagittarius serves as a good time to direct the forces of vision and inspiration towards the goals of attaining a sense of wealth and well being. Tiny Tim (of Charles Dickens fame) was a character who was not disappointed by the lack of food on his table at Christmas because he recognized the sacredness of sharing the company of his loved ones. Don't let the complications of others' expectations spoil your own sense of attainment and satisfaction with life itself, and for the people with whom we have the privilege of sharing that life. Simple pleasures can bring prosperous joy. Sagittarius emphasizes travel, sports, and philosophy: all those things which require adaptable enthusiasm. There are many ways of seeing and many directions to look.

Mercury square Jupiter (occurring Nov. 18 – 27.) While this aspect is occurring it may be best to hold off on requesting a job position, asking for a raise, or signing any binding contracts concerning long term investment and payment schedules. This aspect has a tendency to create expensive misunderstandings concerning investments. Bank loans are most likely a large hassle at this time.

November 23rd Sunday

Solar Eclipse
New Moon in Sagittarius

Moon square Sun	2:59 p.m. PST	5:59 p.m. EST
Moon in Scorpio goes V/C	11:27 a.m. PST	2:27 p.m. EST
Moon enters Sagittarius	1:02 p.m. PST	4:02 p.m. EST
Mercury square Mars	7:14 p.m. PST	10:14 p.m. EST

Venus sextile Uranus begins (see 11/25)

There is light at the end of the tunnel, but of course this tunnel is a little longer than we expected. Be extra cautious while the Moon in Scorpio is void-of-course during the day, as accidents or violent outbreaks, among other things, are likely to occur. By 1:02 p.m. PST / 4:02 p.m. EST the Moon enters Sagittarius. Today's **New Moon in Sagittarius** (Moon conjunct Sun) also brings a **solar eclipse**. Solar eclipse energy sets a dark tone in mood for some folks and it is wise to apply caution with regard to emotional disturbances during this time. Fortunately Sagittarius energy helps us to move forward and maintain our vision through dark times of the soul. In fact, for some folks this is a very inspirational place for the heart, when deep philosophical and contemplative states of being bring better insights. There is no question that we have undergone more than a few tests to make it through this season. As for New Moon in Sagittarius, this may very well be a good time to begin planning a trip. It's a time to open up to new opportunities in an inspired and upbeat manner. This may be just the time for some restless folks to make a breakthrough and start new exercise programs, look into new philosophies of life, and apply a bolder sense of exploration.

Mercury square Mars (occurring Nov. 18 – 30.) Hold off on making risky comments and be careful not to misinterpret information as being hostile while Mercury squares Mars for the third time this year. Inflammatory statements abound, and this would be a good time to be careful to think before you speak. See March 28 for more details on Mercury square Mars.

November 24th Monday
Moon in Sagittarius
Mercury conjunct Pluto   6:12 p.m. PST   9:12 p.m. EST

Today we are all going on a trip. Where are we going? Beyond the usual bounds, of course. The Moon newly waxes in Sagittarius and there is hope in the wings. Today, there is very definitely a planetary alignment taking place. It consists of five celestial bodies (Sun, Moon, Mercury, Pluto, Venus) in the sign of Sagittarius. At best, we can expect enlightening, stimulating, generous, and broad-minded moods. At worst, there will be indiscreet, flippant, rash or erratic behavior. Overall we are thoroughly in a position to explore loads of possibilities and foster a broader sense of global community and connection. It's a small world indeed. Sagittarius says: "I see." Look for the signs.

Mercury conjunct Pluto (occurring Nov. 21 – 29.) Mercury conjunct Pluto brings out power issues in our life. The greater powers and struggles in our lives are spoken about and communicated in a wide variety of ways. The areas of our lives requiring transformation and sacrifice, struggle and challenge, now bring us to the point in our sojourn where we can talk about those hardships (i.e., war, recession, disease, loss and illness.) These hardships have forged our own characters and inner strengths. There will be much talk of power, who has it, and who doesn't. Getting in touch with the power that has created us is what all this talk is about. There is an old saying: "If the King at midday says 'it is night', the wise man says 'behold, the stars!'" Recognize that the path each one of us travels brings out both our strengths and our weakness. How we reveal or apply our power, particularly in conversation, is the key to this conjunction.

November 25th Tuesday

Moon in Sagittarius goes V/C	10:57 a.m. PST	1:57 p.m. EST
Moon enters Capricorn	12:31 p.m. PST	3:31 p.m. EST
Venus sextile Uranus	10:20 p.m. PST	1:20 a.m. (11/26) EST

Midday brings us another brief void-of-course Moon interlude as the Moon shifts signs. Some folks might end up getting lost or completely sidetracked for a short while. By 12:31 p.m. PST / 3:31 p.m. EST, the Moon enters Capricorn and our moods come down to earth -- or is it up to earth? Capricorn is the achiever; hence, not only do we wish to get grounded, but now we are aspiring to climb to some higher ground. Capricorn Moon brings focus and determination into the spirit of the day.

Venus sextile Uranus (occurring Nov. 23 – 29.) More unconventional love tendencies appear, as Venus sextile Uranus brings an opportunity for love related matters to break through the imprisonment of crystallized habit. Use this opportunity to work out frustrations with loved ones and to reconcile differences by applying love and accepting divergence, giving freedom and slack to our loved ones, without being ourselves oppressed. Radical or unusual kinds of love can be very refreshing at this time. Here is also an opportunity for the rebellious aspect of art to breakthrough and be recognized.

November 26th Wednesday

Moon in Capricorn goes V/C	7:52 p.m. PST	10:52 p.m. EST
Mars square Pluto	3:17 p.m. PST	6:17 p.m. EST
Venus enters Capricorn	5:07 p.m. PST	8:07 p.m. EST

Moon in Capricorn provides our moods with a steady persistence to meet important goals and make progress with our work. Let the progress of your work shine and take joy in your accomplishments. A very busy new month awaits us, and this is a good time to make some headway. After 7:52 p.m. PST / 10:52 p.m. EST, the Moon is void-of-course and it is best to lighten up on obsessive work practices after this point; very little progress is likely to take place come late evening.

Mars square Pluto (occurring Nov. 14 – Dec. 20.) Mars emphasizes all forms of action, while Pluto represents the transformational powers of destiny. These two planets in the square position spell out the potential for trouble with regard to our actions. Strong disruption between generations is likely to occur at this time. This aspect does imply that this is a more likely time for an "attack" to occur from power-driven sources. Actions or conflicts concerned with higher powers are likely to backfire. It is best not to bluff those of a higher or unanticipated authority at this time. The hurdles of taking action in hopes of creating a transformation may be very dangerous. This may be a particularly difficult time to fight addiction; it is also the most crucial time *not* to give up the fight.

Venus enters Capricorn (Venus in Capricorn: Nov. 26 – Dec. 20.) Now Venus' love energy will be rooted in its travels through the stoic and serious forces of Capricorn. Venus in Capricorn reveals an attraction for the staunch and ardent duties of accomplishing goals. There is a love of stability and predictability that occurs with Venus in Capricorn. This type of expression creates stable ground for the development of relationships, and the general course of affections will be oriented towards impressing your loved ones with how hard you are working to provide for them. Venus in Capricorn inspires a love of work and a desire to work hard towards the achievement of goals. This is the time when many people are more attracted to gaining momentum on getting in shape physically in order to build stamina. Getting in shape on a career level also has an appeal these days of Venus in Capricorn. This is not commonly considered a good placement for Venus in a person's birth-chart, given that the nature of one's love life is often compromised for material and social convenience. Without a more creative set of circumstances at work (in the chart) this type of person's love is often plagued with coldness or indifference, and is somewhat calculating and materially oriented. This is not always true though the complex makeup of people is full of variations of these themes. Whatever the case may be, Venus in Capricorn is most likely to bring out a more serious approach to love matters in general. It is important to show respect and exhibit maturity in matters of love if we are to be taken seriously by loved ones while Venus is in Capricorn.

November 27th Thursday
Thanksgiving Day (USA)
Moon enters Aquarius   1:48 p.m. PST   4:48 p.m. EST

Throughout the morning, Moon is void-of-course in Capricorn. Serious moods may turn out-and-out grumpy, and there may be a tendency towards the typical void-of-course-moon disruptions of delays, setbacks, and minor misunderstandings. This just may involve another trip back to the store, and other annoying mundane episodes. By 1:48 p.m. PST / 4:48 p.m. EST, the Moon enters Aquarius and the science of a time-honored tradition wins out. Expect with all of its splendor and pomp, a classic set of Thanksgiving Day (USA) concerns as the Moon shifts over to Aquarius. Social etiquette is likely to be emphasized or discussed at some point. Aquarius brings out the need to face ourselves and learn things about who we are. As a general rule, Aquarius people are not always completely or solely family oriented. They consider themselves more a part of the global family or the extended family of their choosing. With the Moon in Aquarius, the holiday spirit opens our minds and our dinner tables to all kinds of fascinating, controversial and unusual travelers and conversationalists.

November 28th Friday
Moon in Aquarius
Sun sextile Neptune begins (see 12/3)

This is a good time to work on innovative ideas and projects. Aquarius influence emphasizes reaching out towards a body of light and information which will benefit everyone. The Moon in Aquarius changes our concepts, ideas, and work ethics as we begin to see how much easier we can make life and our workload through an innovative approach to our work. Aquarius calls for the need to breakthrough outmoded methods of achieving progress, and sets the precedent of what we accept as fixed scientific knowledge.

November 29th Saturday

Moon in Aquarius goes V/C	4:46 p.m. PST	7:46 p.m. EST
Moon enters Pisces	6:25 p.m. PST	9:25 p.m. EST

Mercury sextile Uranus begins (see 12/1)

The rebel in all of us needs to let loose today. Its Saturday, Moon is in Aquarius; this has been one amazing and challenging month, and it's almost over. The time has come to get in touch with some personal freedom. Something brilliant and unusual is needed to appease our restless moods. Experimenting with a new way of doing things or approaching matters differently brings a welcomed new perspective. Novelties, games, books and challenges of the mind are special points of interest. This evening the Moon enters Pisces and our outlooks become quite a bit more tranquil and reflective. Artistic fun and culinary delights bring joy.

November 30th Sunday
Advent begins

First Quarter Moon in Pisces
Moon square Sun   9:16 a.m. PST   12:16 p.m. EST

We end this month with the **First Quarter Moon In Pisces** (Moon square Sun.) During this time, moods are easily impressionable. A drifting, spacey, dreamy sort of consciousness leads to strong psychic awareness. Music, art, and poetry fill the senses with creative intuition. Unhappy people may turn to intoxicants to escape their troubles. Passive, cheerful, and kind sentiments will be greatly appreciated. Deep meditation and spiritual practices will empower the imagination at this time. Abstract concepts are everywhere. Mystery, fantasy, enchantment and make-believe are high on the reader's and moviegoer's priority lists. More tranquil practices might include a long meditative walk in pleasant places near water.

December 1st Monday
Moon in Pisces
Mercury sextile Uranus   9:53 p.m. PST   12:53 a.m. (12/2) EST

The final month of 2003 is initiated today with the Moon waxing in Pisces. This lunar energy attempts to delight us with a serene and surprisingly mellow quality of mood, despite the obvious and predictable mayhem that December holidays bring. This is a good time to reflect and work out the troubled part of our spirit with beautiful crafts, creative and artistic projects and sweet, cheerful, uplifting music. As for celestial traffic beyond the Moon, we are fortunate to now reach a time when there aren't quite as many hidden or non-exact aspects that are active all at once. For the next couple of weeks we will experience considerably less celestial activity than we've been used to in the summer and autumn months. The buildup of so much activity over this year is beginning to influence us, and we are now more in a state of reaction to past events rather than being overwhelmed by direct or current planetary aspects and events. From so many conflicting and daunting shifts comes a less active and warmly welcome break. There will be exceptions to the rule; sometimes the quieter lulls bring out the loudest responses to the inner and outer turmoil we are experiencing individually. The aspects (though fewer) that are occurring at this time are affecting certain individuals more harshly than others. At least, not as many of us are overwhelmed or affected right now, and some of us absolutely thrive during this less active period of hidden celestial influences or planetary aspects within orb. Granted, by the third and fourth weeks of this month, the celestial traffic will be pumped back up to full volume once again, so enjoy (or persist through) the first two weeks wisely.

Mercury sextile Uranus (occurring Nov. 29 – Dec. 5.) This aspect represents an opportunistic position for the voices of rebels and revolutionaries to be heard. Here is an opportunity for brilliance to be enhanced. This aspect brings news of change, radical change, and this serves as a good time to exercise the more radical side of our beings with a message holding the potential to free others. Some may act on this aspect with wild abandon, creating an effect of repelling and offending, while for others this radical communication will represent freedom from a particular kind of slavery that has held them back. Note: this aspect is taking place for an extended period of time due to the retrograde pattern of Mercury (set to go retrograde on Dec. 17th), and will happen again on December 30th.

December 2nd Tuesday
Moon in Pisces goes V/C   1:39 a.m. PST   4:39 a.m. EST
Moon enters Aries   2:56 a.m. PST   5:56 a.m. EST
Mercury enters Capricorn   1:34 p.m. PST   4:34 p.m. EST
Venus opposite Saturn begins (see 12/6)

This morning, the Moon enters Aries and picks up the pace on a Mars-ruled Tuesday as we gird our loins for battle. Aries Moon energy fills the day with hustling and bustling. This is a time to do things for the self as well as for others. As ever, Aries Moon moods often preoccupy us with the need to stand out or to be on top, and to notice who is in control of situations and just how they're handling it. There is an eagerness or sometimes even aggression present at times, yet there is youthful inspiration overall, and a drive to get things started.

Mercury enters Capricorn (Mercury in Capricorn Dec. 2 – 30.) Mercury in Capricorn affects the general course of communications with an enterprising emphasis on negotiations. Mercury is the negotiator, and this effort is most seriously emphasized while this versatile planet, encompassing our realms of communications, goes through the determined persistence of Capricorn energy. Mercury in Capricorn brings out an emphasis of communications on the accomplishment of goals. The overall expression of communications and news begins to focus on more down-to-earth issues, and quite often there is a very serious tone to our discussions. Mercury in Capricorn also emphasizes communications on issues such as commercial and corporate progress, market control, the attainment of goods and resources, unions, task forces, and the necessity to exercise control when tasks require discipline. To attain goods we must use each other's services. Are we really being fair or are we just using each other? Does it matter? Make sure you're getting something out of your own attempts to market yourself or promote those around you. If you're *not* doing a service *just as a favor*, make sure that is understood. Everyone has a job to do and the incentive to do that job must be solid. Communications on matters of control are the key to Mercury in Capricorn.

December 3rd Wednesday
Moon in Aries
Sun sextile Neptune   3:35 a.m. PST   6:35 a.m. EST
Sun square Jupiter begins (see 12/10)

Aries Moon continues to build up our energy levels as it steadily waxes towards fullness early next week. Starting up new projects, getting motivated, and leadership are emphasized today.

Sun sextile Neptune (occurring Nov. 28 – Dec. 8.) This is a particularly opportunistic aspect for those Sagittarius people celebrating birthdays this year from November 28th through December 8th. These Sagittarius folks are experiencing an opportunity to awaken in the realm of spirituality and creativity. There is an awareness of the self that goes deep here, and these birthday people are likely to be particularly spacey and difficult to reach while this phenomenon of great depth is occurring. This will be your year, birthday folks, to explore personal opportunities of spiritual growth. This is a good time for these folks to get away from it all, find a sanctuary in which to meditate and open up to some valuable answers with regard to old questions that are haunting them. These folks are in a place that gives them an opportunity to better understand the work of their path, but this is probably only true if they act on their intuitive sensibilities individually, without the influences of others. This will be your year, Sagittarius birthday folks, to enhance your intuition by tapping into it while it's happening. Look within!

December 4th Thursday

Moon in Aries goes V/C	12:52 p.m. PST	3:52 p.m. EST
Moon enters Taurus	2:30 p.m. PST	5:30 p.m. EST

There is a busy shuffle that continues throughout the morning with the Moon in Aries. By 12:52 p.m. PST / 3:52 p.m. EST, the Moon goes void-of-course for about an hour and a half. This time may be filled with impatient outbursts, delays, and, quite possibly, accidents due to people moving too fast and not watching where they're going. By 2:30 p.m. PST / 5:30 p.m. EST, Moon enters Taurus and the pace becomes more grounded with a steady but practical, more realistic set of focuses. Taurus Moon puts us in tune with a great deal more sensibility. Practical concerns such as the cost of living and the expense of the holidays begin to penetrate. Waxing Taurus Moon is an exceptional time to work on raising money and to handle banking needs and expenditures. A master plan to finance this month's expenses and produce what is needed is a good move on this Taurus Moon.

December 5th Friday

Moon in Taurus
Sun conjunct Pluto begins (see 12/11)

Taurus Moon often focuses our attention on the matter of having or not having what we need to get by. Of course there is also the matter of what we *want* in order to make the pending holidays festive. Money management and money related issues are very strong this time of year, especially when the Moon is in Taurus. This heavily waxing Taurus Moon also sets the stage for a lot of concern with regard to the handling of valuables and goods. There is a strong emphasis building up at this time on the need to transport, ship, move and haul all those backbreaking goods of the physical world. The physical work of schlepping material goods is unavoidable. A stubborn determination to take care of business pervades our moods. Slowly and steadily, let the Taurus bull's consummate pace keep the labor from being overtaxing.

December 6th Saturday

Moon in Taurus
Venus opposite Saturn   4:03 a.m. PST   7:03 a.m. EST
Venus trine Jupiter begins (see 12/11)

A Taurus Moon Saturday kicks off the first weekend of the month with the strong desire on the part of many people to acquire what they need in the way of money, goods, and services. In this heartland of the economic world, the Taurian drive is to have and to own, to manage, procure, produce and perpetuate valuables, riches and staple goods. The drive to shop and buy is overwhelming. The message is out there: shop-till-you-drop-it's-Christmas-time! Taurus Moon is an appropriate aspect since it lends to our moods an earthy and stubborn determination to get things done right. Sensible buyers do not waste their energy on overpriced gifts. Quality and value are important. Simple and practical gifts are a time honored tradition.

Venus opposite Saturn (occurring Dec. 2 – 10.) Be careful not to bite off more than you can chew, especially with regard to irresistible attractions. This aspect is taking place for a second time this year. For more details on Venus opposite Saturn, see January 28th.

December 7th Sunday
Moon in Taurus goes V/C   1:54 a.m. PST   4:54 a.m. EST
Moon enters Gemini   3:26 a.m. PST   6:26 a.m. EST
Full Moon Eve
Mercury opposite Saturn begins (see 12/13)

This morning, the Moon enters Gemini and now the lunar energy level is pumped up to maximum capacity; in other words – its Full Moon Eve! This is a time to talk matters over. There will be lots of phone calls made today. Gemini Moon hovers brightly, shining on our moods which reflect on our attempts to sift through all those full ideas and thoughts that have been reoccurring in the last month. This is a frivolous, fun, silly, and fickle time for some, and for others there is the tendency to be burned out by too much information. A myriad of details needing attention have now worked themselves up into an alarming crescendo. It will take some serious thought in order to figure out how to put all these puzzling details of our lives into a workable and comprehensible order. Happy Full Mooning!

December 8th Monday
Full Moon in Gemini
Moon opposite Sun   12: 37 p.m. PST   3:37 p.m. EST

Throughout the day the **Full Moon in Gemini** (Moon opposite Sun) emphasizes conversations, talks, sales, discussions, secretarial chores, and writing. This is a time of built-up emotional energy, usually brought on by mental stress, while there is a strong need to converse and be heard. The Moon already reached its peak of fullness this afternoon at 12:37 p.m. PST / 3: 37 p.m. EST. The full lunar expression of Gemini is accentuating the reflective awareness that all of us have our own unique ways of seeing things. Sagittarius Sun reminds us of our challenge to develop as well as to examine our own individual philosophies. Collective consciousness surfaces in countless forms of media and often conflicts with personal philosophy. Gemini keeps us looking at the two sides of every coin – or philosophy. Gemini seeks all the possible details while Sagittarius strives for the bigger picture. Full Gemini Moon is classically a very busy and swiftly moving time. The Gemini persona keeps our feelings occupied, possibly scattered or frazzled, and actively striving for answers to things we're curious about. Now is the time to give birth to these ideas. Find some answers to the questions you haven't yet anticipated. Investigate the imagination for further details. Record your ideas, share them with others, put them in writing.

December 9th Tuesday

Moon in Gemini goes V/C	2:48 p.m. PST	5:48 p.m. EST
Moon enters Cancer	4:11 p.m. PST	7:11 p.m. EST

Throughout the morning, the post full Gemini Moon begins to wane down while the affects of the fullness can still be felt. The depth of this fullness begins to rattle our overtaxed brains. Despite this, the pace of active thought is still rolling, and progress can be made in the world of communications, discussions, debates and conference calls. By 4:11 p.m. PST / 7:11 p.m. EST, the Moon enters Cancer, and our moods are geared toward caring for and nurturing the tender parts of our being. The fullness of our emotional experience can be felt, and this evening will be a time to comfort, ease, and pamper the heart. A warming drink of something delicious and a caring companion's listening ear would be a fine way to top off the evening. Tonight , home is where the heart is, and this place gives us an edge – the ability to bend the forces of the universe in our own particular way to suit our needs. In this environment we can drop our social pretenses and express how we really feel. It is essential for us to find some sort of emotional outlet. The healthy home environment, or place of the heart, is a place of refuge that nurtures, soothes, protects and reassures.

December 10th Wednesday

Moon in Cancer		
Sun square Jupiter	2:59 a.m. PST	5:59 a.m. EST

Today's Moon in Cancer leaves many folks feeling somewhat withdrawn, and they are likely to be absorbed in their feelings. Moods emphasize feelings, and mother moon now wanes as we seek refuge from the cold and harsh elements of the world. Nurturing and restful space and moments of peace are what people feel like having today, but previous disregard for the transformational aspects of difficult events leads to an urge to vent strong feelings now. Remember: feelings pass. Troubled feelings flow best when properly expressed and released, as opposed to retained and dwelled upon.

Sun square Jupiter (occurring Dec. 3 – 17.) Sun square Jupiter is particularly affecting those Sagittarius people celebrating birthdays from December 3rd through the 17th. This aspect is creating difficulties and obstacles with regard to the prosperity of these folks. The act of getting ahead financially or just staying on top of current financial shifts may be difficult for these birthday folks. Every aspect touches on some part of somebody's personal life. This aspect may also be affecting many others who are experiencing money or career obstacles through personal shifts. Just about everyone has hard times when trying to get ahead, and this is unfortunately the difficult time for these birthday folks. Apply prudence and diligence, as these traits are the strengths that bring people through this challenge. Obstacles create challenges but not necessarily solutions to the work of maintaining one's welfare. It is your personality (Sun) that is being challenged (square aspect) concerning matters of advancement and opportunity (Jupiter) to live with less than you were hoping for at this time. This may be a time to redefine and redirect personal goals. Certainly this is a time to reexamine what truly brings prosperity to one's desires and needs.

December 11th Thursday

Moon in Cancer goes V/C	10:53 p.m. PST	1:53 a.m. (12/12) EST
Venus trine Jupiter	6:22 a.m. PST	9:22 a.m. EST
Sun conjunct Pluto	9:26 p.m. PST	12:26 a.m. (12/12) EST

We may have it all to do, but that doesn't mean that we all feel like doing it! Crabby feelings can be set off by anything that hits home. People may be territorial or annoyed by subtle intrusions. Some may plead: Oh, please, spare us from the sappy, phoney commercial drive to impede our subliminally agitated subconscious! We already know what we must do to get through this season without being reminded how many more shopping days are left until Christmas! Its bad enough that the hidden aspect of Jupiter square Pluto is taking place at this time. This dance between Jupiter and Pluto never reaches an exact square due to Jupiter going retrograde on January 4th, 2004. This aspect is occurring October 26th, 2003 through January 7th, 2004, and is helping to create economic shortfalls, havoc, and power-driven transformation. Just ride the wave and let it all pass over. For more details on Jupiter-square-Pluto-Non-Exact, see December 22nd. As for Moon in Cancer, the listening ear wins the heart of a talker.

Venus trine Jupiter (occurring Dec. 6 – 16.) Venus trine Jupiter is a auspicious and prized aspect that allows for a greater potential to receive gifts of love. This favorable aspect last happened in April and is now occurring for a third time this year. See January 21st for more details on Venus trine Jupiter.

Sun conjunct Pluto (occurring Dec. 5 – 19.) This aspect strongly affects Sagittarians celebrating a birthday this year from December 5th through the 19th. These Sagittarius birthday folks are experiencing some very heavy changes and challenges of mind-altering proportions. Sun conjunct Pluto affects the core of the personality and diminishes those parts of the self that are weak and can no longer be passed off as capable and certain. Pluto's energy melds with the personality to bring out the strongest points of one's character, the very best that a Sagittarian can muster. Pluto removes all impurities of fear by transforming the old self into the new self through unpredictable trials. The weak and inadequate parts of the personality must be destroyed without destroying Sagittarius' own integral power. This is a time for our birthday Sagittarian friends to take hold of change; take this opportunity to make some personal breakthroughs and apply caution. This may be the time to address personal areas of weakness and empower the self with truth and strength of will, even if it means learning to downsize with dignity, or sacrificing sentimental old habits for a greater cause. Meanwhile intense issues of birth, sex, illness and death challenge the Sagittarius personality. For these Sagittarius birthday folks, Pluto crossing over the natal sun transforms not only the personality, but the overall person. Don't get hung up on determining the good or evil behind the use of power. Learn to harness your own power willingly and responsibly while great transformation is occurring in your life. In addition, be sure not to push yourself too hard over these particular years of your life, birthday Sagittarius folks. Pluto's influence will be sure to test you enough without your own self-devised pressures and delusions adding to the setbacks of life. Give in, but don't give up, Sagittarius folks!

December 12th Friday
Moon enters Leo 3:40 a.m. PST 6:40 a.m. EST

Throughout today the Moon in Leo brings out the imaginative, and creative side of our moods. The Sun and Moon are in fire signs; it may appear that someone has turned up the heat. Most of us are readily drawn towards the need to find warmth and affection or just plain attention. Leo Moon draws our attention to personal feelings and desires that need to be addressed and appeased. While some are content to make this a thoroughly relaxing day of self indulgence, others are intent on sharing the Christmas spirit with full-blown theatrics and sheer animal magnetism. In the spirit of giving, start with the self; be sure to make the effort to give yourself something you need today. Do this, and the energy and vitality that you give yourself will shine through by example – it will be a gift of light for others to share. From a sense of satisfaction and assurance, the expression of affection brings peace and happiness.

December 13th Saturday
Moon in Leo
Mercury opposite Saturn 6:14 a.m. PST 9:14 a.m. EST

Creative, fiery and entertaining showmanship fills the atmosphere on this Leo Moon Saturday. The waning aspect of the Moon reveals the need to work things out with the kids and the family. It is hard to shop around and not see things which are needed for one's self. This is a time when we examine what makes us unique by seeing the things we identify with. Many folks tend to find for others what they really would like for themselves. That's okay – a gift is indeed a reflection of the self.

Mercury opposite Saturn (occurring Dec. 7 – 27.) Due to the retrograde pattern of Mercury, this aspect is occurring for an extended period of time and will repeat again on December 21st. This aspect can sometimes create an obsessive coverage by the news media who do an overkill job on reports concerning deaths, endings, a new establishment of control, or any type of important or sensational event. News is easily taken seriously at this time, and it is important to some people not to joke about timely matters at this alarming stage. The god Mercury is famed as an exceptional negotiator and is often thought of as a trickster and a thief. Be careful where you choose to draw the lines and what you agree to when you're involved in your negotiations, or you may be the one to end up feeling as if you've been had.

December 14th Sunday

Moon in Leo goes V/C   12:05 p.m. PST   3:05 p.m. EST
Moon enters Virgo   1:07 p.m. PST   4:07 p.m. EST
Sun square Mars begins (see 12/29)

This morning, the Leo Moon keeps us focused on personal needs. It may be time to clean up the appearance a little bit, and put the beastly parts of the identity back into an acceptable semblance of the self. By 12:05 p.m. PST / 3:05 p.m. EST, the Moon in Leo goes void-of-course for an hour – just enough time for some folks to indulge in a minor identity crisis. By 1:07 p.m. PST / 4:07 p.m. EST, the Moon enters Virgo and many folks may decide to withdraw into a much more analytical perspective on matters. This may be a time to reassess our resources, and focus on adapting to the wide range of demands and services requiring our attention in the vital weeks to come.

December 15th Monday

Moon in Virgo

The waning Moon in Virgo brings out moods of shimmering clarity with a reluctance to spend money on commercial goods which have escalated in prices. Simple resourcefulness will go far. The positive aspect of Virgo Moon calls for some keen perception, purity of intent, and a head-to-toe check on health. This is a time of deduction, of placing importance on logical and methodical application of reason. There is no wisdom in negative feedback; positive or constructive criticism is the kinder way to illustrate a point. The Moon passes through the mutable earth sign of Virgo during this time of the mutable fire sign of the Sun, the way of peace and success comes through the application of caution and the intake of inspired vision.

December 16th Tuesday

Last Quarter Moon in Virgo
Moon square Sun   9:42 a.m. PST   12:42 p.m. EST
Moon in Virgo goes V/C   9:49 a.m. PST   12:49 p.m. EST
Moon enters Libra   7:46 p.m. PST   10:46 p.m. EST
Mars enters Aries   5:24 a.m. PST   8:24 a.m. EST
Mercury-trine-Jupiter-Non-Exact begins (see today)

The **Last Quarter Moon in Virgo** (Moon square Sun) calls for the release of emotional currents which are often caused by our doubts. This release or expression can sometimes come in disruptive ways. Virgo Moon affects the general course of moods with the need to create protective defenses, often causing skeptical, analytical, or even cynical interactions with others. This is a time to be aware, what one is protecting may quite possibly be an ill of some kind that may actually need to be banished and released. These are the Sun in Sagittarius days; applying the vision of how one wants to see their future self is not an easy task, especially if poisonous and debilitating addictions are involved. Often the Sagittarian projects selfhood outwardly in order to envision the demands of an expanding spirit. That same Sagittarian awareness is just as capable of traveling inward and perceiving the needs of the inner self. Let the doubts and fears of your life be flushed away at this time, so that through clarity you may achieve the benefits of your visionary picture of health, wealth, and well being.

Mars enters Aries (Mars in Aries Dec. 16, '03 – Feb. 3, '04.) Today Mars enters Aries and will remain in Aries through Feb. 3rd, '04. Mars, the planet of action and masculine drive and force, is at home in the rulership of Aries, and initiates activities in the most forward and direct manner possible. Mars is the god of war in mythology; often Mars related experience is generated through our impulses, our anger and rage, our fear and compulsion, our need to confront and bring forth the primal force of energy and zeal that is our ability to take action, our spark of life. This planet, now in Aries ,boosts the lives of Aries people and gives them both the energy and the incentive to take action in their lives, and there are undoubtedly heated matters going on in their lives as well. Mars' influence generates activity and heat which can often appear explosive under pressure. Aries people are reminded to keep a cool sense of control at all times, and to build on their crucible of energy with a direct sense of clarity and purpose. Aries folks can strike now while the iron is hot, but use caution: be aware of fires, potential accidents, and fevers. Capricorn and Cancer folks need to be especially cautious as Mars now squares to their natal sun, causing the events around them to seem personally abrasive and particularly maddening at times. Libra people may be aware of extreme fiery activity in their lives with Mars opposing their natal sun. The other fire signs of the zodiac may benefit too. Leo and Sagittarius people are experiencing the favorable trine of Mars to their natal sun; this gives our fire sign friends a boost of energy, some hot and some all too hot. Fire signs have within them the means to naturally identify with the forces of Mars activity in their lives. However, even when one is in one's element, the relentless spirit of Mars must be carefully tempered in their busy lives, or (guess what) they'll burn out! A lot goes on with Mars in Aries, so when the strain becomes too absorbing, remember to rest now and then.

Mercury-trine-Jupiter-Non-Exact (occurring Dec. 16 – 18.) This aspect begins today but ends December 18th due to Mercury retrograde (see Dec. 17.) Mercury trine Jupiter does NOT reach an exact trine and it occurs for only two days. As a general rule, we are blessed to have Mercury trine to Jupiter. This aspect often brings good news that usually assists us to advance somehow. There are prosperous gifts found in the tidbits of information that are circulating at this time. Beware though, Mercury is about to go retrograde tomorrow. Information can surely get mixed up at this time. Quick! BEFORE Mercury goes retrograde, be sure to let Santa know what you really want for Christmas!

December 17th Wednesday
Moon in Libra
Mercury goes retrograde   8:01 a.m. PST   11:01 a.m. EST
Sun sextile Uranus begins (see 12/21)

Libra Moon emphasizes such focuses as, libraries, teaching, research, intellectual pursuits, law and justice. This serves as a good time to apply ourselves to assist others and to create harmony among loved ones. This may seem especially tricky to do now that communications are about to be strongly affected by Mercury retrograde. Many adjustments will have to be made today.

Mercury goes retrograde (Mercury retrograde Dec. 17 – Jan. 6, '04.) Mercury retrograde periods take place for an average of three weeks, and this phenomenon occurs three times a year, leaving us with a total of nine weeks out of the year of unrequited communication attempts. We will end this year just as we began it (January 2nd, 2003) with Mercury retrograde in the sign of Capricorn. This is actually the fourth time Mercury is retrograde this year, since this particular retrograde period overlaps into the year 2004. Keep plans and tasks as simple as possible during this time and be sure all messages are carefully relayed. Retrograde Mercury can really set us into a tailspin at this holiday time of year, causing simple communication mixups, which costs us precious time, right when we want to get so much done. Pay particular attention to what you promise and commit yourself to; Capricorn is a somewhat hazardous place for retrograde Mercury, causing numerous misunderstandings which may appear somewhat serious in intent, or perhaps even manipulative in nature. Be aware of the tendency to be convinced to do something that might disrupt your own harmony or personal mindset. On December 30th the retrograde Mercury will enter Sagittarius, and our communication mixups are likely to center around travel and transportation. It is wise to be cautious and diligent when arranging travel plans this holiday season. Anticipate contingencies! Prepare a back up plan. While Mercury is retrograde, it is best to ask for a confirmation or a repetition of instructions so you're sure your message is clear, properly received, agreed to, and understood. This is a good time to make communication attempts more than once or twice, and be persistent as well as patient. Be aware of the tendency to be confronted with long verbose sagas which attempt to explain rather simple ideas and often waste precious time. Whenever possible, avoid signing big contracts or making important or life altering decisions during Mercury retrograde periods. When relaying ideas, take a moment to internalize thoughts before openly relaying them. Important matters require extra attention, and it may be beneficial to take the time to see to it that others are also paying attention. The close of the first week of January will be a time when so many unsettled communication matters will begin to be addressed in a much clearer fashion.

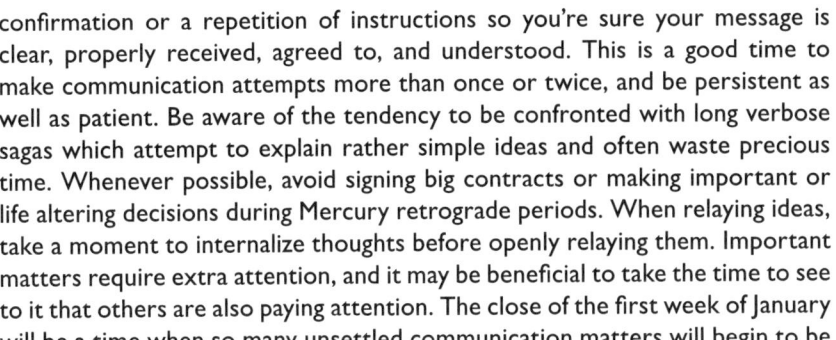

December 18th Thursday
Moon in Libra goes V/C   10:39 p.m. PST   1:39 a.m. (12/19) EST
Moon enters Scorpio   11:20 p.m. PST   2:20 p.m. EST

Today's waning Moon in Libra focuses our moods on maintaining balance. Balance becomes essential and everyone is trying to create a balance no matter what it takes. Those that are more acutely aware of the need for balance are steeped in a world of imbalance. Moon in Libra focuses our moods on the importance of teamwork and the interaction of our friends and loved ones. Friendships and partners play big roles on days like today. Be careful not to get caught up in too many balancing acts in an attempt please everyone.

December 19th Friday
Moon in Scorpio
Venus sextile Mars begins (see 12/25)

There is beauty, sensation and an intensified field of awareness at work. The events of the day may seem laced with strong doses of emotion. A waning Moon in Scorpio calls to us to let go of strong destructive tendencies, and challenges us to cease hurting ourselves and others in order to transform our lower impulses into higher aspirations. Under supportive circumstances, this is a good time to let go of the pain you've been concealing. Sexual activity is the tension reliever many will seek.

December 20th Saturday
Hanukkah
Moon in Scorpio goes V/C   11:43 p.m. PST   2:43 a.m. (12/21) EST
Venus enters Aquarius   10:33 p.m. PST   1:33 a.m. (12/21) EST

The spirit of Scorpio Moon gives us the awareness of deeper, more subtle levels of emotional interplay. The Pluto ruled sign of Scorpio puts us in touch with transformation. Our emotional fields are now undergoing a transformation process which allows us to work through the darkness of this time. The Moon wanes darkly while the Sun in Sagittarius has reached its last day. Not only is this a dark time of the Moon, it is the brink of the shortest day of the year. Insights run powerfully and very profoundly for some folks during this seemingly dark time of the soul.

Venus enters Aquarius (Venus in Aquarius: Dec. 20, '03 – Jan. 14, '04.) Venus in Aquarius creates a fondness for invention, eccentric pleasures, and social life. Venus in Aquarius puts the focus of attraction and adoration on illuminating kinds of knowledge and on brilliant humanitarian causes and exploits. There is an especially strong attraction to invention, all types of invention, and to the ways new technologies will amaze us, particularly with regard to science and the point-of-no-return computer world. It is more likely to be a conducive time for the love life of Aquarius people, whose affections and esthetic pleasures can be enhanced and made whole at this time. Scorpio and Taurus people may notice that love related focuses are causing tension in their personal lives – too many complex issues. Lest we forget, Mercury is now retrograde as well, causing those ill-timed communication problems and misunderstandings. Leo people may become acutely aware of their own personal needs for love and beauty in their life. Leo, as a general rule, can never get enough love and affection, but may be particularly aware of this while Venus is opposing their natal sun this month. Venus in Aquarius is a prime time to perfect and enhance our love of humanity, and to break down the barriers of useless and destructive prejudice and of the stereotyping of our differences.

CAPRICORN

Key phrase "I USE "
Cardinal Earth Sign
Symbol : The Goat

December 21st, 2003 — January 20th, 2004

December 21st Sunday
Winter Solstice
Ursids meteor showers
Moon enters Sagittarius   12:16 a.m. PST   3:16 a.m. EST
Sun sextile Uranus   3:33 p.m. PST   6:33 p.m. EST
Mercury opposite Saturn   10:35 p.m. PST   1:35 a.m. (12/22) EST
Sun enters Capricorn   11:04 p.m. PST   2:04 a.m. (12/22) EST

The Sun and the Moon are currently in the throws of their final voyage through Sagittarius this year. Much later tonight on the west coast (11:04 p.m.), the Sun proceeds into Capricorn, but for now we travel through the shortest day with the Sun still in Sagittarius. The Moon wanes darkly on this shortest day and longest night of the year. From this place of darkness, a spark of hope ignites our dreams. Pensive moods give birth to rich insights.

Sun sextile Uranus (occurring Dec. 17 – 26.) This aspect particularly affects those Sagittarius folks celebrating birthdays this year from December 17th through the 26th. These birthday Sagittarius people are under the direct influence of Uranus in a sextile position to their natal sun. At this time, and during this year, these people are being given an opportunity to release some chaotic steam and reach for aspects of freedom that have eluded them recently. This will be your year to make radical breakthroughs, birthday Sagittarians! There is *no* holding back those creative changes in the midst of unavoidable chaos so go for it! Let change be your inspiration to develop a better outlook on life.

Mercury opposite Saturn (occurring Dec. 7 – 27.) The retrograde Mercury now crosses back over in exact opposition to Saturn once again – this is now a repeat performance of December 13th. The quality of communication seems perhaps macabre and (at times) heavily burdened with a serious tone demanding we pay attention to the confusion currently frustrating our communication attempts. There is an obsessive drive in our thoughts to focus on the news and on messages being spread around concerning matters of closure, deaths, endings, or perhaps even commitments towards a new establishment of control. When Mercury is opposite to Saturn, media coverage and our thoughts are acutely intertwined with time and timely matters. Be careful where you choose to draw the lines and what you agree to when negotiating. If at all possible, it is best to wait until Mercury has gone direct (after January 6th) in order to negotiate final decisions concerning very important matters. Some attempts at getting messages across may very well have to be repeated after that time anyway. On January 21st, this aspect will repeat itself for the final round, allowing for a more formal kind of closure to occur with timely negotiations taking place right now.

Sun enters Capricorn (Sun in Capricorn Dec. 21, '03 – Jan. 20, '04.) Spark up the lights; It's **Winter Solstice!** Throughout the darker and colder regions of North America, hibernating creatures huddle silently in the stillness of the longest night. In the starlit cities and rural cabins, the spirit of the celebration commences, the Yule log of transformation burns brightly in the hearth of everyone who knows: The Sun King returns! At a time when the somber peak of winter's darkness resides, when we anticipate it the most, he returns from the ashes of the longest night. This is the time of Capricorn, ruled by restrictive Saturn. Sun in Capricorn days bring on stern, ardent determination to manipulate the physical world into a whirlwind of banquets, feasts, attainments of grandeur, and major economic shifts. Sun in Capricorn is the time to step out onto grounded plateaus, and to attempt the fulfillment of goals with focused objectives and determination. Capricorn represents the omnipotence of persistence and determination. Busy energy picks up with even a bit more perk and speed. Jack Frost is nipping. A grounded kind of energy takes the stage, and the new season reveals a consciousness of taking control and being in charge of the hardships and perils of winter's storms. The more austere picture of Capricorn goat consciousness is revealed to us through the high and lofty attainments that Capricorn disciplines demand. No mountain is too high for the true archetypal Capricorn, and the focus of this season is always placed on accomplishing and fulfilling the highest of goals and achievements. The working pace for the New Year is set here and eventually evolves into a determined and persistent focus on making grounded progress. Capricorn emphasizes corporate growth, the creation and maintenance of institutions, construction and development, and the use and control of industrial services and equipment. Capricorn urges us not to give up. Many outstanding Capricorns are devoted to their careers and lifestyles with unyielding tenacity. Even when their careers have plummeted to all-time lows, these hardy characters and leaders persist in order to achieve the impossible and build empires out of their domains. Happy Birthday Capricorns, as you progress towards the roundup of another birthday challenge, and meet the New Year with the same old enduring and grounded persistence. Capricorn days of the Sun are splendid times to focus on goals, and to discipline one's nature to make daily tasks add up to something worth accomplishing. Although tedious and often predictable, the Capricorn nature dictates they will get the job done, and then some! Needless to say, the Christmas holiday shuffle is on strong now, *ho ho ho.*

December 22nd Monday

Moon in Sagittarius goes V/C   11:29 p.m. PST   2:29 a.m. EST
Moon enters Capricorn   11:55 p.m. PST   2:55 a.m. (12/23) EST
Jupiter-square-Pluto-Non-Exact   Time   N/A

Sagittarius Sun days may now be behind us, but the Moon still remains in Sagittarius. A dark Moon such as this brings introspective vision. Jupiter is the ruling planet of Sagittarius and emphasizes joviality, exploration, and prosperity. For some folks, prosperity and joy are difficult to find at this time.

Jupiter-square-Pluto-Non-Exact (occurring Oct. 26, '03 – Jan. 17, '04.) Jupiter is currently squaring to Pluto within a one degree orb. This aspect will not reach an exact square; nonetheless it is still very strong. For the past couple days it has been at a standstill. In approximately four days, this Jupiter almost-square Pluto aspect will begin to dissipate and this harsh and lengthy dance between these two planets will end on January 17th, 2004. Jupiter represents prosperity, and plays a big role in the ebb and flow of our expenditures and economy. Pluto represents power structures and the transformations we undergo to maintain them. The square aspect brings obstacles. The weary heart must wade through this economic uncertainty with a positive vision of what it will take to break through the obstacles and achieve prosperity.

December 23rd Tuesday
New Moon in Capricorn
Moon conjunct Sun   1:43 a.m. PST   4:43 a.m. EST
Mercury square Mars begins (see Dec. 26)

We now awaken to the day of the **New Moon in Capricorn** (Moon conjunct Sun.) Whew! It was dark there for awhile, but the stiff upper lip now begins to hint the curve of a contented smile. We are ready to begin raising some light again. New Moon in Capricorn urges us to create new goals and set new heights for ourselves. In the marketplace, there is the classic busy shuffle and serious, determined moods abound. The pace picks up again, and a great deal more is likely to be accomplished today than the past few days have allowed. This is a grounding and much more stable time for us; it is also uplifting and challenging at the same time. Let the blessings of your heart fill the gap when the sadness of missed loved ones creeps in. Strength of will is enhanced by the bounty of love in one's heart. Let the gifts of those we've loved from Christmas past bring renewed strength. Let the new love of this time bring fond new memories to carry over to the Christmas seasons to come. New Moon brings new light – rejoice! Don't expect to get a whole lot done on Christmas Eve. The long void-of-course Moon will probably generate slow progress.

December 24th Wednesday
Christmas Eve
Moon in Capricorn goes V/C   5:52 a.m. PST   8:52 a.m. EST

Today, for the entire day and night, the Moon in Capricorn will be void-of-course. This is not good for our procrastinating friends and kin who have left themselves no margin for error on today's schedule. If you've left yourself with a long list of things to do today, and you're serious about making it through the list, be sure to prioritize your tasks and be realistic. This is not the time to set yourself up for disappointment. This will be a day of confusion, delays, weather setbacks, obstacles and misunderstandings, and many change of plans are likely to occur. With this void Capricorn Moon, many people may find themselves unwittingly trampling all over other people's feelings. It doesn't help that Mercury has been retrograde (see Dec. 17), and that communications are tricky to get across effectively. This could actually be a very lovely, grounded, kicked-back sort of day if there aren't a whole lot of important tasks that need to be done. As for Old Saint Nicholas, have no fear. The watch for Santa's sleigh on the radar screen begins late tonight and just thirteen minutes past midnight PST / 3:13 a.m. (12/25) EST, the Moon enters Aquarius. Those exceptional humanitarian feats that this jolly figure has been known to accomplish will be well within his abilities with the newly waxing Aquarius Moon. Santa might be a little behind schedule, but as always, he'll get the job done! Cheers!

December 25th Thursday
Christmas

Moon enters Aquarius	12:13 a.m. PST	3:13 a.m. EST
Venus sextile Mars	5:29 a.m. PST	8:29 a.m. EST

Sun conjunct Mercury begins (see 12/26)
Mars square Saturn begins (see 1/1/04)
Venus conjunct Neptune begins (see 12/30)
Sun opposite Saturn begins (see 12/31)

Aquarius Moon brings a brilliant, exciting, unusual, and joyous Christmas. This is a time when we reach out to everyone we know and learn from them. It's a great time for giving. Aquarius Moon brings out strong feelings for our fellow humans and a love for all humanity. Charity events and humanitarian deeds are greatly emphasized this Christmas. New technological toys and learning tools will be a big hit today.

Venus sextile Mars (occurring Dec. 19 – 31.) This favorable aspect comes to us on Christmas day like an opportunity knocking on love's door. Venus emphasizes the vibrations of love, magnetism, and also sensuality. Mars' influence emphasizes the awareness and application of action, movement, involvement, and also harnesses uplifting kinds of strength and vitality. Through simple acts of love and caring, our morale is heartily boosted. This week, many love matters are being stirred up; Venus reminds us to draw towards ourselves the pleasures we desire. Mars is reminding us to apply effort, and to generate energy for ourselves and our loved ones. All of this Venus and Mars energy is a blend of opportunistic harmony contributing to the beauty and aesthetic pleasure ignited by this green and red holiday.

Peace on Earth

On this Christmas day here is my gift to you: Peace on Earth! This motto remains the cry of loving hearts; it is a dream, a hope, a rarity, a demand, and an epigram and a maxim carried through the centuries comprising the millennia. It doesn't have to be a rarity though; we can find peace within ourselves. The so-called enlightened ones have done it, so why not everyone? We are fortunate to know this phrase well, but few folks will deny the surmounting chaos surrounding us remains the fascination of us all. This is a turning point for humanity. We are the ones chosen to carry the torch into the 21st century. For starters, peace comes from within. The best way to contribute to the song of Peace-on-Earth, is to emulate Peace itself. A challenge? You bet it is! But NOT impossible. How can you express Peace if you aren't feeling it? Even if you were to fake it, how can it be manifested with any kind of exuberance when the biting and howling dissatisfied world out there bombards you with chaos? The murmur of humanity and all its wailing about for life and death appears to keep us from reaching into ourselves and finding peace where we are broken or lost. There are times when we do feel broken, and a sense of being broken requires the process of healing. Peace is healing. Feeling inadequate about the conditions life has imposed on you does not make you weak. Each and every individual has the strength within to find Peace. We have reached the age of knowledge, and we have discarded the repression of recent centuries. Now we are being given the opportunity to own up to things about ourselves that the dominions of the world have held over our heads for centuries. Freedom is the cry of the New Aeon. There is so much attachment to which we commit ourselves as humans. Those who have learned to intermittently disengage from their personal attachments have learned well the lesson of letting go. As humans, we are bound for change; this requires letting go as well as learning to attain. This has been the way of our ancestors, but the troublesome struggles to possess and to control still haunt us. Welcome to the age of Aquarius. This is the place of human discovery. The human race is younger than we think and older than we know. Love unites us, and Peace comes from inner assurance and a spiritual connection to the higher self. There are twelve signs in the zodiac and each of them has their own phrase. **Aries, I am (peace)** – **Taurus, I have (peace)**, **Gemini, I think (peace)** – **Cancer, I feel (peace)** – **Leo, I will (peace)** – **Virgo, I analyze (peace)** – **Libra, I balance (peace)** – **Scorpio, I create (peace)** – **Sagittarius, I see (peace)** – **Capricorn, I use (peace)** – **Aquarius, I know (peace)** – **Pisces, I believe (peace.)** We all have our own ways of finding Peace, but few of us know how to find it regularly. Christmas is a time that helps us to remember this human expression of PEACE. Peace on Earth is your gift to yourself. Although you can't pretend that evils aren't occurring here on the planet, you can find Peace within. Starting with self-respect, you CAN bring peace to yourself. Peace is the counterbalance to facing the warrior part of the self, and it IS possible to have one with the other. Take a deep breath and call Peace inside!!! Make it your gift to yourself today, and commit to finding Peace everyday! It's doable! With Peace in your heart, there is Peace on Earth. Keep it here! Ignite the Peace torch.

December 26th Friday
Kwanzaa / Boxing Day

Moon in Aquarius
Mercury square Mars   12:53 a.m. PST   3:53 a.m. EST
Sun conjunct Mercury   5:11 p.m. PST   8:11 p.m. EST

The warmth and regenerative quality of yesterday's upbeat Moon in Aquarius is still glowing in the hearts and moods of many people as they make their way thoughtfully into the day. This is Boxing Day. Shopping on the day after Christmas is what Boxing Day represents to most of modern North America, but it's actually a British tradition. The custom has its roots in this time after Christmas when extra gifts are boxed up and traditionally given to household employees and other service workers. Some relentless shoppers think of it as the time to box up those inappropriate gifts and take them back to the stores for exchanges. Other folks may use this time to share their extra gifts with friends and extended families.

Mercury square Mars (occurring Dec. 23 – 29.) Under the influence of

Mercury square Mars, this is not a time to lose one's temper! For details on this aspect, which is now taking place for the final time this year, see March 28th.

Sun conjunct Mercury (occurring Dec. 25 – 29.) This is a most common aspect which creates a much more thoughtful, communicative, and expressive year ahead for those Capricorn people celebrating birthdays this year from December 25th – 29th. This is your time (Birthday Capricorns) to record ideas, relay important messages, and pay close attention to your enterprising thoughts as they are touched by Mercury, creating the urge to speak and be heard. Your thoughts will reveal a great deal about who you are at this time and in the year to come.

December 27th Saturday

Moon in Capricorn goes V/C   2:57 a.m. PST   5:57 a.m. EST
Moon enters Pisces   3:10 a.m. PST   5:10 a.m. EST
Mercury sextile Uranus begins (see 12/30)

The Moon enters Pisces and our moods are filled with artistic flare and great enthusiasm. This is a superb time to be entertaining, as the waxing Pisces Moon undergoes positive aspects throughout the day allowing many of us to enjoy the course of events. Effervescent drinks and festive holiday surroundings enliven the imagination. Meditative moods also give us a relaxed and comforted feeling. Psychic awareness is strong today. This is a good time to recharge the spiritual batteries with some activity that puts us in touch with our divinity.

December 28th Sunday

Moon in Pisces goes V/C   4:03 p.m. PST   7:03 p.m. EST

The Moon in Pisces gives our moods a more flexible expression as we ease up even more on the mental tension brought by the past week. Our intuitive sense has deepened now and we seem to have a great deal more perception. Waxing Pisces Moon encourages us to build on our imagination. Pisces Moon energy brings amicable and sentimental moods, and a sparkling and vibrant quality exists in our overall demeanor. The ups and downs of our moods tend to fluctuate frequently on a waxing Pisces Moon. At 4:03 p.m. PST / 7:03 p.m. EST, the Moon goes void-of-course and we are likely to be quite a bit more abstract in our way of feeling.

December 29th Monday

Moon enters Aries   10:08 a.m. PST   1:08 p.m. EST
Sun square Mars   9:57 p.m. PST   12:57 a.m. (12/30) EST
Mars sextile Neptune begins (see 1/5/04)

We're stepping up the pace unquestionably now with the vibrancy of the waxing Aries Moon. This gives an energetic flare to our moods on this post-holiday Monday. Although the tempo and beat of the Aries Moon brings this energy, it also brings feisty, impulsive, and sometimes argumentative tendencies. This is particularly true while Mercury is still retrograde until January 6th, 2004.

Sun square Mars (occurring Dec. 14, '03 – Jan. 16, '04.) This aspect particularly affects those Sagittarius and Capricorn born people celebrating birthdays from December 14th, '03 through January 16th, '04. This aspect creates the illusion that obstacles are constantly getting in the way of the actions (and will) of these people. This may be a time when harnessing energy seems like a chore. It may serve as a good time for these people to lighten up on their expectations of themselves for awhile, and not let such setbacks get in the way of enjoying life. Relax! In time, it will be easier once again to get your personal goals and your willpower into a state of action. Expect a year of having difficulty relating to various events as they occur; this is not that unusual, given the times. Since this year may bring the tendency for accidents and mistakes, this will be a good time for these birthday folks to learn a great deal about how to pace themselves and to work through the obstacles in order to perfect personal visions and goals.

December 30th Tuesday

First Quarter Moon in Aries
Moon square Sun	2:03 a.m. PST	5:03 a.m. EST
Uranus enters Pisces	1:15 a.m. PST	4:15 a.m. EST
Venus conjunct Neptune	9:24 a.m. PST	12:24 p.m. EST
Mercury sextile Uranus	1:31 a.m. PST	4:31 a.m. EST
Mercury enters Sagittarius	11:52 a.m. PST	2:52 a.m. EST

Today we reach the **First Quarter Moon in Aries** (Moon square Sun), and our moods are generally up beat, outgoing and forward. Waxing Aries Moon activates, warms up and vitalizes our moods, giving us the incentive to forge our way forward. There is inclination towards being self-motivated and the active ones among us are certainly on the prowl. Aries Moon inspires us to take bold new steps as well as instilling confidence and the warrior spirit. First Quarter Moon in Aries serves as a good time to apply diligence with inspired ability, and to initiate new projects that will carry through the wInter.

Uranus enters Pisces (Uranus in Pisces: Dec. 2003 – March 2011.) Uranus is all about raising our consciousness in an expedited and sometimes overwhelming manner. Today Uranus bids farewell to Aquarius and will not return here again for nearly eight more decades. Uranus in Aquarius last affected us in the post-World War One era, creating a world of invention which changed our history and human levels of expertise immensely. Since 1995, Uranus in Aquarius has brought to us a radical change in the advancement of technology, which once again ties humanity together in a much more eye-opening and advanced fashion. Uranus, after all, is the ruling planet of this expression of Aquarius, and it is here where we have always seemed to surprise ourselves with the reality of the unimaginable. As we head into the days of Uranus in the sign of Pisces for the next eight years, this promises to bring radical change to our religious institutions. This time sweeps our consciousness with an awakening to our belief systems and spiritual lifestyles. Chaos moves through and challenges our beliefs, our spiritualism and our place of worship. We all received some clue as to what this phenomenon is like (this past year) since Uranus first wandered into the early degrees of Uranus back on March 10th. Uranus then moved through Pisces up until September 15th, when the retrograde motion of Uranus brought it back into the late degrees of Aquarius for the last time this cycle. With Uranus now in Pisces, there may well be a dramatic attempt at cracking down on Piscean expressions such as addiction, escapism, and unconventional forms of worship. Such attempts will probably backfire since Uranus is not much into being contained, and the level of knowledge we have harnessed at this point will allow us to defend our beliefs in a much more awakened manner. This all emphasizes our need to confront the emotional hardships of facing our mortality. New and radical fascinations and expressions can be expected to develop in the world of psychic research, occultism, art, poetry, movie making, plays, and music. Those who treasure their beliefs as an intricate part of their lifestyle are likely to see great change and possibly challenges to their spiritual lives. Metaphysical endeavours are likely to be tried and tested in ways we would never have imagined. Uranus was last in the sign of Pisces from 1919 – 1928, and this was probably one of the most dramatic decades of United States history. It was evidently a time of breakthrough for women's rights, political scandal, thriving drug trade and mobster activity, and economic upheaval: a place where the old and new clashed like never before. Upheaval occurred alright, especially in church where the raising of hemlines revealing the ankles, raised eyebrows at the pews. Don't forget – that was before television came along and when church attendance was very high. Pisces rules the mutable waters, encompassing our fascination with elixirs and the spirits commonly known as alcohol, and that time of Uranus in Pisces brought the daunting but exciting era of Prohibition. People found freedom by escaping to the movies (a breakthrough time for silent pictures), bootlegging liquor and, foremost, whatever it took to appease the senses while surviving the hardships imposed by various kinds of emotional upheaval. A radical movement sweeps across our deepest spiritual convictions with Uranus in Pisces now occurring once again in a whole new modern setting. This time will be interesting, no doubt. For more information on Uranus in Pisces, see March 10th.

Venus conjunct Neptune (occurring Dec. 25, '03 – Jan. 4, '04.) These two very feminine planets are currently aligned as a higher and lower octave of each other, creating a very fluid and open expression of femininity. See March 12th for a recap on Venus conjunct Neptune.

Mercury sextile Uranus (occurring Dec. 27, '03 – Jan. 5, '04.) This aspect last took place on Dec. 1st (extending from Nov. 29 – Dec. 5.) This week, we get to undergo the process all over again while Mercury remains retrograde. This aspect represents a time of opportunity for rebels to speak out, except their voices will undoubtedly be muffled by the relentless quality of messages being misinterpreted (as hostile or chaotic) while Mercury is retrograde.

Despite all this, here is an opportunity for our thoughts to be enhanced in a manner that hasn't been addressed before. This aspect brings news of radical change, delivering a message that holds the potential to free others. This process becomes more internalized since Mercury retrograde tends to turn our thoughts inward, and it may seem difficult to translate some of the more profound concepts mulling around in our heads into a comprehensive dialog. Just as it was back at the beginning of the month, some folks may act on this aspect with wild abandon, creating an effect of repelling and offending, while for others this radical communication will represent freedom from a particular kind of slavery that has held them back.

Mercury enters Sagittarius (Mercury in Sagittarius Dec. 30, '03 – Jan. 14, '04.) Mercury which is currently retrograde (see Dec. 17) now goes back (from our geocentric view) into the late degrees of Sagittarius. The planet of communication, information, and news is once again expressed through the sign of expansion, exploration, and vision. While Mercury is retrograde (until January 6th) through the mutable fire sign of Sagittarius, communications are likely to be thwarted with regard to people's travel plans. Travel routes are likely to be closed down, detoured or difficult to find due to weather, trouble with airline companies, holiday traffic congestion and void-of-course lunar phases. If you plan to meet someone, especially in a busy public terminal, have a back up plan for an alternative place and time when schedules fall by the wayside and cell phones (for whatever reason) fail to work. Don't get frustrated: this is normal holiday mayhem appearing more amplified than usual. Just know this quality of life is to be expected and there is little anyone can do to change it. Fortunately, Mercury has already been retrograde for a couple of weeks and only has another week to go before it resumes course on January 6th, '04.

December 31st Wednesday

Moon in Aries goes V/C	6:27 p.m. PST	9:27 p.m. EST
Moon enters Taurus	9:02 p.m. PST	12:02 a.m. (1/1/04) EST
Sun opposite Saturn	12:57 p.m. PST	3:57 p.m. EST

Just as sure as a great number of traditionalists are preparing to ring in the New Year, the cluster of celestial events that have been taking place this final week of the year are keeping the pace rolling. Throughout the day, people are rushing about, and anxious to get here and there, to do this and that. By 6:27 p.m. on the west coast / 9:27 p.m. on the east coast, the Moon goes void-of-course. Aries void-of-course moon could be rather daunting or overwhelming for some, especially those who must push their way through crowded events. Moods are geared towards the ever popular "me first" attitude; coupled with the fact that not everyone can actually be first, the nasty, uncompromising and inconsiderate wanderers in the crowd are going to create some aggravation. By 9:02 p.m. on the west coast, the Moon enters Taurus and the final three hours of this festive evening bring a grounded, sensual, and pleasurable quality. It isn't until two minutes after midnight that the folks on the east coast will find themselves in this mood setting. After all the pushing around in Times Square, the approach of midnight, and the commencement of the New Year with the final two minutes of a high-spirited Aries Moon, New Year's day begins tomorrow with the Moon in Taurus, and for those who love such things the celebrations and parades will no doubt be beautiful and pleasurable sights.

Sun opposite Saturn (occurring Dec. 25, '03 – Jan. 6, '04.) This aspect particularly affects those Capricorn people celebrating birthdays from December 25th, '03 – January 6th, '04. These birthday folks are undergoing personal challenges with regard to patience, leaving them feeling acutely aware of who and what is in control. They are particularly aware of the crucial factors concerning time, limitation and timing. This challenge represents the necessity to persistently be on top of timely matters that impinge on one's sense of control, discipline, and accuracy. Factors may have worked themselves up to an alarming crescendo during the phase of one's life when Saturn opposes the natal sun. This challenge will pass over time, but in the year to come it reminds those affected by it (particularly Capricorn birthday people) to take a good look at what does matter in their lives, and to appreciate life itself. This may be a time of sacrifice, loss or compromise. This is certainly a time of coming to terms with what is real and most important in life. Saturn represents those aspects of life that we are willing to work for and maintain. Just because there is an acute awareness of timely struggle does not mean that it is time to give up, or to just throw away what has been laboriously achieved by the application of one's will. Saturn represents our sense of discipline and the exercise of effort and focus. Here we learn about our limitations, and our strengths are also realized. This is a good time for these birthday folks to conserve energies and take losses and difficulties in stride. Through the tests of this time, a stronger human being emerges to take on the future tests with greater ability and confidence. Running away from hardship and destroying everything in the process will only make life more difficult later. Abolish fear! Face it now. Handle it now and throughout this year! This is your time, Capricorn birthday folks, to act responsibly! Remember, your Capricorn nature can handle this, given the fact that Saturn is your ruling planet, and being challenged by your own ruler is something you are likely to handle better than most signs of the zodiac. It's nose to the grindstone as usual, and you may be passing this test without even noticing there is one!
Cheers to All! Bright Blessings, And Happy New Year!

Special Moon Sign Guide Supplement for Mother's Day:

And now for a segment of commentaries on Mom. This is written for Mother's Day, and the Moon speaks to us about the Mother in rich ways. She who gives, and She who nourishes; She who toils to give life and preserve it, She who instinctively knows how to reach the core of our feelings... She is Mother, the door of life and the first one there for us. Nature and Earth are connected with the feminine archetype of Mother and so is the Moon whose influence affects our moods and our emotional shifts and changes throughout life. Her art is the science of reflection, the reflection of the heart. She has a dark side and a bright side and She recognizes that very thing in us. Some of us truly understand this and in different ways have fulfilled the role of Mother. Knowing how to reach the heart is a process of knowing how to care. Everyone has an emotional core that needs food and sustenance. The Mother nourishes a part of Herself by nourishing Her child. She also sacrifices a great part of Herself in this act of love and heartfelt generosity. She gives for the sake of giving and not for reward or approval. Not everyone has the purity of this archetypal picture of their own mother, or of their own experience of nurturing. The dark side of the emotions can run just as deep. Look up the Moon sign under which were born and read about how your mom related to you personally in your tender youth as the bonds of motherhood unfolded.

Moon in Aries: Your mom let you be exactly who you are. You always came first. Her relationship with you always came first. She let you run into things, head first of course, and knew instinctively that you are a survivor. Perhaps she's had high expectations of you as a warrior and encouraged you to be first in all that you do. Emotionally, she instilled courage and a pioneering spirit. She was always showing you new things and charging you with great impulses to reach out and explore. Your mom's presence was a deep and alluring inspiration. Sometimes her manner may have seemed forceful. Sometimes she may have been naive or pushy, hot headed or quick tempered. How about impatient? Your emotional relationship was no doubt head strong and all of this is a reflection on your own emotional path in this life. Your first impressions of life with mom gave you what it takes to be an open and expressive explorer of your feelings.

Moon in Taurus: Your mom wanted you to have the finest... The warmest, the cleanest, the driest, the newest. All those words end in 'est', turn it into a prefix and you get an 'est'-imate. She wanted you to have the best that life could buy and was always estimating how much it was going to cost her. Mom wanted you to have. She may not have always given you what you wanted but right from the start she recognized the value of your needs and gave you the best options of life in her power. All this was given to you in a very practical and beautiful way. She showed you nature and gave you a sense of being down to earth. On the down side, here exists the emotional toils of great sentimentality. Emotionally, your mom may have been possessive, like she owned you. Letting go of you was a hard task, but all young babes must grow. Whether sensitive or stubborn about it, there she was nurturing you with her loyalty and fulfilling your earthly needs. Though rarely she may have doubted it, the sparkling lights of your eyes told her you possessed a great value for all the world to one day see.

Moon in Gemini: Your mom bonded with you through your thoughts as well as your emotions. She always seemed fascinated with what you were thinking. There was some emotional importance placed on your apparent intelligence and she strongly wanted you to develop your thinking process. She presented you with dual options and choices. For you, variety was the spice of life. She gave lots of games and toys and details for you to comb over and experience. She kept busy keeping up with you as well as staying one step ahead. On some level your mother's relationship and bonding dealt with brightness and intelligence. Together through your bonding process you were always thinking about things and bonding on the emotional plane through some process of logic. Your mother was like your playmate, as immensely curious about you as you were of her. You were always studying the details of each other. On the down side, mom may have instilled nervous or mixed emotions at times, sending cross messages and mixing up your wires. Over all, your mother played a large role in your early development by encouraging and inspiring your inexhaustible thought process.

Moon in Cancer: Moon rules Cancer. Your mom ruled your emotional realm deeply. She always touched the core of your heart with her own emotions. She knew exactly how to nurture and care for your emotional as well as your physical hunger. She instilled deep feelings in you. Your bond may have been so strong that the two of you never let go of the Mother/Infant connection and your mother may still psychically possess the infant child that lives within you. As a result you can always tell when Mom is thinking of you, influencing your decisions, particularly on how to nurture and care for yourself. She always knows when you're sick. Even though she may have already passed on into the next world, or no longer sees you, your mother has found a way to be there with you again and again. Mom always has a way of being present in your emotional core. The Cancer Moon relationship quite often causes moodiness and the down side is the tendency to hang on to worries and fears. "Don't worry, be happy". Celebrate Mom and the Mom within! Cancer is a fine place for your moon!

Moon in Leo: Your mom took great pride in your arrival! She instinctively desired that all the world would one day bow to you. She loved to show you off and placed your shining character in the limelight of every event. Mom was emotionally tied into the very regal and self-assured side of your being. She knew how to nurture your ego. There is a wild side to you that she intuitively served and encouraged with her heart. Heart to heart you and your mother identified with life in a very colorful and lively way. Your mother's influence on your emotions has been so empowering that to this day you have strong feelings about the importance of standing out and being special, being properly served, and being acknowledged for your efforts in the world. The down side of this relationship may be that your mother always put you on the spot. Emotionally there may be a constant struggle to perform and perfect your act in order to achieve and receive the kind of affection and acknowledgment that your mother got you hooked on. Don't let your emotions be stifled by stage fright; if it feels good let it shine. Your ego has enough juice, thanks to Mom, to endure those hard blows of criticism.

Moon in Virgo: Quite possibly your mother was like the Virgin Mother. Yours was, for her, an immaculate conception and she cared for you with meticulous wonder. Everything she handed you had to be analyzed, sterilized and investigated with regards to your health and pureness of well being. She had strong feelings about your small and delicate, infant youth and was probably constantly concerned for your safety, cleanliness and comfort. As a result you adopted the emotional tendencies of being careful, fastidious and concerned with cleanliness and order. She showed you how to touch the physical world in a gentle fashion and be thorough with your assessment of how things work and function. Through this relationship you may have been touched with a strong need to analyze your emotions constantly, making sure that it's always safe to feel what you're feeling. Your mother may have instilled shyness, or modesty that makes it hard to share feelings openly. Your own feelings can be less inhibited when you know you have taken the precaution that your mother instilled to create a safe environment in which to express yourself and let go of your doubts and fears.

Moon in Libra: Your mom took it upon herself to create harmony and beauty and a strong basis of love to draw from in your emotional relationship. With Libra, relationship is the key, and your mother poured on the love with diligent attempts to nurture your core while acclimating your feelings towards dealing with the real world intelligently. When you were a young infant, your Mother was careful not to expose you to too much at once, always concerned not to imbue you with too many impurities. Her main concern was to assist you to respond to the love she gave you and send it back like a cherub of light. Balance was the obsession your infant care was based on. It was important for her to know that her affections for you were well received and that you were capable of responding to love. In this empowering attempt to make you a strong human being with warm, compassionate wisdom, your mother possessed high hopes concerning your welfare beyond the precious stage of infancy. Regardless of how she performed her motherly duties, she concerned herself dearly with your learning process and education. On the other hand, she may have had great expectations of you, and may have fancied you a strong leader with an iron fist behind the glove of diplomacy and social tact. In areas of your relationship that were not harmonious there may have been a strong drive for you to prove yourself socially, even as a young child. Your mother has sought a library of wisdom for you because she was able to recognize your great thirst for beauty and your great hunger for love.

Moon in Scorpio: Great passion and intensity fills your emotional core and although she may have had dominant ways of expressing it, your mother was profoundly touched by her love for you. After all, Scorpio represents sex, birth, and death, a big part of what we involve ourselves with emotionally. Scorpio Moon relationship with mom indicates that she might of had some secrets kept from you at birth. There is a further mystery attached to your connection with your mom. She may have died when you were born or very young. She may have had some extraneous circumstance which intensified your nurturing process and her role with you as a mother. She was protective and fiercely proud of you although she may have had strange ways of expressing it. Perhaps she had to give you up for adoption and her pain through life as a result of your separation may easily have been just as horrific as your own pain through life. Your mother's influence instilled strong psychic and intuitive power to your emotional base. She gave you a powerful sense of recognizing danger and for some, a fascination with death as well as life. Your emotional development is often toying with the edge and pushes you to depths of expression that few attempt on the emotional plane. Indeed your mother gave you a passion for life, a true reflection of her own expression.

Moon in Sagittarius: Since the day you were born your mother brought out deep philosophical and visionary perspectives that influenced your moods and emotional development. She kept you moving in a restless, adventurous and inspired fashion. Perhaps she traveled with you a lot as an infant. She wanted you to have the stars and beyond. It was important to her to expose you to everything she could as soon as you were able to digest it all. She nurtured you with high hopes and focused on developing you in as many advanced ways as possible. On the emotional plane your mother gave you the driving desire to go beyond simple feelings and pull up a deeper picture of why we are here and what our purpose for existing is about. Emotionally, you are loaded with a tremendous amount of electrical energy which can shift and blend in a powerful and profound way. Thanks to this Mom relationship of yours, you have the capability to obtain great visionary insights and a wide range of perspectives and awareness.

Moon in Capricorn: Your mother's love nurtured you in a very dry, stoic and practical manner. Your mother wanted you to have the world and be adept with every little responsibility that comes with it. Foremost, she wanted you to be ready and equipped for life and she meant business. She took her motherhood seriously and you were the product of her hard work which sought to produce and maintain a useful and functional new person in the world: You! Many theorize that Capricorn is not an adept sign for dealing with emotions. Capricorn Moon people are thought to be hard driving, work-obsessed people who often spare the indulgence of emotions and sentiment. On the contrary, Capricorns in general have deep caverns of emotions well concealed and protected like their counterpart, or opposite sign, Cancer. The down side is that your emotional drive is geared towards an obsessive work ethic and it may be very difficult for you to know how to relax and express your feelings freely. It may have been very important for your mother to express her affections by providing you with conventional, practical and basic needs rather than emotional vibrations and interaction. Raising you was a job, but she was there to perform her role as Mother in a way that would harden you to the harsh realities of the turbulent emotional tides of life. The cardinal earth sign of Capricorn teaches us about provision, sustenance and the use of our resources. Mom has provided you with a firm emotional base to endure great hardships and trials.

Moon in Aquarius: Your mother gave birth and life to you with the profound understanding of what it means to be the water bearer; the symbol of Aquarius. It was her humanitarian duty to raise you with knowledge and expose you to as much knowledge as is humanly possible to acquire. It was important to your mother to have you wake up to the world around you and adapt to learning at an accelerated rate. Your emotional core adopted this outlook of taking on the brightest and most idealistic route toward altering the perspectives of your fellow man. Your emotions place emphasis on the giving and the sharing of your knowledge with a generous heart. She sensed and knew you were brilliant, and took it upon herself to educate you at every turn in as many ways as possible, in a diverse, worldly and culturally adept manner. She encouraged you to share and get along with others from a very young stage of life. On the down side, mom may not have given you the emotional or physical stimulus that a young infant needs to feel secure in the world. Most of your drive towards giving to others may be in part due to your own quest for love and knowledge. This is not to say your mother didn't love you, it just means that her love may have been displayed in an intellectual way rather than emotionally. This is fairly true for all the air signs of the Moon (Aquarius, Gemini and Libra) as the pressure on our emotions to operate in a logical manner brings the bearer to some extraordinary places in their emotional scope. To this mother, knowledge is often a matter of fact, and an essential path towards the maturation of your emotional development. As a result, you feel a strong need to help others and to spread the knowledge you have as swiftly and effectively as possible.

Moon in Pisces: Your mom truly believed in you. She gave you rich insights about life that your emotional character is constantly shifting through. The Pisces Moon, like the other water moon signs Cancer and Scorpio, gives you a strong psychic edge that frequently amazes yourself and others. Pisces gives you the added edge of adaptability to all your impressions and all your psychic inclinations. Your mom had a dreamy, instinctual and very imaginative emotional bond with you. Her kind, sympathetic and receptive tones and gestures towards you gave you a deep sense of compassion and creative intuition. Your mom sensed your artistic side and gave you lots of room to explore the creative part of your being. She gifted you with a flare for the feminine approach to the emotional realm. When things went wrong, your mother usually handled it well around you because she was acutely aware of your strong sensitivity and impressionability. The down side of your relationship may have been caused by an over sensitivity that existed in your bonding process. She may have attempted escapism of the Mother-role or simply often spaced out when it came to nurturing you in the ways that you needed it. There really is no logical way to put a finger on the heart-beat of how the mysteries of this miraculous bond works. Regardless of how you may look back on your mother's influence upon you, she sacrificed much of herself to serve your needs and she carried a strong faith in who you showed yourself to be from the very start.

Sekhmet